Identities, Cultures, Spaces

Identities, Cultures, Spaces: Dialogue and Change

Edited by

Fernando Kuhn

CAMBRIDGE SCHOLARS
PUBLISHING

Identities, Cultures, Spaces: Dialogue and Change,
Edited by Fernando Kuhn

This book first published 2013

Cambridge Scholars Publishing

12 Back Chapman Street, Newcastle upon Tyne, NE6 2XX, UK

British Library Cataloguing in Publication Data
A catalogue record for this book is available from the British Library

ISBN (10): 1-4438-4610-4, ISBN (13): 978-1-4438-4610-3

TABLE OF CONTENTS

LIST OF ILLUSTRATIONS

LIST OF TABLES

INTRODUCTION

IDENTITIES, CULTURES, SPACES: DIALOGUE AND CHANGE

FERNANDO KUHN

Far from being the subject of consensus, the term "globalisation" is perceived by some authors to refer to a contemporary process, while others view it as an older phenomenon, or perhaps as one stage in something overarching (Robertson 1992; Osterhammel and Petersson 2005); indeed, Wallerstein (1974, quoted in Robinson 2007, 128) regards globalisation as "virtually synonymous with the birth and spread of world capitalism." Hirst and Thompson (1996, 197, cited in Sklair 1999, 155), for instance, see "no fundamental difference between the international submarine telegraph cable method of financial transactions [of the early twentieth century] and contemporary electronic systems." Conversi (2010, 37) mentions authors who affirm that "the Roman Empire entailed forms of globalisation," or that "Genghis Khan, 'the world conqueror' and 'the emperor of all men,' inaugurated the pattern of 'modern' globalisation" (citing Weatherford 2004, 16), and that "long-distance contact during late antiquity" can "be described as 'incipient globalisation'" (citing Harris 2007).

This "current" (stage of) globalisation has been described since the 1980s (cf. Martell 2007) and 1990s (cf. Robinson 2007) by a number of authors, including Giddens (1990), Robertson (1992), Held (1995), Waters (1995) and Hannerz (1996). Giddens (1990, 64) defines it as the "intensification of worldwide social relations which link distant localities in such a way that local happenings are shaped by events occurring many miles away and vice versa," while Robertson (1992, 8) calls it "the compression of the world and the intensification of consciousness of the world as a whole." Similarly, for Held (1995, 20), globalisation is

> the stretching and deepening of social relations and institutions across space and time such that, on the one hand, day-to-day activities are increasingly

> influenced by events happening on the other side of the globe and, on the other hand, the practices and decisions of local groups can have significant global reverberations.

Waters (1995, 5), in turn, views globalisation as:

> a social process in which the constraints of geography on economic, political, social, and cultural arrangements recede, in which people become increasingly aware that they are receding and in which people act accordingly.

Finally, according to Hannerz (1996, 17), "in the most general sense, globalisation is a matter of increasing long-distance interconnectedness, at least across national boundaries, preferably between continents as well."

At the beginning of the second decade of the twenty-first century, many aspects remain controversial. If, as Held and McGrew (2007, 1) observe, the events of 9/11 were considered for many globalisation sceptics as "the beginnings of a peculiar return to 'normality' in global politics, as geopolitics, violence and imperialism … reassert themselves with a vengeance," then the present financial crisis and the challenges it brings to the integrity of the European Union and its common currency further strengthens the arguments of authors like Ferguson (2005), Saul (2005) and Rosenberg (2005), for whom "globalisation is over."

This atmosphere of uncertainty—combined with economic indicators which may suggest some kind of reversal of the conditions that had originated, favoured or characterised globalisation—cannot, however, undo many of the effects produced by the process of globalisation, which are manifest in the political, economic and cultural spheres. But even in the improbable event of "de-globalisation"—with the revocation of all treaties and agreements, and the imposition of all sorts of commercial barriers and cultural filters, and the interruption of communication systems that have been allowing people to interact on a worldwide scale, such as the Internet and mobile phones—the unprecedented cultural contacts that have formed in recent years as a consequence of the circulation of people, contents and goods will surely influence cultural practices for a long time. "Cultural globalisation," or the cultural dimension of globalisation, remains a topical phenomenon, not only because of the "state of culture in transnational motion—flows of people, trade, communication, ideas, technologies, finance, social movements, cross border movements, and more" that result from globalisation (Shome and Hedge 2002, 174), but also because the "clashing and mixing of culture" does not occur exclusively "across the boundaries of nation-state societies, but within them too," as noted by Featherstone and Lash (1999, 1). As is the case with the term "globalisation," there is no consensus about what is to be understood as "cultural globalisation." According to Castells (2009, 117), the term refers to "the emergence of a specific set of values and beliefs that are largely shared around the planet." Nijman (1999, 148) perceives it as "an acceleration in the exchange of cultural symbols among people around the world, to such an extent that it leads to changes in local popular cultures and identities." As Movius (2010, 6) observes, the globalisation of culture is "familiar to almost everyone" and is often considered as "tantamount" to the globalisation of the media. For Hopper (2007, 188), it is most appropriately taken to be "a catch-all term or concept to describe international, transnational, regional, local and global developments that have a cultural dimension, as well as counter-developments such as forms of cultural consolidation."

Robinson (2007, 140) offers a comprehensive description of the divergent views concerning the ways in which globalisation and cultures relate to one another.

> Cultural theories of globalisation tend to line up along one of three positions (Tomlinson 1999; Nederveen Pieterse 2004). Homogenisation theories see a global culture convergence and would tend to highlight the rise of world beat, world cuisines, world tourism, uniform consumption patterns and cosmopolitanism. Heterogeneity approaches see continued cultural difference and highlight local cultural autonomy, cultural resistance to homogenisation, cultural clashes and polarisation, and distinct subjective experiences of globalisation. Here we could also highlight the insights of post-colonial theories. Hybridisation stresses new and constantly evolving cultural forms and identities produced by manifold transnational processes and the fusion of distinct cultural processes. These three theses certainly capture different dimensions of cultural globalisation but there are very distinct ways of interpreting the process even within each thesis.

Most of the contemporary debate concerning cultural globalisation suggests that the traditional notion of "culture"—or "a culture" (Gupta and Ferguson 1997, 1), which is understood as "a separate, individuated cultural entity, typically associated with 'a people,' 'a tribe,' 'a nation,' and so forth" (Stocking 1982, 202–3, in Gupta and Ferguson 1997, 1)—is obsolete. A number of authors have questioned the notion of culture as "based on social homogeneity, ethnic consolidation and intercultural delimitation" (Brancato 2006); as "a more or less publicly shared, internally homogeneous and distinctive system of patterns, symbols, or meanings" (Lamb 2000); as a "bounded whole" (Dahl 2008, 30) with "stable borders" (Sandkühler 2004, 81); or as something with "physical borders and which builds on the past" (Eriksen 1993, 10, in Dahl 2008, 30). They have also questioned "the idea that a world of human differences is to be conceptualised as a diversity of separate societies, each with its own culture" (Gupta and Ferguson 1997, 1), a vision that, according to Appadurai (1992, 35–36), "incarcerates" the native in a fixed "way of thinking that admits no fuzzy boundaries and is splendid in its internal consistency" (cf. Raheja and Gold 1994, 2) and assumes, as Lamb (2000, 3) notes, "that all members of a culture more or less agree with each other, just as people of one culture are also set off, uniquely different, from people of other cultures."

Instead, "culture" has increasingly been conceptualised as a process (Baumann 1999; Rosaldo 1993; Geertz 2000; Moore 2004; Craith 2004), "a polymorphic symbolic dimension of social construction and reproduction in multicultural and transcultural societies" (Steingress 2010, 4). "Culture" also has been experiencing a continuous de-territorialisation (King 1991, in Kearney 1995; Lie 2002; Brancato 2006) and re-territorialisation in places not related to its origins and traditions.

A similar debate surrounds the concept of "identity," once defined as, for instance, "the consciousness or the feeling of belonging to a social network or a locality or an area and the feeling of oneness with these" (Heller 2011, 5). As Hall (1996, 3–4) posits,

> The concept of identity deployed here is therefore not an essentialist, but a strategic and positional one. That is to say, directly contrary to what appears to be its settled semantic career, this concept of identity does *not* signal that stable core of the self, unfolding from beginning to end through all the vicissitudes of history without change; the bit of the self which remains always-already "the same," identical to itself across time. Nor—if we translate this essentializing conception to the stage of cultural identity—it is that "collective or true self hiding inside the many other, more superficial or artificially imposed 'selves' which a people with a shared history and ancestry hold in common" (Hall 1990) and which can stabilise, fix or guarantee an unchanging "oneness" or cultural belongingness underlying all the other superficial differences. It accepts that identities are never unified and, in late modern times, increasingly fragmented and fractured; never singular but multiply constructed across different, often intersecting and antagonistic discourses, practices and positions. They are subject to a radical historicisation, and are constantly in the process of change and transformation. We need to situate the debates about identity within all those historically specific developments and practices which have disturbed the relatively "settled" character of many populations and cultures, above all in relation to the processes of globalisation, which I would argue are coterminous with modernity (Hall

> 1996b) and the processes of forced and "free" migration which have become a global phenomenon of the so-called "post-colonial" world. Though they seem to invoke an origin in a historical past with which they continue to correspond, actually identities are about questions of using the resources of history, language and culture in the process of becoming rather than being: not "who we are" or "where we came from," so much as what we might become, how we have been represented and how that bears on how we might represent ourselves. Identities are therefore constituted within, not outside representation.

In a context where, on one hand, the linkages between culture and identity become "more problematic as the sources of cultural production and dissemination increase" (Featherstone and Lash 1999, 1), and on the other hand, "globalisation has been perhaps the most significant force in creating and proliferating cultural identities," as Tomlinson (2003, 16) affirms, the importance of "space" as a third, influential factor in the equation cannot be ignored. The reconfiguration of cultures and identities tends to manifest in—or in spite of—a given spatiality, be it, as in the categorisation provided by Heller (2011, 6), "an administrative or a physically delimitable section of the surface of the earth," or "a space of action determined by the ranges of activities of the people," or a "space characterised by the perception of the people," varying in "size, shape and features"; or even virtual/digital, mental/imaginary.

This volume addresses issues that arise in the field of multidisciplinary research, where cultures, identities and spaces intersect: spaces where cultures and identities interact and overlap; spaces where they are shaped and consolidated; spaces through which they are separated; spaces to which they adapt; spaces into which they echo and spread; spaces imperceptibly contained within other spaces, where cultures and identities coincide. From the macro- to the micro-level, from the collective to the individual, from the real to the constructed, then to the imagined and back to the real, from isolation to integration, a wide range of topics that make up the field are contemplated in the chapters presented here.

In "Cartographies of Transculturality: Region as 'Dialogue Zone,'" Fernando Kuhn approaches the dynamics of cultural interaction by means of a conceptual analysis of the notions and discourses of "culture" and "identity," as well as their presumed extensions. Observing the influence of shared spatialities in the forging of commonalities, he proposes the concept of "dialogue zone" and suggests the regional scale—in its multiple dimensions—as a reference for "understanding," "defining," and "mediating" the interactions of "cultures."

Kuhn presents the idea of "spheres of interaction," a categorisation consisting of "spaces (landscapes and courses)" and "vectors (language, science, arts, media and sports)." Adopting Europe as a reference, in light of the diversity of its configuration and the efforts invested in its integration, he provides examples of how these spheres of interaction are being materialised and examines the effects brought about by the increasing mobility of people and contents.

In "Homely Sites and Landscapes as Elements of Regional Identity," Sulevi Riukulehto describes the evolution of the concept of identity as it has been elaborated in the context of distinct disciplines, from logic and philosophy to sociology and political science, from mathematics and geometry to psychology and ethnology, and shows how such discourses have been adopted and put into typologies and used as categories, following a trajectory that commences with the logic formulation of the "identity of exact sameness" ("A=A," i.e., "an object is exactly the same as itself") and culminates with the economist's view of identity as a rational and momentary choice.

Highlighting the many kinds of definitions that emerge when identity is taken as "a quality of people" rather than merely "the quality of a place or of an object," Riukulehto directs his focus to the regional sphere, reflecting on its significance for the process of identity formation and the transition between individuality and collectivity. At this point, he introduces the concept of "homely landscapes"—a three-level model representing "the complex entity of natural, human-made and mental environments that an individual recognises to be his own"—and proposes it as "an opening to define and to model the deeper meaning of regional identity."

In "Multiculturalism: The Ideology of the New World Order," Siyaves Azeri exposes his critical view about the discourse of multiculturalism, in which he identifies an ideology at work in the service of capitalism, despite its alleged "humanitarianism." For Azeri, the multiculturalist approach adopts an inadequate premise while "attributing an immutable essence to 'culture'": instead of being examined as a dynamic process involving social relations in a social-historical context, "culture" is analysed under the scope of "an association of arbitrary elements," implying that "culture is a meta-historical, self-contained category or form."

Warning of the risks posed by what he calls "this fetishistic view of culture," Azeri observes that "multiculturalism and cultural relativism function as ideological apparatus in the hands of the most reactionary regimes around the world and their 'progressive' apologists" in order to "politically justify their being and their politics as the representation of certain cultural and traditional values that also allegedly determine the being of people." If all practices are accepted and respected in the name of an established "culture," "tradition" or "cultural value," what happens to individual human rights inherent to those who, inside such "culture," simply do not agree with its values? When people are no more "citizens that have certain equal rights and duties regardless of their sex and race," but "members of this or that ethnicity, religion, sect, tribe, linguistic community"? Turning his attention to such dilemmas, Azeri reflects on the motivations behind the discourse of multiculturalism and its implications.

In "Defining Urban Integration through Active Participation of Rural Migrants," Z. Ezgi Haliloğlu Kahraman presents a case study carried out with the involvement of seventy-five rural migrants living in three distinct neighbourhoods in Ankara. Before detailing the methodological framework conceived and employed to gather and interpret these migrants' impressions and experiences of the process of urban integration, Kahraman revisits previous conceptualisations of urban integration, which include "assimilation, accumulation, unification, acculturation, placement, interaction, identification, adaptation, cultural pluralism, and multiculturalism." She also enunciates and examines eight "dimensions of integration": background, economic, cultural, social, political, physical, institutional and personal.

A comprehensive map of attributes of urban integration (forty-five in total, condensed into sixteen categories or "factors") emerges as Kahraman reveals the data obtained in the research. Combined with the historical perspective that the author brings to analysis of the rural-to-urban migration process in Turkey, such data provide a valuable tool not only for seeing the whole picture at the micro-level of the districts of a big city like Ankara, or at the national level as a question supposedly pertinent to "Turkish culture," but also for contributing to the debate around more universal issues of migration, as in the case of the questions raised by Azeri.

In "Territorializing Spiritual Values: Notions of 'Belonging' and 'Possessing' in the Context of the Controversy over Max Brod's Legacy," Markéta P. Rubešová analyses the German–Israeli dispute over the legacy of Max Brod and (by extension, since Brod was the guardian of his legacy) Franz Kafka. Both writers were born in Prague (currently in the Czech Republic, but at that time a part of the Austro-Hungarian Empire), to Jewish families; both were German speakers, producing literature in German. In light of concepts of identities and their frontiers, and considering the dynamics between belonging and possessing, Rubešová directs her focus to decoding the rhetoric used by their opponents, "that part of the public discourse that makes conscious or unconscious use of national, cultural and political rhetoric in order to justify their claims."

Investigating what may have been the identity(ies) of Kafka, how his personal history connects to the Czech Republic, Germany and Israel, and how he is still perceived in these countries, as portrayed by printed media, Rubešová observes that the "case of the diverse interpretations of Kafka's personality and legacy constitutes an interesting meeting point of notions of individual and collective identities"; a perfect "battlefield" for the attempts of appropriation—or "territorialisation," as she calls it—as identified and described by her.

In "Science and Society in a Utopian Map," Marianna Forleo examines Edwin Abbott Abbott's *Flatland, a Romance of Many Dimensions*, written in 1884. Considered a metaphor for British society at that time, the romance is narrated by a square called "A. Square," who lives in "Flatland," a two-dimensional world inhabited by geometrical figures. His (Square is a male character) life changes when a Sphere intersects the Cartesian plane, detaches him from it and lifts him "in [the] Space, giving A. Square the opportunity to see his plane world from above and to get perceptible proof of the existence of height."

Forleo highlights the cultural transition operated by such (intercultural) contact (mainly, but not exclusively this one, since Square is also introduced to other unexplored dimensions, like "Pointland" and "Linealand"), a transition that is similar to the one experienced during the Victorian age at the end of the eighteenth century, when "England was the centre of a scientific and social revolution" and "people established a new relationship with Nature thanks to the machine": this way, "industrialisation led to a social revolution that upset the secular hierarchy and human relations and brought about a new picture of the world."

Analysing the use of scientific language as a tool for the explanation of the world in utopian texts, as well as the description of utopian cities, Forleo reflects on the successive recreations of the notion of "space"—including its conception as a "mental place"—and the dimensional and intellectual relativity of the most diverse contexts in which "signs of a new culture" can rest hidden.

In view of what Schuerkens (2003, 212) calls "one of the most significant tendencies of the twenty-first century," that is, "the interdependency of the world caused by many transnational relations, processes and flows," it must be expected that studies involving the questions that permeate these chapters become more and more interrelated, increasing their complexity. Sreberny-Mohammadi (1996, 19) writes that:

> Attempts to clarify the scope and meaning of culture, to identify and understand the new forms of identity, and to study the role of the media as sites of production of meaning and as disseminators of particular kinds of cultural products, will remain central to developing the analysis of the processes of globalisation.

With the reflections, ideas and topics proposed here, this volume hopes to be contributing to this task.

CHAPTER ONE

CARTOGRAPHIES OF TRANSCULTURALITY: REGION AS "DIALOGUE ZONE"

FERNANDO KUHN

Millions of people travel every day. In 2011, according to data from the United Nations World Tourism Organisation, the number of international arrivals reached 983 million, corresponding to 2,693,150 travellers per day (UNWTO 2012). Going to the workplace, attending business meetings, visiting family or friends, and studying are frequent reasons for travelling. But there is also tourism: and in this respect, a great, and increasing, number of people travel without being motivated by any professional or personal obligation.

As a powerful economic activity involving a wide range of distinct interests, the tourism industry possesses many tools and strategies to make a place "attractive"—as has been noted by authors such as Gold and Ward (1994), Ward (1998), Kirshenblatt-Gimblett (1998), Kotler et al. (1999), Palmer (1999) and Kotler, Haider and Rein (2002). But whatever the quality of the efforts designed to "convert a location into a destination" (Kirshenblatt-Gimblett 1998) or the real uniqueness of a given place being marketed, the fact is that not everyone is attracted by places portrayed as representing "the encounter between past and future," as "East meets West," or as displaying the convergence of civilisations. Such mottos would never work if there was not also, for certain kinds of people, some prior interest in experiencing such differences. Tourism is thus an example of how many people, all around the world, are curious about and open to establishing some kind of interaction with the "diverse."

During their stays—which are frequently short—tourists generally catch no more than a glimpse of the way locals live. Having the opportunity to share their streets, sights, weather and food for a few days, such visitors can hardly imagine the feeling of "ownership" or belonging to that place (except in cases where their personal interests and careful planning provide them with a full set of references about the places to be visited). But what should one say about people living in neighbouring areas who do indeed share at least some aspects—such as landscape, language, architecture or musical style—of what is normally called "culture"? Can we say that people belonging to close "micro-cultures" integrate the same "culture"? Do they share the same identity, or maybe "fragments" of identity? And furthermore: What is still unique and absolutely non-shared, or non-shareable, in the contemporary society of an increasingly globalised world?

Notions and limits of culture

As is widely known, "culture" and "identity" are not terms that have a generally agreed definition. The classic definition by Edward Burnett Tylor (1871), for instance, explains "culture" as "that complex whole which includes knowledge, belief, art, morals, law, custom, and any other capabilities and habits acquired by man as a member of society." For Boas (1930, 79), it "embraces all the manifestations of social habits of a community, the reactions of the individual as affected by the habits of the group in which he lives and the product of human activities as determined by these habits."

Hall (1997, 2) offers a comprehensive description that seems particularly appropriate to any discussion involving the limits of cultures:

> "Culture" is one of the most difficult concepts in the human and social sciences and there are many different ways of defining it. In more traditional definitions of the term, culture is said to embody the "best that has been thought and said" in a society. It is the sum of the great ideas, as represented in the classic works of literature, painting, music and philosophy—the "high culture" of an era. Belonging to the same frame of reference, but more "modern" in its associations, is the use of "culture" to refer to the widely distributed forms of popular music, publishing, art, design and literature, or the activities of leisure time and entertainment which make up the everyday lives of the majority of "ordinary people"—what is called the "mass culture" or the "popular culture" of an age. High culture versus popular culture was, for many years, the classic way of framing the debate about culture—the terms carrying a powerfully evaluative charge … In recent years, and in a more "social science" context, the word "culture" is used to refer to whatever is distinctive about the "way of life" of a people, community, nation or social group. This has come to be known as the anthropological definition. Alternatively, the word can be used to describe the "shared values" of a group or of a society—which is like the anthropological definition, only with a more sociological emphasis.

In times when "the world's societies are too systematically interconnected to permit any easy isolation of separate or independently functioning systems," as Clifford (1993, 61) observes, the comprehension of "culture" as an unfinished and incomplete result of dynamic processes permanently in operation, has gradually emerged as an alternative to the traditional vision, based on "social homogeneity, ethnic consolidation and intercultural delimitation" (Brancato 2006), and which conceives human beings as "cultural" or even "territorial" and "national" subjects, "bearers of a culture, located within a boundaried world, which defines them and differentiates them from others" (Grillo 2003).

This new "processual" discourse of culture (Baumann 1999, 90), in which "cultures and communities are seen as constructed, dialectically from above and below, and in constant flux," and which puts emphasis on "multiple identities or identifications whose form and content are continuously being negotiated" (Grillo 2003, 160), has favoured the rise of a diversity of views regarding the dynamics of cultural interactions.

As Lähdesmäki (2010, 21) observes, while in a non-academic context the concepts of multiculturalism, interculturalism, cross-culturalism, transculturalism, cultural dialogue, cultural pluralism and cultural mosaic "have often been used as synonyms, or the contents of the different concepts are difficult to distinguish from one another," these several ways of discussing, defining and representing the focus of cultural diversity "criss-cross in academic and everyday discussions."

While for Benessaieh (2010, 19), "interculturality is often used to express the right to difference in relations of a dualistic nature between minorities or marginalised cultures and the majority or dominant cultures … which have historically tended to be tense or conflictive," for Guerrero Arias (in Stolle-McAlister 2007, 165, and as quoted by Medina-Lopez-Portillo and Sinnigen 2009),

> interculturality is not the simple coexistence of different cultures, but rather the sharing of these cultures in their difference, and sharing is only possible from living everyday life among culturally differentiated communities, each with its own and distinct meanings of existence. It implies dialogical meetings and a continuous relation of alterity between concrete subjects, among human beings endowed with distinct visions of the world, among those that produce symbolic exchanges of senses and meanings.

The term "transculturation" was formulated by Ortiz while analysing Cuban history and society and has been continually revised "to accommodate its utility as a critical tool in literary and cultural studies, postcolonial studies, and anthropology" (Logan 2005–6, 43). Originally, it was applied to express:

> the different phases of the process of transition from one culture to another because this does not consist merely in acquiring another culture, which is what the English word acculturation really implies, but the process also necessarily involves the loss or uprooting of a previous culture, which could be defined as a deculturation. In addition it carries the idea of the consequent creation of new cultural phenomena, which could be called neoculturation. (Ortiz 1947, 102–3)

Although, as Brancato (2006) notes, "the association of the notion of culture to the particle 'trans-', which suggests ideas as different yet complementary as transit, transfer, translation, transgression, transformation, is not entirely new," it is particularly strengthened in a moment when "groups are no longer tightly territorialised, spatially bounded, historically unselfconscious, or culturally homogeneous" (Appadurai 1991, 191), and the borders between cultures that once were taken as "stable" seem to "evaporate," leading to "the end of illusion that regional borders and cultural identity are congruent" (Sandkühler 2004, 81).

For Brancato (2006), "transculturation," as a model of pluridirectional cultural exchange, may be seen as the predecessor of the newly developed concepts of "transculturality" and its complementary term "transculturalism," although it should not be confused with these.

Trying to "think of cultures beyond the contraposition of ownness and foreignness," and searching for an appropriate concept to deal with the contemporary aspects involved in a discussion about culture, Welsch (1999) examines and discards the concepts of "interculturality" and "multiculturality": the former, once it "seeks ways in which … cultures could nevertheless get on with, understand and recognise one another," for still proceeding "from a conception of cultures as islands or spheres"; the latter, for the fact that in spite of taking up "the problems which different cultures have living together within one society" and seeking "opportunities for tolerance and understanding, and for avoidance or handling of conflict," it proceeds "from the existence of clearly distinguished, in themselves homogeneous cultures," and favours the rising of "regressive tendencies which by appealing to a particularist cultural identity lead to ghettoisation or cultural fundamentalism" (Welsch 1999, 196–97). And Azeri (2013, 90, this volume) goes beyond this, classifying multiculturalism as an instrument for the "attack against certain basic human rights."

For Welsch (1999, 197), cultures assume a new form that "is to be called *transcultural* insofar that it *passes through* classical cultural boundaries. The concept of transculturality … seeks to articulate this altered cultural constitution," and is able "to cover both global and local, universalistic and particularistic aspects" and to fulfil "the globalising tendencies as well as the desire for specificity and particularity" (Welsch 1999, 204).

As Sandkühler (2004, 82) explains, this concept assumes that, instead of "homogeneous unities with stable borders," cultures "emerge and change through the dynamics and complexity of flexibly coexisting networks between persons," functioning like "*agendas* within which one thinks and according to which one wants to act in solidarity with others, because more than one person is convinced of its worth for the shaping of life."

For Benessaieh (2010, 15–16), what makes "transculturality" different from "transculturation," "multiculturalism" and "interculturality" is the fact that its concept catches accurately "the sense of movement and the complex mixedness of cultures in close contact," while it also describes "the *embodied situation of cultural plurality* lived by many individuals and communities of mixed heritages and/or experience, whose multifaceted situation is more visible under globalisation."

Thus, "transculturality" seems to be a useful analytic tool in reflections involving a number of situations where other concepts are not so easily applicable: as when Rosaldo (1994, in Kearney 1995, 557) poses the pertinent question of "what happens to notions of cultural uniqueness when individuals acquire cultural repertoires that are binational?"; or when immigrants living their lives across national borders have to "respond to the constraints and demands of two or more states" (Glick Schiller et al. 1995, 54); or when, as Meredith (1998, 3) observes, "postcolonial does not mean that 'they' have gone home … 'they' are here to stay, indeed some of 'us' are them, and therefore the consequential imperative of relationship negotiation"; or, also, when "culture" itself becomes "increasingly deterritorialised" (King 1991, in Kearney 1995; Lie 2002; Brancato 2006), in what Kearney (1995, 557) calls a "nightmare" for contemporary cross-cultural correlational studies, as a consequence of the constantly increasing extension and pace of global diffusion of information; and when, in the same sense, once "large numbers of people, no longer rooted in a single place, go to great lengths to revitalise, reconstruct, or reinvent not only their traditions but their political claims to territory and histories from which they have been displaced" (Glick Schiller et al. 1995, 52), "culture" is "reterritorialised," i.e., it "takes roots in places away from their traditional locations and origins"—a phenomenon that "embraces a series of processes ranging from diffusion from their origin across borders (spatial, temporal and cultural) to establishment in a new place in a new form" (Short and Kim 1999, 78, quoted in Lie 2002).

Transcultural identities

In suggesting how "transculturality" can be understood, Benessaieh (2010, 29) refers to a "cross-cultural competence, a cohesive *identity* that transcends frontiers or time, or a plural sense of self for individuals and communities who see themselves as continuously shifting between flows and worlds, rather than *identifying* with a single, monolithic culture."

As was mentioned above, similar to what happens with "culture," the term "identity" is understood in several senses. Calling it an "elastic concept," Jamieson (2002) refers to a number of researchers who have commented on the diverse uses being made of the term. Authors from a range of disciplines in the field of social sciences have claimed that despite being widely used and discussed (increasingly since the 1960s and 1970s, as Weigert (1983) notes), its occurrences are rarely based on a determinate conceptualisation. According to Oring (1994, 211–12), "definitions of 'identity' are vague if not absent entirely." "Identity," as perceived by Brubaker and Cooper (2000, 1), "tends to mean too much … , too little … or nothing at all." For Triandafyllidou and Wodak (2003), "studying identity, be it ethnic, cultural, linguistic, national or regional, in the contemporary context becomes troublesome" due to "a whole range of social and cultural forms that co-exist uncomfortably with existing definitions of social identity."

Gleason (1983) writes:

> Today we could hardly do without the word identity in talking about immigration and ethnicity. Those who write on these matters use it casually; they assume the reader will know what they mean. And readers seem to feel that they do—at least there has been no clamour for clarification of the term. But if pinned down, most of us would find it difficult to explain just what we do mean by identity. Its very obviousness seems to defy elucidation: identity is what a thing is! How is one supposed to go beyond that in explaining it? But adding a modifier complicates matters, for how are we to understand identity in such expressions as "ethnic identity," "Jewish identity," or "American identity"?

Examining the distinct meanings frequently associated with the term, Brubaker and Cooper (2000) argue against its use also as a *category of analysis* instead of solely a *category of practice*, and employ the term "nation" as an analogy: "'Nation' is a widely used category of social and political practice … But one does not have to use 'nation' as an analytical category to understand and analyse … appeals and claims" made in the name of "nations" (Brubaker and Cooper 2000, 5). The problem, according to the authors, is "not *that* a particular term is used, but *how* it is used," and depending on "the context of its use and the theoretical tradition from which the use in question derives," "identity" itself emerges as a "richly ambiguous" concept.

Brubaker and Cooper (2000) propose the partition of "identity" into a number of processes and conceptual tools, expressed in "less congested terms," such as the categorisation and identification of self and others, the sense of self-understanding and the construction of feelings of commonality, connectedness, groupness or belonging with other. Despite agreeing with such disaggregation of the term, Jamieson (2002, 509) observes that:

> Many theoretical traditions within sociology do indeed offer accounts of identity that itemise a package of processes. Moreover, authors who theoretically stress the fluidity of identity often also acknowledge and attempt to explain everyday common sense perception of continuity of self, and a not unusual sense that many people have of always being "much the same." It remains widely taken for granted that some sense of continuity of self, the anticipation of a future and a memory of the past, is intrinsic to the human condition and this is often implicit, if not openly acknowledged in much sociological theory. A combination of diversity and fluidity on the one hand and of core and continuity on the other is not a paradox for sociological traditions that discuss the social construction of "the self." The concept of "the self" makes it clear that people have only one self but many aspects of self-identity. Moreover, there are some clues in long established traditions of sociological work concerning why some aspects of the self are more primary or core than others.

"Identity" may mean simply "the consciousness of the feeling of belonging to a social network or a locality or an area and the feeling of oneness with these," as defined by Heller (2011, 5). But as Neumann (1993, 210, in Kuzio 2001, 345) points out, it is "inconceivable without difference." Thus, it can refer to "the ways in which individuals and collectivities are distinguished from other individuals and collectivities in their social relations," as Jenkins (1996, 4, in Georgalou 2009, 110) proposes. Armstrong (1982, 5, in Kuzio 2001, 345) even argues that "groups tend to define themselves not by reference to their own characteristics but by exclusion, that is, by comparison to 'strangers.'"

According to Georgalou (2009, 110), it bears two basic meanings: "the one has to do with absolute sameness, while the other encompasses a notion of distinctiveness which as Triandafyllidou and Wodak (2003, 210) acknowledge, 'presumes consistency and continuity over time.'"

The concept of identity adopted by Hall (1996, 3–4)

> accepts that identities are never unified and, in late modern times, increasingly fragmented and fractured; never singular but multiply constructed across different, often intersecting and antagonistic discourses, practices and positions. They are subject to a radical historicisation, and are constantly in the process of change and transformation. ... Though they seem to invoke an origin in a historical past with which they continue to correspond, actually identities are about questions of using the resources of history, language and culture in the process of becoming rather than being: not "who we are" or "where we came from," so much as what we might become, how we have been represented and how that bears on how we might represent ourselves. Identities are therefore constituted within, not outside representation.

In a transcultural perspective, this "process of becoming," which combines "diversity and fluidity" with "core and continuity," can be seen as a context that "blends the preservation of the affective ties of the home culture with the acquisition of instrumental competencies required to cope successfully in the mainstream culture" (Suárez-Orozco 2004, 193). Welsch (1999, 204) affirms that "transcultural identities comprehend a cosmopolitan side, but also a side of local affiliation (cf. Hannerz 1990). Transcultural people combine both."

Spaces of transculturality

The discussion of such processes in which encounters and interplays of cultures and identities take place seems inherently associated with the idea of "space," which, according to De Certeau (1984, 117, quoted in Lie 2002, 4), can be viewed as "a practised place." Pratt (1991, 34) introduces the concept of "contact zones," defined as "social spaces where cultures meet, clash, and grapple with each other, often in contexts of highly asymmetrical relations of power, such as colonialism, slavery, or their aftermaths as they are lived out in many parts of the world today." In another work, Pratt (1992, 6) deploys the term to denote "the space of colonial encounters, the space in which peoples geographically and historically separated come into contact with each other and establish ongoing relations."

Bhabha (1994, 218) points out that "the non-synchronous temporality of global and national cultures opens up a cultural space—a third space—where the negotiation of incommensurable differences creates a tension peculiar to borderline existences." Hollingshead (1998) observes that "many places and people exist ambivalently in 'displaced' or 'under-recognised' third spaces—located within in-between forms of supposed difference." Nederveen Pieterse (2009, 72) discusses the "interstices," or sites of "intersticial emergence" (Mann 1986), informal spaces inhabited by diasporas, migrants, exiles, refugees, and nomads. Lie (2002, 7) quotes Turner's definition of "liminality," as "potentially and in principle a free and experimental region of culture, a region where not only new elements but also new combinatory rules may be introduced" (citing Turner 1982, 28), a context where "new ways of acting, new combinations of symbols, are tried out, to be discarded or accepted" (citing Turner 1977, 40). Crang, Dwyer and Jackson (2003, 441) conceive of "transnationality" as "a multidimensional space that is multiply inhabited and characterised by complex networks, circuits and flows." Heller (2011, 7) refers to border areas as "areas of interference ... which are marked by overlaps and coincidences of cultural phenomena and activities of different groups of population and of reciprocal relations between these groups" and whose populations develop a specific identity for this border area—a process that Heller (2011, 7) calls "interferentiality."

Lie (2002) compiles a number of terms frequently employed to allude to these "spaces of intercultural communication" or "zones of transcultures," such as "borders," "boundaries," "borderlands," "border zones," "cultural fronts and frontiers." Banerjee and German (2010, 26) bring up the "distinction between countries, which have borders (border is defined as a geographic territorial limit or a geopolitical boundary) and cultures which have frontiers (frontier is defined as a socio-cultural limit/boundary)" as drawn in the then forthcoming work by Buzzi and Megele (2011).

Lie (2002, 18) argues:

> Blurred genres (Geertz 1973), cultural interplay, cultural mélange, cultural bricolage, métisse, mulatto, glocalisation (Robertson 1995), pluralism, syncretism, universalism… We seem to be running out of concepts to address the same. But […] what is of interest to our discussion here is the idea of cultural mixing through a process of encounter and negotiation. The mix is not only in-between cultures, but also in-between what we now have termed the global and the local, or the processes cultural globalisation and cultural localisation. Furthermore, this cultural mixing often takes place, as we have seen, in bordered spheres, zones characterised by inbetweenness, borderlands or, based on Turner's theory of liminality and situated within

the field of anthropological communication studies: "liminal/oid spaces of intercultural communication."

Lie (2002, 20) calls "hybridised transculturality" the "state of intercultural transformation" when "the space transforms into a participatory negotiated hybrid space of cultural forms and elements. It is a state of equality … characterised by lived and integrated differences." In such a context, according to Lie (2002, 20), "instead of emphasizing similarities the different cultural elements have come to be known, accepted, shared and lived by the different cultural groups. The entanglement has formed a new culture."

Steingress (2010, 6) points out that the "new spaces of cultural production and experience" that define "transcultural hybridisation" appear as a "consequence of a new life-style that is not limited by borders of national culture" (brought by "post-national cultures") and "of social relations that characterise social reality in postmodern society and allow transcendent cultural production and experience" (citing Alexander 2003). In the same way, Heller (2011, 7) admits that "interferentiality is not restricted to border areas." Kennedy and Roudometof (2001, 22) also affirm that "just like people, cultures can and do migrate, increasingly assisted by electronic communications and the mass media in addition to being carried through inter-personal social exchanges," so leading to the formation of "communities of 'taste,' shared beliefs, or economic interests" and makes transnationalism "necessary, unavoidable and advantageous," a "built-in feature of the cultural, social, political and economic lives of many people everywhere."

An example of this kind of communities emerging from transnational practices—those adopted by backpackers with origins in highly educated middle class backgrounds—is offered by Binder (2003, 5), who introduces the term "globedentity" to describe "a type of identity construction that not only refers to the individual but reflects the world (globe) in this identity."

According to Morley and Robins (1995, 1), once the flows of people, culture, goods and information have pulled the natural limits of communities or nations beyond physical boundaries (such as geographical distance, seas or mountain ranges), we must start thinking "in terms of communications and transport networks and of the symbolic boundaries of language and culture—the 'spaces of transmission' defined by satellite footprints or radio signals—as providing the crucial, and permeable boundaries of our age."

Third space, contact zone, liminality… Basically, what occurs within such territories and configures them as "spaces of transculturality" is the convergence of identities, cultures and place (thus converted into space).

This is an encounter that, according to the context and the interpretation, can be primarily viewed as involving some kind of conflict, dominance, imposition and its consequent adaptations (the third space perceived as an "arena" where different cultures struggle); or, instead, this intersection can be taken as a continuous exchange, a dialogue—of experiences, tastes, ways of life, beliefs—favoured by the discovery of alterity and diversity, as well as the desire or need for widening horizons, be them social, cultural, financial or whatever (the same spirit that makes people interested in attending fairs, festivals, expositions, conferences)—surpassing the feeling of being "limited by the size of our world" (Forleo 2013, 145, this volume).

While suggesting that major museums loosen their "sense of centrality" in an effort to assume the nature of "specific places of transit, intercultural borders, contexts of struggle and communication between different communities," Clifford (1997, 212–13) apparently employs the term for the two situations, defining "contact zones" as "places of hybrid possibility and political negotiation, sites of exclusion and struggle," but also as "an intermediate zone of coexistence in which people, who originally were geographically and historically separated, meet." Therefore, both visions—third place as "arena" or "fair"—do not necessarily exclude the aspects that are more visible with respect to the other one; nevertheless, conflict and dialogue are rarely focused on simultaneously. The very notion of "contact zone" is clearly inclined to the former, once it evokes colonial and slavery periods.

Conversely, it is the latter vision that lies behind many concepts regarding the "third space." Also discussing the role of museums, Gere (1997, 63), for instance, proposes they be seen "as a node in a network of interactive relations, where culture, communities and people can meet and exchange ideas," and supports the notion of the "dialogic museum" (elaborated by Wei Tchen in Karp, Kreamer and Lavene 1992), described as "a cultural free space for open discussion."

As MacDonald (1992, 161, also quoted in Gere 1997, 63–64) notes, "the globetrotting mass media, international tourism, migration, and instant satellite links between cultures are sculpting a new global awareness and helping give shape to what Marshall McLuhan characterised as the global village." Within this context, a number of factors are operating to emphasise the importance of actions and perceptions involving the notion of "dialogue." These factors include the rising of "communities of taste" (as observed by Kennedy and Roudometof 2001); the increasing appeal of cultural alterity (tourism as a means of constructing identity, as discussed by Picard (2004) and Alonso

González (2006)) and ethnic diversity ("ethnoscape" being sold "as spectacle," according to Shaw, Bagwell and Karmowska 2004); the growing importance of the revenues attracted by the tourism industry and, consequently, the "reinvention of the city as a 'destination,' rather than a domicile" (Holmes 2001, 37); and the multiple efforts carried out in order to promote districts, cities, communities, regions and nations (as discussed by Kotler et al. 1999; Kotler, Haider and Rein 2002; Kearns and Philo 1993; Gold and Ward 1994; Ward 1998; Kirshenblatt-Gimblett 1998; Fainstein and Judd 1999; and Shaw, Bagwell and Karmowska 2004). Although these factors may not play out in the sphere of international relations, they do at least concern the situations of people's everyday lives.

That is the case, for instance, for what Bishop (2011, 637) calls "foodscape," while describing Singapore's Orchard Road, a place of "convivial cosmopolitanism" that embraces "a heterogeneity of food outlets … and ethnic origins of food," where "the heterogeneity is embodied and defined by spatial/temporal architectures and rhythms of everyday practices" and "multiple uses, identities, and relationships are played out through complex micro-regions of time and place." Ahluwalla (2003, in Duruz, Luckman and Bishop 2011, 599) refers to food markets, food halls, hawker centres, street stalls, ethnic cafes, coffee shops as places where people from distinct backgrounds "converge to buy and sell food, conduct business, share news and information, as well as to engage in various social, cultural, religious and political practices." For Duruz, Luckman and Bishop (2011, 599), these are "spaces in which rigid, racialised identities are disrupted by physical intimacy and exchanges, and where older colonial forms are being reworked and recaptured to reflect new cosmopolitan experiences."

Aside from descriptions related to musical and literary practices, "dialogue" is defined by the *Merriam-Webster Dictionary* as:

> *a*: a conversation between two or more persons; *also*: a similar exchange between a person and something else (as a computer)
> *b*: an exchange of ideas and opinions <organised a series of *dialogues* on human rights>
> *c*: a discussion between representatives of parties to a conflict that is aimed at resolution <a constructive *dialogue* between loggers and environmentalists>

In its turn, the *Free Online Dictionary, Thesaurus and Encyclopaedia* draws from the *American Heritage® Dictionary of the English Language* the same definitions of "a" and "b," while adding a usage note to the effect that: "In recent years the verb sense of *dialogue* meaning 'to engage in an informal exchange of views' has been revived, particularly with reference to communication between parties in institutional or political contexts. Although Shakespeare, Coleridge, and Carlyle used it, this usage today is widely regarded as jargon or bureaucratese." The same website also quotes "-Ologies and -Isms" (The Gale Group 2008), which defines the term as "a frank exchange of ideas, spoken or written, for the purpose of meeting in harmony."

For the *Oxford Dictionary of British and World English*, "dialogue" as a noun means, "a discussion between two or more people or groups, especially one directed towards exploration of a particular subject or resolution of a problem," while as a verb it is explained as to "take part in a conversation or discussion to resolve a problem."

The *Cambridge Advanced Learner's Dictionary and Thesaurus* presents the term as "formal talks between opposing countries, political groups, etc.," whereas for the *Longman English Dictionary Online* it is a "a discussion between two groups, countries etc." Finally, the *Macmillan Dictionary* calls it "a process in which two people or groups have discussions in order to solve problems."

In summary, "dialogue" is understood as a conversation, a discussion, or an exchange of ideas and opinions. It is established by people, groups, institutions and countries, and usually it involves an attempt to achieve an agreement to solve problems, exchange views, or simply meet in harmony. When such conditions and intentions prevail at the convergence of space, (distinct) cultures and identities, this "third space" of negotiation is converted into an area of dialogue. Rather than the concept of the "contact zone," which tacitly suggests the presence of some form of conflict, the notion of "dialogue zone" assumes that the advantages derived from a cosmopolitan conviviality are recognised, desired and pursued by those who take part in it.

Mapping the dialogue zone

If translated into mathematical terms, the idea of a third space might sound as simple and basic as a definition of the "intersection of sets," which according to the *American Heritage® Dictionary* can be understood as "a set that contains elements shared by two or more given sets." The representation of two circumferences overlapping in a shadowed area seems a temptingly powerful analogy to suggest that shared spatialities may favour the interaction of identities and "cultures"—a term that, as Jack and Phipps (2005, 11) observe, "used metonymically, is also a commonplace and useful shorthand for referring to peoples and nations"—

and by means of this everyday negotiation of diversity (Amin 2004), lead to the forging of commonalities in the course of time.

The image can be useful for purposes of generalisation, but distinguishing the contours of such areas and measuring the extensions of "cultures" is obviously not so simple. Jessop et al. (2008, 390) highlight the attempts carried out by scientists from distinct disciplines over the last three decades to elaborate an adequate account of sociospatial relations and their reorganisation after being transformed by "the crisis of North Atlantic Fordism, the intensification of 'globalisation,' and the concomitant restructuring of inherited geographies of capital accumulation, state regulation, urbanisation, social reproduction, and sociopolitical struggle," resulting in four specific "spatial lexicons": territory, place, scale and network.

Jessop et al. (2008, 390) remark that during the 1980s, "places" started to be increasingly understood "as relationally constituted, polyvalent processes embedded in broader sets of social relations," in opposition to the previous view, that considered them merely as "fixed, areal, self-contained, and more or less unique" units of sociospatial organisation. At the close of this decade, attention turned to "the claim that the Westphalian nexus between national territory and sovereignty has been subject to 'unbundling'" (citing Agnew and Corbridge 1994; Taylor 1994) and to "discussions regarding the changing territorialities—and, more generally, the spatialities—of statehood followed" (citing Brenner et al. 2003). In the 1990s, Jessop et al. (2008, 390) continue, "efforts to decipher how inherited global, national, regional, and local relations were being recalibrated through capitalist restructuring and state retrenchment" led to a turn to scale, which addressed "processes of scale-making and scale-jumping, and their impact on the hierarchical (re)differentiation among various intertwined forms of sociospatial organisation such as capitalist economies, state institutions, citizenship regimes, and urban systems." Finally, networks and their "transversal, 'rhizomatic' forms of interspatial interconnectivity" came into focus, especially in "investigations of commodity chains, interfirm interdependencies, governance systems, interurban relations, and social movements," stimulating theoretical debates concerning "the conceptualisation of emergent network geographies and their relation to inherited territorial, place-based, and scalar formations" (Jessop et al. 2008, 390–91).

According to Thrift (1998, quoted in Paasi 2002, 806), "however different the accounts of globalisation may be, the notion of region is central to each of them." If globalisation can be understood as an increase of flows of people, goods, money, information, images and technology

(Featherstone 2006, 389), an "intensification of worldwide social relations which link distant localities in such a way that local happenings are shaped by events occurring many miles away and vice versa" (Giddens 1990, 64), the impact of the "global space," taken "as the space of the afar, the abstract, the virtual, the encroaching, the hegemonic" (Amin 2004, 33), over "the space of the intimate, the familiar, the near, the embodied" that constitutes "the local" (Amin 2004, 33), provoked, in reaction, "the reinforcement of … localism" (Nederveen Pieterse 2009, 70), a response materialised in a growing interest in "the local," which has become visible as a resistance, as the source of particularities and variety, and as what gives sense to individuals and communities (Braman 1996, 27). "Regionalisation" emerges in the context of the relative weakening of nation-states: now pressured by demands from above and from below in matters concerning economies, markets, media, societies and cultures, they transfer their sovereignty to "transnational regions" while delegating their competences to the local spheres (Bayardo and Lacarrieu 1999, 17) and to "sub-national regions." "Globalisation," thus, "encourages macro-regionalism, which, in turn, encourages micro-regionalism" (Cox 2005, 147)—both processes are usually called "regionalisation" (Bechev 2004, 77–79).

Often used by geographers as synonymous with "place" (Pred 1984; Johnston 1991; Allen et al. 1998; also quoted by Paasi 2002, 806), the term "region" has been employed to allude not merely to a given scale between the local and the national (Paasi 2002, 806), but to a wide range of geographic, administrative and organisational levels as well—"dimensions," as enumerated by Kuhn (2012): supra-municipal, sub-state or sub-provincial; supra-state, supra-provincial or sub-national; autonomic; supra-national or sub-continental (Basque Country, Istria, Magreb, Lapland, Scandinavia, EU, Mercosur); supra-continental (Mediterranean, Asia-Pacific Economic Cooperation, Middle East and North Africa (MENA, in the coinage of the World Bank)); and geo-cultural or geo-linguistic (Sinclair, Jacka and Cunningham 1996; Straubhaar 1997)—crossing the borders of nation-states, but not necessarily as a continuous physical territory (Latin America, Arab World, Asian Diaspora, Lusophone Community) dimension.

Ashbrook (2011, 874) defines "region" as an entity that "may be delineated by culture, function, shared identity, institutions, politics, or combinations of these criteria," where these are aspects that shape space and are subject to contestation by different actors. Ashbrook (2011, 874) quotes Bechev (2004, 84), for whom "regions are invented by political actors as a political programme, they are not simply waiting to be discovered."

Amin (2004, 33), detailing the "compositional forces" that appear as a consequence of globalisation and "are transforming cities and regions into sites immersed in global networks of organisation and routinely implicated in distant connections and influences," emphasises the growing importance of "a relational reading of place that works with the ontology of flow, connectivity and multiple geographical expression, to imagine the geography of cities and regions through their plural spatial connections," causing them to be "recast as nodes that gather flow and juxtapose diversity, as places of overlapping—but not necessarily locally connected" and seen "with no automatic promise of territorial or systemic integrity … without prescribed or proscribed boundaries" (Amin 2004, 34).

Not surprisingly, "boundaries" also arouses new reflections. Mentioning the complexity of the question of whether "a place/region/territory should be understood as a bounded unit," Paasi (2002, 807) notes that:

> As in the case of state territoriality (Taylor 1994), the various organisations, institutions and actors involved in the institutionalisation of a region may have different strategies with regard to the meaning and functions of the region and its "identity" (cf. Allen et al. 1998, 34). "Regions" may be open to economic or cultural processes and concomitantly territorially governed. Some people may identify themselves passionately with the region, others may have a less affective attitude, while some may raise strong resistance to hegemonic spatialised identity narratives and practices. Thus a region/place may be bounded in some sense but not in others. The idea of a boundary as a dividing line is just one possible conceptualisation that has guided (political) geographical thinking since the institutionalisation of the field.

Commenting on the description, provided by Caldo (1996, 285), of geographical identity as an "identity relationship that links a given community to its lived space," Pollice (2003, 107) agrees that "the lived space should be regarded as that moment of integration that combines the physical dimension of geometrical space and the social dimension of relational space," meaning that in such case,

> space is not only "the scenario of human action," but the "representation" of human action, and it condenses the values of the culture that is produced in it (Caldo 1994, 17) … In fact, the territory is precisely a relational space that grows in time as the product of a process of cultural sedimentation; the engine of this process is the identity relationship between a community and the space occupied by the community. As a matter of fact, the space becomes the territory of an actor as soon as it is involved in a social relationship of communication (Raffestin 1983). Later on, Dematteis (1995) explains this definition: a territory is a land that functions as a

> medium of communication, a means for work, production, exchange, co-operation. (Pollice 2003, 107)

Once boundaries are seen to "occur not only at the 'edges' of regions, but are to be found everywhere within them" (Paasi 2002, 807), "region" seems to be (or to comprehend or represent) the place, territory, scale and even network that best conforms to the idea of an area where dialogues take place—as well as all "the intense everyday negotiation of diversity … associated with the exposure to cultural, social, experiential and aspirational difference among those who share a given regional space" that Amin (2004, 39) talks about. Heller (2011, 6) goes to the extent of comparing it to "space" when he says that:

> "Space related identification" is a process during the course of which an individual or a group acquires and shows affiliation to a space or a region. "Space" or "region" is understood as follows: 1, an administrative or a physically delimitable section of the surface of the earth; 2, a space of action without such kinds of borders, that is, a space which is determined by the ranges of activities of the people (space of action); 3, a space characterised by the perception of the people (space of perception); this space can vary concerning its size, shape and features.

Region as dialogue zone

If region can indeed be interpreted as a sphere of mediation embracing what is "inside" (in the "locational" sense), "beside" (in the territorial sense), "above"/"below" (in the scalar sense) and "transversal" (in the interspatial sense); a zone into which multiple spatialities of distinct natures—physical, digital, temporal, mythical—converge; where commonalities are elicited from a continuum of shared experiences; where a diversity of cultural practices and identification processes interplay, contrast and eventually merge, and such conviviality is favoured, encouraged or even induced—if region can indeed be so recognised, then this regional sphere can be recognised as a "dialogue zone," an instance of transculturality.

There have been a number of initiatives designed to generate economic and cultural integration in recent years, especially those involving regions and nation states. Mercosur, Unasur and the European Union are probably the most ambitious. In the first case, however, as Kuhn (2008, 111) notes, despite efforts such as the Protocol for Cultural Integration, signed in 1996, "there is much criticism of the fact that Mercosur has been constituted essentially to promote the economic relations among its members, neglecting other kinds of interaction" (citing Caldeira 1997; Martín-Barbero 1999; Calderón and Szmukler 1999; Ansaldi 2001)—although authors such as Abínzano (2007, in Hauck 2007) do affirm that the most important results achieved by the bloc have been cultural rather than economic. After researching the diffusion of news involving the bloc itself and its member countries by the main newspapers from each country, Kuhn (2008) concludes that relations involving Mercosur and its members are primarily economic and observes that the objectives of the bloc were renewed and reformulated under the scope of the Unasur (South American Union of Nations), an entity that was founded in May 2008 by all South American countries (excluding overseas territories of France and the United Kingdom), with the declared intentions of building "an integration and union among its peoples in the cultural, social, economic and political fields, prioritising political dialogue, social policies, education, energy, infrastructure, financing and the environment, among others."

While in South America there are still many actions to be performed in pursuit of more effective integration, in Europe the process is far more advanced. The conception and implementation of integrative policies at the most varied levels, combined with the aims of preserving its inner rich diversity and favouring distinct kinds of interactions, make the European Union a unique reference point when it comes to envisaging the dynamics that operate in the formation of a dialogue zone.

The European project, however, is also subject to severe criticism, and the "eurosceptical" discourse has been proving its electoral appeal for years. Grundy and Jamieson (2007, 664) observe that social scientists seem divided over the significance of a still-not-settled "European identity" in everyday lives and its possible effects for social cohesion: some stress it as "a stepping stone in progress from divisive nationalism to an inclusive global citizenship," while others see "Europe" as "remaining an empty category meaning different things to different people and nothing much to many, consequently of little consequence for social integration."

Van Reybrouck (2011, 3) argues that "the only 'real' Europeans are those who are highly educated, who travel a lot, who are cosmopolitan, who live in the cities and read Eurozine" (a network of European cultural journals), and the reasons have to do with the "abstract," "bureaucratic," "Kafkaesque" and "multilingual" nature of the European Union: "all European languages are official languages … it means that no one ever talks to anyone … there is no common forum." He concludes that "There is no European public space" (2011, 3).

For Leggewie (2009), a European society will not be able to develop a political identity before the instauration of a common historical consciousness applied to the whole continent. This would allow European memories to be divided between European nations as a "shared memory," instead of dividing European nations off from one another, provoking a "memorial divide." According to Eder (1995, 213), such a "collective learning process in which collective memories are mirrored and related to each other in a new way" could lead to the creation of "a particular 'We' beyond the 'We' created by membership in a community."

Drakulić (2011) draws an ironic picture of a hypothetical "Museum of the European Way of Life," called "Euroskansen" in allusion to the Skansen open-air museum in Stockholm. "Currently under construction"—due to the economic, political and social collapse brought by "the profit-driven economy," "the expensive EU bureaucracy," "the refusal to admit and to integrate immigrants, a workforce that because of the ageing population was much needed," "the adoption of the dominant concept of endless economic growth, as well as deregulation and outsourcing," and the prevalence of "infotainment, consumerism and individual concerns," all combined with "the financial and ecological crisis"—Euroskansen "will provide the main source of income for the population of the Old Continent" when in 2050 its guided tours will introduce tourists from all over the world to the "paradise lost" of hospitals with free medical provision, public schools and low-cost public transport, bookstores, newspaper kiosks, free public lectures and seminars"—a "brilliant idea for how Europeans could survive, maintaining their way of life and even profiting from it!"

The irony is revealing of a "European way of life" that is somehow shared and which probably includes diversity, as Shevchenko (2011, 2) affirms when claiming that Ukraine has a European nature. The example of what one can find in a short walk from the Mickiewicz monument in Lviv to Serbian Street or from the Armenian Church to the Roman Cathedral ("Polish or Russian songs," "Jewish jokes," "a Budapest-style goulash," "a Munich-style Eisbein," "a shot of Czech Becherovka or Austrian Marillenschnaps") may indeed capture a feeling of Europeanness, but then the same could be said about many European cities being Asian. It is particularly useful, however, to endorse what Delanty (2007, 3) perceives as a "hyphenated notion of civilisation" constituting a "plural phenomenon," the need to redefine the notion of "three historical Europes" (Western Europe including "the wider colonial context"; Central Eastern Europe including "the engagement with Russia and the wider Slavic dimension"; Southeastern Europe including "the Ottoman, Byzantine, and

Slavic heritages") into a vaster civilisational area, taking into account the many common strands that shaped each of them.

Schlögel (2004, 2) discerns the resurgence, "more strongly than ever," of historically different regions throughout Europe, indicating that the once-polarised continent of the Cold War has dissolved into a multipolar Europe, with its "differences, these centrifugal forces, and also with this strength"—areas like Northeast Europe around the Baltic Sea "bearing the stamp of the Hanseatic League"; Southeast Europe, the area influenced by Istanbul, including part of the Black Sea region, the Aegean Sea and the Balkans, extending as far as Bucharest and Sofia, and even the south of Russia, the Crimea and the Ukraine; Eastern Europe "in the real sense, i.e. the Russian Federation, Belarus and the Ukraine"; Central Europe, "the region which cannot be precisely defined ... towns such as Milan and Vienna, Budapest and Bratislava, Warsaw and Vilnius, Lemberg and Cracow, Prague and Munich," where a "strong consciousness of a communal history and tradition that is open to modernisation still prevails"; Western Europe "with its centres of Brussels, Luxembourg, Strasbourg ... London, Paris and Amsterdam, with the great 'Blue Banana' axis from Manchester via the Rhine and Frankfurt am Main to Marseilles, Barcelona and Turin": and Southern Europe, the area influenced by Rome (Schlögel 2004, 2–3).

While this feeling of Europeanness is not restricted to the countries that comprise the European Union, perceptions concerning the bloc itself have been changing since its foundation according to the orientation of its policies and under specific circumstances. De Jager (2009, 3) analyses the dominant metaphors used to describe the supposed nature of the European Union:

> Since the establishment of the European Coal and Steel Community, the project Europe has been evolving towards a state at the European level: a United States of Europe. The European integration process has therefore been characterised by an aim to weaken the position of the member states and to erase national borders. The European Commission therefore increasingly focused on regions during the 1980s and 1990s, and the European project was therefore often described as a Europe of the regions or a new medieval Europe. The creation of a common market with economic and social cohesion was followed by acts and policies to demarcate, border and protect the common European space. This has inspired scholars, politicians, the media and artists to describe the EU as a fortress Europe. Especially scholars have conceptualised the EU's attempts to govern external territories, in order to keep its own internal space safe and stable, as a Europe as an empire. The metaphors are thus not isolated concepts but part of a development of constructing and naming the

European project in which the project seems to evolve towards a replication of the nation-state.

Particularly in what concerns regionalisation, the greater part of the expectations stirred by the imagery of a "Europe of the Regions" were not confirmed (Deas 2004; Hepburn 2007; Painter 2008). According to Hepburn (2007, 2), when in the early 1990s the European Union began to bring regions to take part in its decision-making processes, it was interpreted by regional political actors as "a political, constitutional or economic goal that enabled the realisation of their specific territorial interests," instead of "a uniform theory or pattern of regional engagement in Europe," and the frustration of such demands for autonomy led them to become more eurosceptical. Nevertheless, Painter (2008, 5) notes that whilst the Committee of the Regions "fell a long way short of reconstituting the European Union as anything approaching a federation of subnational regions," in some respect it indeed institutionalises a long-standing enthusiasm for regionalisation inside the bloc.

In the same way, Deas (2004, 3) highlights the advances introduced by policies expressed in the European Spatial Development Perspective (ESDP), that, however incomplete, "proclaimed the view that the EU's future economic, social and political development should be based on the development of horizontally integrated geographic territories rather than on vertical sectors" and the Interreg Community Initiative, intended to prepare border areas for a community without internal frontiers by means of the development of transnational "mega-regions."

Regions—and especially cities—are also exalted under the auspices of the European Cities of Culture programme, which celebrates them as cultural getaways. As Amin (2004, 20) points out, the stimulation of "a 'consumer' cosmopolitanism" inspired by "the virtues of world music, minority ethnic food and festival, regeneration based on multicultures and multiethnic public spaces, and the exoticism of the stranger" helps to reinforce the local economy through new consumption, besides demonstrating "an openness to multiculturalism and multiethnicity."

Such policies and their effects, combined with a number of commonalities already present in the individual or collective imagery or truly experienced in memory and in daily life, as well as the interactions taking place in an increasing diversity of situations, are aspects that distinguish Europe as being an extraordinary context for the observation of transcultural dialogues in process—either taken as a region itself or as an archipelago of regions overlapping in their distinct dimensions.

What we are referring to here may be a city's "sublocal" district that starts receiving migrants from rural areas (as in the case discussed by

Kahraman 2013, this volume); or a city like Copenhagen that compounds with Malmoe the transnational Øresund region; or geocultural/geolinguistic regions in a dispute over the legacy of a writer from a city currently pertaining to a third country and heritage—as in the situation described by Rubešová (2013, this volume) involving Franz Kafka and his "dialogue" with these three traditions; the supranational union comprising twenty-seven countries known as the "European Union," or supra-continental organisations like the Union for the Mediterranean, which encompasses these and sixteen more nations from Africa and the Middle East; the original European continent, with or without including the Asian part of Russia and Turkey; and a variety of different possibilities.

These malleable regionalities—malleable enough to be conformed to within specific but frequently uncertain territories, expanded into imagined affiliations and permeated by flows of every nature—acquire the condition of "third spaces" where cultures and identities meet. While hosting such encounters, they define, mediate and shape them, by means of their ontological geographic, historic, economic, administrative, social, cultural, environmental configuration.

Would it be possible to trace the dynamics of the dialogues that result from such encounters? To map and picture them according to a model taking into account both aspects involving territory and place as those respecting scalar linkages and the fluid connectivity of networks?

The following attempt assumes that dialogues are induced and manifested in ways that fit into a classification. The term "spheres of interaction" is suggested in order to encompass and describe a range of expressions disposed in categories, which consist of "spaces" (divided into "landscapes" and "courses") and "vectors" (divided into "idioms," "science," "arts," "media" and "sports"). It employs for preference examples pertaining to the European Union, sometimes extending into Europe and beyond, but in a few cases other regions are portrayed with the aim of making the example clearer.

Spheres of interaction

"Spheres of interaction" are conceived as the zones in which dialogues occur, presenting either a spatial or a diffusional, vectorial nature. Here, "spaces" are understood as "physical" and relatively permanent structures available for being shared due to the simple fact that "they are there"; it is where occurs a primary, incidental and unavoidable contact with a natural or cultural legacy and with other people who also "happen to be there." "Spaces" comprehend "landscapes" and "courses." "Landscapes" include geographical and architectural aspects invested of a sense of familiarity which may incorporate and evoke identity ties with that particular place. "Courses" are routes that, besides constituting "landscapes," represent a platform (a "bridge") for the convergence of diversities, circuits through which differences circulate and for this reason become the first thing to be held in common.

"Vectors" presuppose a (mental, electronic, digital) movement of ideas, knowledge, forms of expression, and the predisposition for a (secondary type of) contact: "idioms," "science," "arts," "sports" and "media" originated from other contexts ("cultures") may be assessed or not, consumed or not; and when their contents reflect the dialogue itself, it can be said that they are inviting a further (tertiary) type of contact. The examples provided below focus on this latter kind of vector, for the reason that they are not so frequent.

The influence of landscapes in the production of identities is recognised by many authors (Kaplan and Herb 2011, 351; Cusack 2007, 101). For Häyrynen (2000, 16, quoted in Kaplan and Herb 2011, 351), each landscape image "would evoke a geographical area, each region a narrative, thus triggering national pride, melancholy or aesthetic appreciation." In this regard, Schrenk (1999) underlines the contribution of architecture. Riukulehto (2013, 58, this volume) introduces the concept of homely landscapes—"the complex entity of natural, human-made and mental environments that an individual recognises to be his own"—as a tool to define and structure regional identities.

Cusack (2007, 101) proposes "riverscape" as an analogy to "landscape" in order to highlight how rivers have become points of reference in the representation of "national landscapes," considered in view of the fact that a number of regional and national capitals "are built around and closely identified with a particular river, which may come to signify the nation." Being often associated with life and regeneration as well as the passage of time, rivers "have been appropriated as symbols of national vitality," besides providing "an excellent metaphor for the uninterrupted 'flow' or 'course' of national history" (Cusack 2007, 101).

Rivers can also be considered as "courses," in the same sense as oceans, railways, highways, roads and trails are routes for the circulation of diversity. "Courses" can also be non-signalled trajectories that are fixed in a collective memory, as in the Australian aboriginal peoples' practices reported by Bruce Chatwin in *The Songlines*. Braman (1996, 30) sees their "migratory, communal, and aural orientation towards place" as "an example of construction of the local through travel and through a sharing of songs and stories with other groups in a traditional society."

There are a lot of examples of "courses" that due to a variety of historical factors have been impregnated by a "mythical" aura: the U.S. Route 66, with its 2,448 miles (3,940 kilometres) from Chicago to Los Angeles; the imprecise Pan-American Highway, connecting Prudhoe Bay (Alaska) to Ushuaia (Argentina); the Trans-Siberian Railway, with its 5,753 miles (9,259 kilometres), crossing seven time zones between Moscow and Vladivostok or Beijing, in a journey that attracts many foreign tourists and takes eight days to complete; the Orient Express train service between Paris and Istanbul; the Danube river, which crosses seven European countries with its 1,770 miles (2,850 kilometres)…

Among "courses," probably the most famous and rich of meanings is the "Silk Road," but, as Thorsten (2005, 303) explains, "there can be no 'actual' living memory of the Silk Road, just as there is sensu stricto no 'Silk Road.' The expression … was first used in 1877," and "silk, moreover, was only one of the commodities exchanged throughout extensive networks, never a single 'road.'" Anyway, popular narratives diffused in the most varied forms and discourses of tourism and diplomacy, according to Thorsten (2005, 301), have not only transformed it into "fashionable nostalgia, expressing longing for a perceived time when universalism was a norm," but it has also come to signify "belonging to the newest trade and political networks across Asia."

A plan announced by the European Union and designed to improve connections between different modes of transport throughout the bloc includes the implementation by 2030 of a core network of corridors crossing the EU, and a comprehensive network feeding into it to be finalised by 2050. The ten corridors—linking Helsinki to Ravenna, Warsaw to the Midlands, Algeciras to the Ukraine border, Hamburg to Nicosia, Helsinki to Valetta, Genoa to Rotterdam, Lisbon to Strasbourg, Dublin to Brussels, Amsterdam to Marseille, and Strasbourg to Constanta—are expected to become, in time, important routes for the free flow of people and goods, further increasing exchanges and interactions.

As the name suggests, the European Institute of Cultural Routes embraces diversity in its approach to its work. According to its website (<www.culture-routes.lu>), the institution, established in 1997, has been charged "with ensuring not only the continuity but also the development of the cultural routes programme of the Council of Europe." Its actions include collaborating with publishers to explore broad topics like pilgrimage ways, parks and gardens, textiles; producing weekly newsletters with suggestions for ignored heritages and new thematic trails to be discovered; carrying out a work of cultural observation to better inform project carriers about the evolution of pan-European co-operation and cultural tourism; developing conventions for partnerships and objectives aiming at the implementation of projects based on multidisciplinarity; elaborating studies and reports; preparing, assembling and creating exhibitions and publishing and co-publishing multimedia works or products.

Other initiative worth mentioning is EuroVelo, a network of high-quality cycling routes connecting the whole continent, developed by the European Cyclists' Federation. The Iron Curtain Trail, for instance, defined on its website (<www.ironcurtaintrail.eu/en/der_iron_curtain_trail/index.html>) as "a border stretching from the Barents Sea to the Black Sea," is an invitation for people "to retrace and experience the former division of the continent on a 6,800 km cycle track along the length of the former border, combining European culture, history and sustainable tourism," and claims to be contributing "in a lively and very practical way to the creation of a genuine European identity."

Similar actions occur in the areas here considered as "vectors." With respect to "idioms," for instance, the European Bureau for Lesser-Used Languages maintains programmes that encourage mobility and transnational partnerships to motivate participants to learn languages; it also supports Mercator networks of universities on research on lesser-used languages in Europe, and celebrates the European Day of Languages on September 26.

Actions under the heading of "Science" are focused on a range of conferences concerned with collective aspects involving the bloc or the continent (as for instance the "European Tributary States of the Ottoman Empire"), studies programmes (such as the Erasmus Student Network) and exhibitions (such as the "Lost World of the Old Europe: The Danube Valley, 5000–3500 B.C").

"Art," in its most diverse manifestations, has also been favouring and sustaining transcultural dialogues. The Eurovision Song Contest had its first edition in 1956 and since then it has become one of the longest-running television shows in the world, reaching transnational audiences and gathering artists representing more than forty countries. Bolin (2006, 204) compares it to the World's Fairs of high industrialism, affirming that in the same way as these events "promoted the modern nation-states by displaying technical mastery and inventiveness," currently "so too does the Eurovision Song Contest display a nation's mastery and refinement of its culture industry."

Regarding cinema, good examples can be found in movies such as "Donau," "Éxils," "Le Grand Voyage," "Monsieur Ibrahim et les Fleurs du Coran," "Um Filme Falado," "L'Auberge Espagnole," "Ulysses' Gaze" and "Corridor X—The Diasporic Space."

"Donau, Dunaj, Duna, Dunav, Dunarea" ("The Danube"), by Goran Rebic (Austria 2003), is emblematic: it shows a small group of people from different nationalities in a boat traversing the Danube, from Vienna to Sulina. The river is represented both as a landscape and as a course, a means of transportation that puts people in contact—or in dialogue—with distinct realities.

"Éxils" ("Exiles"), by Tony Gatlif (France and Japan 2004), relates the story of two young Parisians who decide to revisit their origins in Algeria, passing through Spain where they have to find work to earn money to complete the journey. Elements representing cultural traditions from these regions are highlighted in the film.

In "Le Grand Voyage," by Ismaël Ferroukhi (France, Morocco, Bulgaria and Turkey, 2004), an old man convinces his young son to accompany him in his pilgrimage from the south of France to Mecca, driving through Italy, Serbia, Turkey, Syria and Jordan, meeting different people and experiencing different habits.

"Monsieur Ibrahim et les Fleurs du Coran" ("Monsieur Ibrahim"), by François Dupeyron (France, 2003), is also about a journey, but of an old Muslin man running a small market in Paris and a Jewish teenager who lives in the same street, to whom he directs paternal feelings. They travel to the Turkish countryside, where the old man introduces his culture to his young friend.

"Um Filme Falado" ("A Talking Picture"), by Manoel de Oliveira (Portugal, 2003), follows a cruise ship heading from London to Bombay with stops in cities permeated by the heritage of ancient civilisations. On board, a history professor tells her daughter about these old cultures.

In "L'Auberge Espagnole" ("The Spanish Apartment"), by Cédric Klapisch (France and Spain, 2002), seven students taking part in the Erasmus programme from different parts of Europe share an apartment in Barcelona, where they become close friends.

"Το βλέμμα του Οδυσσέα/To Vlemma tou Odyssea" ("Ulysses' Gaze"), by Theo Angelopoulos (Greece, 1995), narrates the search, by a film maker, for mythical ancient film reels that supposedly recorded the history and customs of the Balkans. Crossing the region, he encounters his own history.

"Corridor X—The Diasporic Space," by Angela Melitopoulos (Germany, 2006), was conceived as part of "Timescapes," a collective editing project for video. According to its website (<www.videophilosophy.de>), it involves five authors from five countries "that lie along the 'old' European axis between Berlin and Istanbul, and dominated the strategies of the political alliances within Europe before World War I," conforming to a "geographical territory which is becoming a memorical territory" (which the project calls "B-zone"). "Timescapes," in its turn, integrates "Transcultural Geographies," described as "an art and visual research project focusing on the transitory geographies of the Balkans, Turkey and the Caucasus."

"Corridor X" alludes to the above-mentioned Pan-European Corridors (more specifically to the number "ten"), and is a road movie "about a historical transit road connecting Germany and Turkey via Salzburg, Ljubljana, Zagreb, Belgrade, Nis, Skopje, Veles, Thessalonica, and Istanbul." Again according to the project website, it "points to the actual condition" of what used to be "a collective, transcultural space and a common, recollective denominator for migrants from Turkey and Greece" and now is reduced to "a post-war territory in which the situation of mobility and migration has fundamentally shifted toward immobility."

"Corridor X" is also the name of a documentary photo essay presented in 2009 by Davor Konjikusic, a photographer based in Zagreb, about life around the tenth corridor. "Nationale Zéro," by the French collective Tendance Floue, is another example of a photographic work picturing parts of the European Union. Collectively covering the 14,291 miles (23,000 kilometres) of a non-existent highway—the one in the title—over seven months, the ten participant photographers were individually responsible for one section of the journey, mapping out their own route within it, and taking photos every fifty kilometres along the way.

Active in the field of "culture" and "arts," the "Trans Europe Halles—TEH" (<www.teh.net>) introduces itself as "a network of independent cultural centres offering a dynamic forum for ideas, collaborations, and mutual support in the pursuit of intercultural exchange, understanding and artistic freedom." Founded in 1983, it has fifty-one members as well as twenty-one Friend Organisations from twenty-nine European countries, linking cultural actors from Moscow to Amsterdam and from Helsinki to Belgrade. In its turn, "Roots and Routes" is an international network for the promotion of cultural and social diversity in contemporary performing arts and media, by means of educational activities, mobility programmes and stage performances for young music, dance and media talents in diverse European countries.

Also a European network, but of cultural journals, "Eurozine" counts eighty-three partner journals from the whole continent. Launched in 1998, it publishes and translates chosen articles on the Internet, offering its readers a "Europe-wide" overview of current themes and discussions and creating a new space for transnational debate. Its declared "philosophy" salutes European diversity (often "evoked with near euphoria"); dialogue as a means for achieving a common identity; and the spread of political, philosophical, aesthetic, and cultural thought between languages—a "translation of cultures."

With similar objectives, "cafebabel.com" (<cafebabel.co.uk>) claims to be "the first multilingual European current affairs magazine, designed for readers across borders"—it was created in 2001. Investing in participatory journalism and presenting a daily coverage, it represents a channel of expression for what it calls the "eurogeneration," that is "the first generation living Europe on a day-by-day basis thanks to the Erasmus programme, the internet and an increasing level of mobility."

The same concepts behind these two initiatives can be found in the "Euronews" television channel, founded in 1993 under the auspices of seventeen (according to Casero 2001, 11; but "joined by a further eight" according to Chalaby 2005) public television stations belonging to the European Broadcasting Union: the diffusion of a pan-European perspective, a Europe-wide coverage, and the production of multilingual content—its news service is simultaneously available in English, French, German, Spanish, Italian, Portuguese, Russian, Arabic, Turkish, Persian and Ukrainian. However, it has to deal with some specific challenges.

Euronews was shaped as a response to the global influence achieved by CNN with the coverage of international news during the Gulf War two years earlier (Casero 2001; Chalaby 2005; Bourdon 2007). As Casero (2001) remarks, competing in this case means adopting the same format, which involves high costs. When 49% of the company's shares were acquired in 1998 by ITN, a private company from London, Euronews became independent from European political institutions and had to opt for a more commercial logic, which implies more competition. The goal of developing a European identity, equally expensive, had to be set aside.

In criticising the performance of Euronews, especially concerning the matter of European identity, Bourdon (2007, 275) argues that "the reference to Europe as a common space simply cannot function," because "there is no European centre … no European language, not only because of linguistic diversity itself, but also because of a lack of a common sense of time … a common history." In addition, Casero (2001) echoes the arguments of Richeri (1994) and Schlesinger (1996) against the neutral tone employed by Euronews in reporting the news, which in their opinion makes the programmes boring and distant, creating no involvement in the audience.

In opposition, Gripsrud (2007, 486) highlights Euronews's "quite strong presence in both overt and indirect ways in today's European media landscape," and quotes numbers that signify its penetration and financial viability. Gripsrud (2007, 487) observes that pan-European channels "reflect the highly complex map of Europe when it comes to ethnicity, taste and traditions—i.e. culture," thus contributing "in some interesting ways to a partially shared European audiovisual space."

Four years before the creation of Euronews, a cooperation between sixteen members of the European Broadcasting Union and commercial News International's Sky Channel led to the foundation of Eurosport, a successful satellite pan-European channel (Collins 1998; Bourdon 2007, 272) dedicated to the coverage of European and international sporting events in eighteen languages (Chalaby 2005, 166).

As the last vector in this model of "spheres of interaction," "sport" contributes to dialogue on a series of occasions. Although it may lead to conflictive situations, especially when football is in question, it has also been an opportunity for healthy transcultural practices. Even those who cannot attend mega-events like the Olympic Games and the World Cup get involved via media coverage, and this is also true for continental competitions such as the UEFA EURO and the Champions League. On a lower scale, small cities celebrate enthusiastically when their local teams have the chance to take part—as in the Brazilian case—in the Premier, Second, or even Third National League, Prime or Second State Leagues, or in the Brazil Cup, albeit generally for the purposes of taking part in the two eliminatory matches (Kuhn 2009).

Conclusion

As has been seen, some of the examples above result from the implementation of institutional policies, involving planning, coordination and considerable investments, which unequivocally indicates a sense of priority. The remainder can be credited to personal efforts (or "a collective of personal" efforts), equally demonstrating commitment to an idea. The sum of such actions comprises a vibrant, colourful and polyphonic scene that is not easy to find elsewhere.

At the same time, however, and perhaps even in the same places, conflict may irrupt—and economic crises such as the present one always provide the ideal recipe for it. Therefore, concepts addressing the problematic aspects that can emerge in intercultural encounters have not lost their utility, and probably will never lose it. But there is nothing new in xenophobia, there is nothing new in prejudice, and there is nothing new in intolerance, strangeness, distrust. People and peoples are not expected to know, respect and like each other.

What seems relatively new, and even surprising, is that precisely in a moment of extreme interconnectivity and mobility of people, goods and contents, when the world seems smaller, closer and more mixed than ever, and hence when differences supposedly should be aggravated and lead to more discomfort and misunderstanding, an inclusive approach can be so appealing. The initiatives discussed here reveal, above all, not only a disposition for dialoguing, but also for cultivating dialogues. Many of these actions were conceived or stimulated—that is, they are not fruit of unavoidable coincidences, or accidental, forced and harsh "contacts." Europe, or the European Union itself, still may be no perfect Eden for minorities, a land of peaceful and respectful conviviality between people from distinct countries, identities, cultures, ethnicities, or beliefs; but the involvement demonstrated by people and institutions at distinct levels in promoting such values is encouraging. It proves that there is space for hearing and there is space for talking; dialogue is on the agenda.

A whole generation has been growing amidst transculturality, benefitting from it, and experiencing dialogue in their educational and professional practices and more and more in their personal lives as well. On the other hand, "contact," in the conflictive sense, has become multifaceted and fragmented, so many are the ethnicities and nationalities being integrated into contemporary society. Today's threatening "other" can be a future colleague, a future neighbour, a future wife of a brother-in-law, the future owner of a preferred shop. As multiple identities are increasingly being instigated and developed, intolerance tends to imply more difficult choices; it even becomes subjected to negotiation, at least for gathering complicity. Sometimes commonalities may take shape faster than incompatibilities. Dialogue, at the end of the day, may be worthwhile.

As societies seem to be entering a new context wherein the demands, challenges and opportunities concerning identity and cultural diversity begin to deserve more attentive consideration, it may be useful to examine such issues under a distinct framework. Cartographies of transculturality that take into account the concept of "dialogue zone," applied to regional dimensions and based in the spheres of interaction model, as proposed here, offer the convenience of favouring an estimation of the real importance which dialogue has been acquiring in recent years, as well as its potential.

CHAPTER TWO

HOMELY SITES AND LANDSCAPES AS ELEMENTS OF REGIONAL IDENTITY

SULEVI RIUKULEHTO

Identity as a conceptual tool in research work

The concept of identity has strongly differing significations in different branches of science. More than twenty varying meanings and definitions of identity can be found in the research literature. The discourses in natural and human sciences are remote from each other. Obviously, all the discourses cannot be commensurable (Fearon 1999, 4–7; Gleason 1983).

The basic meaning of sameness—identity as expressing the equality of two expressions—is still used in philosophy, mathematics, geometry and logic. One of the basic laws in logic is the law of identity (A≡A). It states that an object is exactly the same as itself. There exists an exact sameness between A and A. The law, of course, is a tautology in nature, but undeniably true. An entity can only be fully identical with itself. Any difference always gives rise to a new, separable identity.

This concept of identity is easy to understand and accept; it is logical and consistent. Things have the same identity if they are exactly identical with each other. Everyone has studied and drawn identical circles and polygons at school as part of basic studies in geometry.

This concept of identity is still largely used in philosophy, but philosophers have also further developed the concept. According to the famous example by David Hume, the identity of a ship obviously stays the same if some single part of the ship is replaced with a new one. It even stays the same if each and every part is substituted one by one (Hume 1739, 326–27). Finally, the identity of the ship is the same even if there is not one original atom in the ship. Hume's notion of identity bears a close relation to the concept of identity in logic and geometry, but his concept is decisively different. The substituting parts may look alike but they are not exactly the same.

In the age of enlightenment, identity took on broader conceptual content, as philosophers like Hume and John Locke used the word when referring to the personality of an individual (Gleason 1983, 910 –11). The two most well-known and referred to classics are Locke's *An Essay Concerning Human Understanding* (1690), and Hume's *Treatise on Human Nature* (1739). The "personal identity" defined by Locke in his essay is an early predecessor of the discourse of identity so common in present-day psychology. Naturally, Locke's concept is still considerably different from the later versions of the concept, but certain similarities can be seen. Separate instances in the literature concerning the identity of an individual have been traced much further back to the Middle Ages (see especially Locke 1690, 162–71 and Hume 1739, 319–34; Akhtar and Samuel 1996).

Identity as we usually know the concept today derives from the main works of the psychologist Erik Eriksson. He was the most important figure in the establishment of this discourse (e.g., Eriksson 1968, 15–25). For Eriksson, identity has to do with one's feelings about one's self, character, goals and origins.

Psychologists have produced an ocean of literature about identity crises and the construction of identity on a personal level. This discourse has been enormously effective in the social sciences. The concept has been widely accepted and further developed in sociology and political science, for example. The range, complexity and differences among the various formulations of the concept are remarkable.

In social discussions identity does not usually mean exact sameness. Usually, identities are taken to be either a social category defined by membership rules, characteristic attributes or expectations; or socially distinguished features that a person takes a special pride in, or accepts as unchangeable and socially consequential. In its most simple form identity is an answer to the question: "Who are you?" (Fearon 1999, 11, 20).

During the last half of the twentieth century concepts of identity were further developed, and parted ways in different branches of social sciences. Identities have been placed into typologies, and these have been used as categories especially in ethnology, sociology and in political science. Such concepts as national identity and ethnic identity serve as examples of the kinds of categories concerned.[1] Political scientists have even developed the concept of state identity: just as individuals are members of social categories, so there are social categories whose members are states (such as the OECD, NATO, the UN and so on). The same kind of identity makes states join together (Wendt 1994).

A different approach has been presented by economists. They have taken identities to be a matter of rational choice: an individual chooses his or her identity from the known alternatives under certain, more or less restricting conditions. For example: in a cricket competition an Indian living in Australia has to choose if he or she is cheering for India or for Australia. Similarly, religious beliefs may be chosen from tens of different alternatives (Sen 2005, 398–406).

The concept of identity is fundamentally changed if identities are viewed as choices. As far as I know, in all other branches of the sciences identities are understood to be relatively stable phenomena.

Choices are made all the time, again and again: coffee or tea? With sugar or without? Which channel? How long a time? The basic character of choice is momentariness. Attitudes, on the contrary, are more fixed but even the strongest attitude may change in seconds. When Chernobyl collapsed, millions of people all around the world changed their attitude towards nuclear power immediately. Institutions are at the other end of the axis. They are changing very slowly—if at all. On the continuum from temporary to permanent, identities are situated somewhere between attitudes and institutions (see fig. 2-1 below). Identity has very little to do with rational choice. An individual cannot change his or her identity momentarily or voluntarily: one day a Caledonian, the other day a proletariat. It seems to me that the economists who emphasise rational choice have partly missed the special nature of the concept of identity.

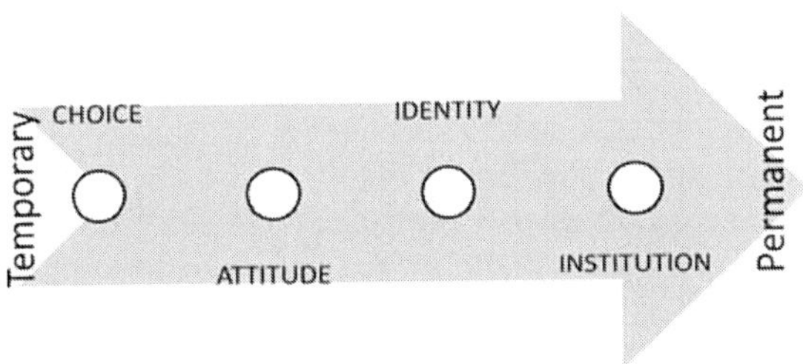

Figure 2-1. *Identity on the continuum from temporary to permanent phenomena.*

The path from the identity of exact sameness to that of momentary choice is long and complicated. There are so many different conceptions concerning identity that some authors prefer not to use it as a research concept at all (instead of "identity," Brubaker and Cooper (2000) recommend substituting concepts such as "identification," "social location," "self-understanding," "commonality" and "groupness.") On the other hand, there have been many attempts to produce syntheses between various conceptions.

A theoretical framework created by Finnish cultural geographer Anssi Paasi has been widely made use of in regional science. His model tries broadly to take hold of the various contents that are presented in the numerous discourses of identities (Paasi 1986; 2000; 2003). The framework is useful if one tries to classify the discourses found in various identity discussions. Paasi distinguishes between the identity of a region and the regional identity of its inhabitants. Two parts can be differentiated in the identity of the region: an objective part (nature, history, etc.), and a subjective part or an image that can be further subdivided into an internal and an external image. These could also be called self-image (internal) and reputation (external). The regional identity of inhabitants, on the other hand, can be differentiated into regional consciousness and regional identification. In regional consciousness Paasi recognises knowledge, emotion and activity. Actually, Paasi's model is a typology in which different kinds of content relating to identities can be recognised at the same time.

The purpose of these kinds of typologies is to structure the concept of identity so that it can be better applied in research work. In reality, it may have the reverse effect: the various discourses, concepts and rationales originating from different traditions may be hard to differentiate from each other. Image, self-image, regional consciousness and identification, the persistence of the place, sameness and whatever else, are interwoven together, and all of them are studied as identities. The neat aim of capturing whole the cluster concept of identities easily results in misunderstandings.

Identity may be defined as the quality of a place or of an object, entirely independent from people, but does this kind of definition make any sense in human science? The concept of identity becomes clearer, more interesting and more useful as a research category if it is reserved for human beings only. There are no identities without people.

If identity is taken to be a quality of people, there still exist many possible ways to further define the concept. Identity may refer to image and to external repute. This kind of identity works as a category in which individual findings are classified. The premise of observation is that people—those of a certain region for example—have similar identities. They are Russians, Germans, Frenchmen or, say, Parisians, Catalonians, etc. Identities may be utilised in analysis as categories into which individual findings are classified. The definition does not necessarily have to be based on regional demarcation. People may be divided otherwise, between proletarians, middle class and bourgeoisie, for example. Often the categories have some administrative basis, and people are dropped into the classes that were anticipated beforehand.

Adherents to another interpretation emphasise the cultural nature of identity. Identity may be dug out from the symbols and codes presented in textual and non-textual sources because it is manifested in discourses, in behavioural patterns and in expectations. This kind of approach is favoured in recent directions in historical and social studies, such as regional history (for "collective identities" in historiography, see: Aronsson 2007, 263–65; Conzen 2001, 91–93; Lancaster 2007, 32–37; Larson 2001, 70, 77; Phythian-Adams 2007, 5).

Instead of being stable, a priori categories, identities can be understood as outcomes in the evolutionary process of individuals. Thus, everybody has a unique personal identity, composed of many elements. This kind of approach to identity is favoured in psychology to the extent that identity, self-image and individuality can hardly be distinguished from each other. In research work the concept of identity should not be restricted to the individual level only (Kaunismaa 1998, 40). Collective identities can be derived from individual identities. Also, collective identities are changing over time and they are useful tools for social scientists and historians: obviously regions can be identified and characterised by the use of regional identities. The evolutionary and procedural nature of collective identities fits well in historiography: both identities and regions are undergoing incessant and mutual change (Cayton 2001, 143–44; Hurt 2001, 175–79).

The significance of the region in identity formation

The region is one of the most important factors on which identity can be based, as it always has an impact on its inhabitants. The environment in which an individual lives may form a steady and lifelong base for that individual. A region (conceptualised as the environment surrounding a human being) forms one's insight and comprehension, thus influencing his or her identity. So, obviously, there exist regional aspects of identity in every one of us. Regional identity is a way to position oneself in the world, but its role and significance may vary widely. It is not the most important basis for everyone. Such factors as profession, age, religion, nation or ethnic background may be more important.

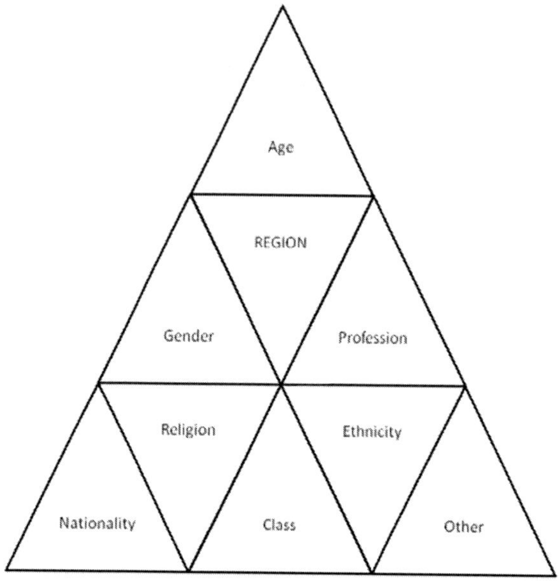

Figure 2-2. *Region as part of individual identity.*

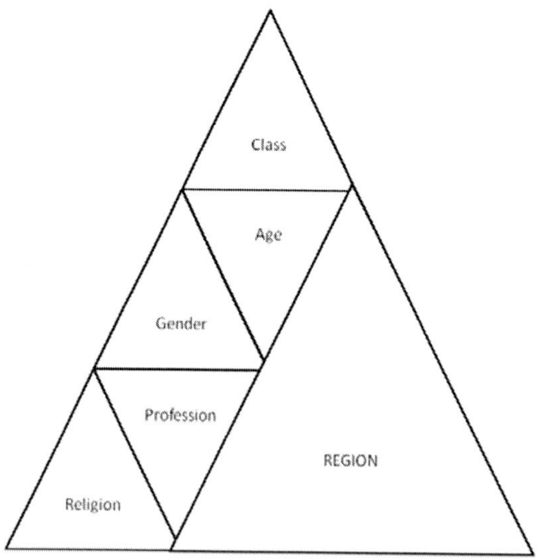

Figure 2-3. *The example of an identity in which the regional element is dominant.*

On a personal level the various ingredients usually blend into each other resulting in a unique, overlapping, individual identity. The role of region in this process is not necessarily decisive for an individual, but it is certainly relevant on a more general level: the people of a certain region seem to have a tendency towards a regular identity. They seem to share parallel features; there are similarities in their identities. If we analysed a certain age group, profession or any other element in personal identity, we would probably obtain the same finding. Although the point of departure in the analysis was personal and evolutionary identities, a collective identity could also be abstracted from the characteristics of all those identities. Over time the general-level collective identity is accumulated in culture. It can be seen in those practices, attitudes and beliefs that are quietly established as the conventional habits of thought. The matter-of-course identity pops up occasionally.

> Family identity is considered when relatives meet each other or when one participates in genealogical association. National identity comes to mind and is under discussion in connection with certain events, such as sport competitions or when one faces citizens of one's home country abroad. Ethnic identity is activated if foreigners or ethnic minorities are discriminated against. In these situations the collective identity is not found or composed out of nothingness but is structured by use of the codes that exist and have become common in culture. (Kaunismaa 1998, 45)[2]

Identity works like the frame-technique in computers: usually the various elements of identity are overlapping one another; some parts are completely hidden. A single occasion may wake up any hidden element and it pops up to the top. Region is one of the overlapping frames in identity. It may be activated all the time, or every now and then.

The three levels of the homely landscape

I have often wondered about the differences that we can find in languages concerning the conceptualising of our relationship to local and regional familiarity and its impact on an individual. Think about such an essential ethnological concept as "Heimat" in German ("hembygd" in Swedish, "kotiseutu" in Finnish, etc.). The concept has long been an essential part of Finnish ethnology (Mäkinen 2000, 19; Tuomi-Nikula 2009). Probably the parallel concept can be found in many languages, but as far as I know there is no comfortable translation for the concept in English or Spanish, for example. "Homeland," "pais natal" or "patria chica" do not cover the whole phenomenon of Heimat, hembygd and kotiseutu. The French "terroir" and "son pays" are closer to the idea of the site in which one was born or in which he or she has lived, and which has influenced one's identity. The concept includes not only the natural environment, but also the cultural phenomena that one has quietly adopted.

Perhaps the same kind of many-dimensional meanings can be linked to the English word "landscape." It is used in its concrete meaning to be the visible features of an area of land. But it is also used when referring to the sphere of intellectual activity. I have heard such expressions as "the landscape of the soul" or "the landscape of the human heart."

I suggest the term "the three levels of the homely landscape" be used to refer to the complex entity of natural, human-made and mental environments that an individual recognises to be his own.

The concept of the homely landscape is a useful tool for defining and structuring regional identities. As a cultural concept it exceeds the mere natural-geographic level of observation. Nature and culture are united in the idea of homely landscape as a coherent living environment, continually changing and developing.

Man has a natural propensity to find a home and to fix himself as part of his immediate surroundings. This propensity is common to everyone. A palace serves as a home for a prince. A homeless beggar becomes attached to his city even if he lives underneath the sky of blue. As we remember from the novel by Mark Twain, neither a prince nor a beggar feels at home if the roles are exchanged.

Every human being has homely sites and landscapes in some form. Homesickness is a universal phenomenon. Even the smallest babies are trying to capture their immediate surroundings in order to become familiar with them. Naturally, a baby first gets to know the closest things and people—usually those that are inside his room and home. Lap, cradle, high chair and child's car seat are landmarks in our first homely landscape. The experiences of early childhood are later extended by newer capture of objects, people and places. Homely landscape is an evolutionary concept: it is the expansion from home to yard, to relatives, to neighbourhoods, to playgrounds, to day-care places and schools.

A growing child gives a special meaning to the people and places next to him. A tie of attachment, or even of love, is gradually developing as one becomes more familiar with their immediate surroundings. It is constructed of three kinds of things, or three elements of the environment, and each of them consists of both physical and cultural features.

The elements are (fig. 2-4): **natural** environment (physical), **built** environment (both physical and cultural) and **mental** environment (cultural). These can also be understood as stages superimposed onto each other, natural landscape being the primary phase on which built environment is based; and both of them form the basis for the mental environment in its manifold social features, such as traditions, language and normative institutions, as described in figure 2-5 (the three stages of homely landscapes have often been present in regional history and histories of migration, although no special attention has been paid to them. See e.g., Pooley 2007, 76; Fernández-Manjón 2010, 111. I have also presented the model of homely landscapes in two conference papers: Riukulehto 2010a; 2010b).

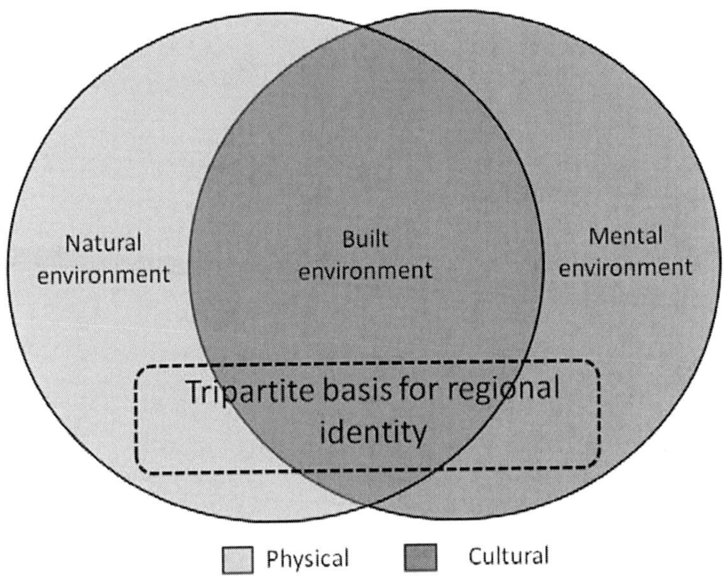

Figure 2-4. *Natural, built and mental environment for an identity.*

The three-stage environment in which we are entirely absorbed offers three kinds of landscapes for the identity of an individual. Thus, correspondingly, we can differentiate **the three stages of homely landscapes** (the tripartite rectangular area in figure 2-4): natural, built and mental.

The first stage in this model is natural environment: soil, water and air with all the species living in it. The natural places, such as familiar lakes, woods, swamps, hills and mountains, form the homely landscape of the first level. It plays an essential role in the construction of identity for an individual.

In reality, natural objects are seldom faced in their purely natural state. Usually we meet them as partly natural but to some extent culturally processed. Man has printed his hand everywhere. A mountain is almost changeless; nostalgic emotions may arise if one returns to the homely mountain area of childhood after thirty years. The feeling of stasis and sameness is impressive. The flat dwarf trees—if there are any—may easily be 200 years of age. Each and every gnarled pine looks exactly the same as in one's childhood. The same familiarity cannot necessarily be obtained on forest land. When returning, the fertile forest of childhood may be an empty clearing or a sapling stand. Familiar landmarks cannot be found.

The changes in the natural environment may cause resentment. A monolithic block of stone or a familiar view to open swamp may have a strong symbolic meaning for an individual. Other people may never entirely understand their deeper significance for that individual. The loss of this kind of natural relic may be hard even for a full-grown man. This is why we frequently see rallies and demonstrations for the conservation or preservation of a tree dominating the landscape, a lake or another nostalgic place.

Our view of homely landscape remains imperfect until we fix the natural details seamlessly with the man-made parts of our environment. A child first takes possession of his nearest area: the home with its daily utensils. More experiences will be caught from the world around: a classroom, a commercial centre or the timber yard of a factory area. The built environment forms the second stage of our homely landscape. It also consists of familiar experiences, feelings and perceptions. Homely landscape is a highly experimental thing.

How does it smell when mum is baking? Or what kind of smell is oozing from cellar, hay barn or fishing boat? Not everyone will know. There are lots of everyday situations that do not exist without the built environment of a certain kind. The one who lives in a different area is left without these experiences. A child is firstly confronted with the built environment: a baby is put into a cradle, not into a forest.

We cannot really think about the totality of our home without the third stage of landscape: the mental one. Besides nature and built environment we are deeply interwoven into a complicated net of traditions, habits and norms. Nobody is born into an empty world. Even an infant understands that mum and dad are not just anybody. They have a special position, a particular role, certain responsibilities and privileges.

The habits of thought, customs and traditions are inconspicuously adopted from neighbourhoods. We silently accept the homely dishes; we dress up like the others do; we adopt the roles of men and women. The third stage of homely landscape may be hardest to identify but it is the strongest of all. Its significance can be profoundly understood when we meet people who speak, behave, dress and think differently. That makes us understand that one hails from somewhere.

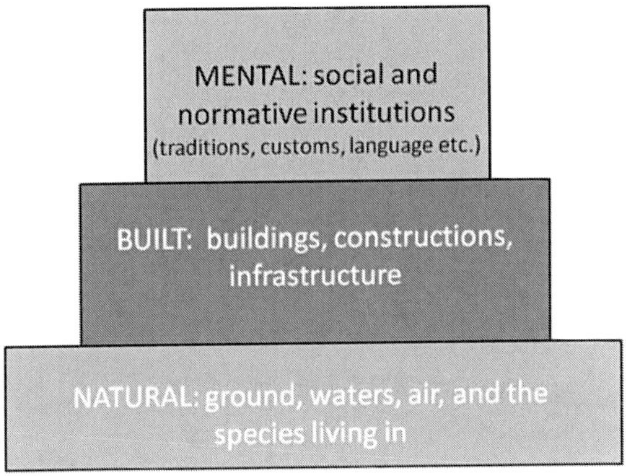

Figure 2-5. *The three stages of homely landscapes.*

The homely landscapes always have a strong effect on us, no matter if they are physical (the ground, water and air—and all the species living in them: forests, seas, mountains, etc.), built (buildings, constructions and infrastructure: roads, fields, factories, schools, etc.) or mental landscapes (social and normative institutions: traditions, language, customs, etc.). Evidently, every identity is under the continual influence of the three stages. The totality that one considers as one's home area always has elements of all three. The three stages of homely landscapes are interwoven into one regional identity.

Usually one does not separate natural, built and mental environment from each other. They form a unit, the entity of living that we are familiar with. Accumulating this entity means the construction of regional identity, or a kind of home-site identity.

The oasis-like areas of familiarity

Children often have a tendency to think that each of us can only have one homely area (Minna Mäkinen (1996) has revealed this kind of tendency in pupils' attitudes towards their homely landscapes in the Finnish municipality of Lempäälä, for example). An adult who has spent his life in one place usually agrees. But nowadays most people move more than once in a lifetime (fig. 2-7). We move repeatedly because of studies, jobs, vacations in summer cottages, etc. The homely landscape of an individual is spreading. The same finding has often been made in migration studies (e.g., Pooley 2007, 77).

Besides the original home of childhood one can have numerous other homes and home sites: a student residence, a do-it-yourself one-family house, a home for the aged, or a traditional life-annuity home. All of them link to reminiscences, relationships, experiences and important places. A newcomer to an area becomes fond of his environment simply by living in and conquering new places and experiences.

We can also have various home sites at the same time, and we can accept all of them as part of our experimental belonging: a home, a student campus and a summer cottage with all of their natural and cultural environments (fig. 2-6). The home site of childhood—once undeniably unique—may lose its position when a new series of homely landscapes are accepted. Each of them is an extraordinary and precious possession for an individual. The successive and parallel oases of landscape do not necessarily exist spatially side by side (Mäkinen 1996, 55–56; Klusákova and Teulières 2008, 326). Finally, one's regional identity is a unique network of fragmentary oases of many homely landscapes.

The oases are dynamic and evolutionary in nature. All of the successive and parallel landscapes have their natural, built and mental environments. Obviously, homely landscapes are not necessarily limited to localism: they may sporadically cover a country, or they may even reach another continent.

In ethnological studies home is usually understood evolutionarily. The circle of familiarity is continually spreading and changing (e.g., Aaltonen 1963, 9). The home area of a nomad or a vagabond may be surprisingly wide. The neighbouring province may look like home if it is seen from a distance. The home site of frontiersmen may spread in many directions: two, three or even four provinces may feel like their own. Migrants often talk about new and old home sites.

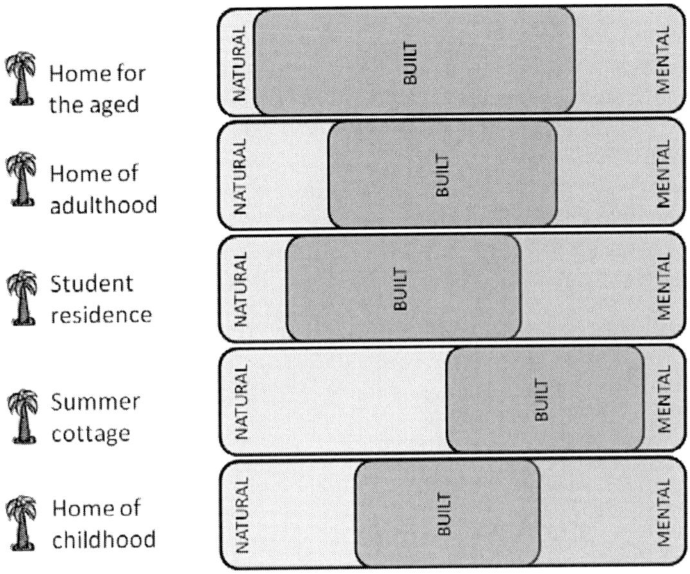

Figure 2-6. *A series of homely landscapes. Each one is composed of natural, built and mental parts.*

The place of birth is not necessarily the only or the most important oasis of homely landscape. Neither is the house where an individual lives. Familiarity is often formed operatively. A summer cottage is easily made part of one's homely landscape simply because a lot of time is spent there. The same goes for clubs, schools and places of work. The most important landmarks may be formed of the natural environment, but more often they are represented by the built environment.

People are always living within a culture. Social relations, friends and relatives complete the picture of the environment as our home. The physical, built and mental stages of homely landscapes are not separate factors but prerequisites and results of each other. Our closest landscapes are full of important reminiscences.

In fact, our environment always has bare spots as well as familiar oases. This is true even for people who have spent their whole life in the same place. Some nearby areas are known thoroughly, others incompletely or not at all. Surprisingly close to one's own home yard may be found places that one has never noticed. In reality, most of us only recognise roadsides and other places in our travelling itineraries. We expand our homely landscapes by these routes.

The oasis of the homely landscape is an illustrative concept. It captures successfully the temporal development of the sense of home district. It creates a mental image of a little human in a big, unknown world. Man is like an explorer filling in the bare spots on his map. He does not necessarily fear travelling outside the oases; his stance is merely curious and ready to learn. It is always challenging to wander outside of these; it is more or less like drifting—but not necessarily being lost. Every now and then one gets to an oasis, a harbour where one does not need to strain.

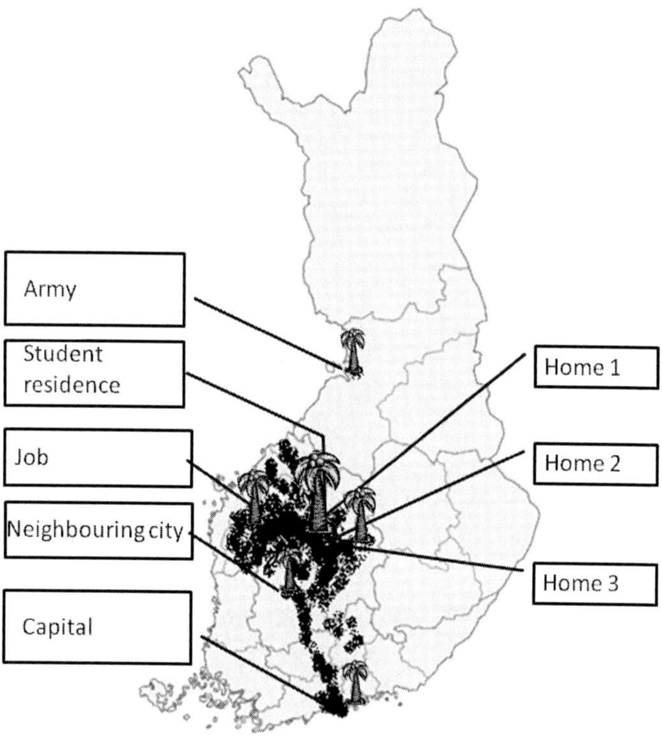

Figure 2-7. *The serial oases of homely landscapes on a map. A specimen from Finland.*

The relation between regional identity and homely landscapes

Identity can be a useful tool in history and other social sciences. Such is the case in regional history when identities are used in order to compare and to clarify differences between regions. Typical regional features and even frontiers can be seen in identities. Most useful are the identity models that do not try to grasp all the identity discourses at the same time. The experiences of homely landscapes serve as an opening to define and to model the deeper meaning of regional identity.

The phenomenon of homely landscapes is universal. People of any age and any place have experiences of their environment and of its three stages. The natural and cultural elements are intermingled in the superposed multi-storey structure of homely landscapes, but they can also be differentiated. We can easily focus our examination on any of these elements: natural, built or mental phenomena of homely landscapes. The entity is evolutionary. Our collection of landscapes is undergoing continual change. Administrative units, such as municipalities, provinces and districts, have a certain role in people's life, but they do not seem to be the most important regional units from the individual's perspective. The tripartite concept of homely landscape opens an interesting and evolutionary angle of vision to the analysis of regional identity. It consists of oasis-like areas of familiarity concerning fragments of natural, built and mental landscapes.

In research work the concept of regional identity, however, cannot entirely be replaced by the tripartite concept of homely landscapes. The point of view is always personal and experimental in homely landscapes: it is always a landscape experienced by someone, or a collective identity that is interweaved from personal experiences.

If we accept the interpretation that the image of a region is defined chiefly from outside—whereas identity is constructed within—the concept of homely landscape is an essential or perhaps even an indispensable tool in the construction of regional identity. It helps us to better understand the significance of region as one of the basic elements of identity. It would be, however, highly fallacious to always equate regional identity with homely landscapes; there are regional identities of much larger perspective than homely landscapes. Lapplandness, the identity of the inhabitants of Lapland, is an example of this. The region is spread over a large arctic area, but not all people with this identity are Lapps. Such are also the national identities, or Europeanness—covering a continent.

In regional studies the term "region" may refer to the content of the study, but it may also refer to the point of view or the geographic definition of the subject. Any identity, if regionally demarcated, can obtain the label "regional."

If a researcher on the basis of his observations is defining the regional identity of, say, an African area, he does not necessarily research homely landscapes at all. Observation may be concentrated on any of the possible ingredients of one's personal identity (gender, religion, age group, etc.); regionalism is therefore a further condition for the research project. The regional focus does not make the people under observation feel more familiar with the area. But, on the other hand, if we study identity specifically from the perspective of people's relation to the place where they are living, we are basically concerned with regional identity. Then the concept of homely landscape may be more definite than that of regional identity. This notion certainly deserves more attention in the historical and social sciences. I hope the concept of homely landscape will also be useful in expanding the research field of regional history.

CHAPTER THREE

MULTICULTURALISM: THE IDEOLOGY OF THE NEW WORLD ORDER

SIYAVES AZERI

There is a trend found in both academic and political circles towards uncritically promoting all cultures and traditions. Some "radical left" figures, groups and organisations are among the most prominent advocates of this trend, despite the fact that the inherent values in these "cultures" and traditional frameworks are mostly misogynist, homophobic, anti-egalitarian and xenophobic. Multiculturalism serves the benefits of capitalism in the era of the New World Order. It not only produces and reproduces social, economic and political inequality and injustice, but also, by attributing a permanent essence to such human products as culture and tradition, it eternalises "racial," "national," "ethnic," "tribal," "religious" and "sectarian" differences as perpetual identities, ghettoises the society and justifies the "Iraqisation" of society.

Multiculturalism does not signify a simple practical or political directedness in reaction to immediate political issues as some of its proponents claim. Rather, it designates a totality of beliefs, a general framework through which humans are conceptualised and are defined in a certain form, are attributed certain properties, and are claimed to have a peculiar identity. Culture, in this picture, is that transcendental paradigm, the magical apparatus that allegedly resolves the enigma of human identity. In this sense, multiculturalism is a theoretical system that produces and reproduces false identities and thus false consciousness. Hence, it is more appropriate to consider it an ideology or an ideological system similar to religion, nationalism, etc.

Multiculturalism also has affinities with identity politics or the so-called politics of recognition. It serves as a theoretical apparatus for determining the "natural material" that is presupposed by identity politics, say, ethnicity, tribe, race, culture, etc. In presenting the political outcome of identity politics as a natural entity, it once again assumes an ideological role; i.e., it turns the relation between cause and effect upside down; it presents the politically recognised entity, say, culture or ethnicity, as a natural entity that needs to be politically expressed. Thus, an analysis of the theoretical framework of the politics of recognition also reveals certain elements central to multicultural ideology.

Methodological aspects

On the methodological level, multiculturalism, in its most general form, represents an unjustified shift from "individualism" to "community-centrism." This unjustified shift, which can be traced in the writings of many multiculturalist (mainstream and leftist) authors, represents the inadequacy of the multiculturalist view in the analysis of culture, which can be labelled as "culture-fetishism." Analysing the commodity as a category of the capitalist mode of production, Marx (1996, 82) states:

> A commodity is therefore a mysterious thing, simply because in it the social character of men's labour appears to them as an objective character stamped upon the product of that labour; because the relation of the producers to the sum total of their own labour is presented to them as a social relation, existing not between themselves, but between the products of their labour.

Marx calls this phenomenon "commodity fetishism." A consequence of commodity fetishism is that the products of human activity appear to them as definite, independent entities. Marx explains this by making an analogy between commodity fetishism and religious beliefs: the phantoms of human thinking start to appear to them as independent entities that enter into a relation with one another and with human individuals.

In political economy, commodity fetishism also appears to conceive capital as an independent entity that belongs to individual capitalists. Hence, the fetishist views capital not as a social relation but as a thing-in-itself. The fetishist conceives general social capital not as the social relation between the capital and the workforce, but as the sum of the individual capital in society.

Culture fetishism

The same fragmented conception is visible in the multiculturalist analysis of culture. Reification and culture fetishism are manifest in the way that culture is analysed as an association of arbitrary elements. The implicit assumption is that culture is a meta-historical, self-contained category or form. The elements that form this category and fill its content are chosen arbitrarily. A quick look at how "sub-cultures" or "cultural identities" are named in, e.g., the USA or Canada is useful. Blacks, for instance, are referred to as African-Americans, and Chinese and other people from the Far East are called Asian-Americans. Natives are called aboriginals or First Nations. People from the Middle East are called Muslims or Arabs. Jews form another category, and so on. What is striking is the random use of and reference to elements of ethnicity, geographical origin, religion and race. Multiculturalism, be it right-wing liberal or left-wing constructionist, attributes essentiality to culture. It neither needs nor can provide a unique, exclusive definition of "culture." The choice of these arbitrary elements that are covered by the blanket-term "culture" is made with respect to the particular—overt or covert—sociopolitical side taken.

The fetishist view of culture and the basic rights of persons, which conceives these products as reified entities, is manifest in the following: "a secure cultural context also ranks among the primary goods, basic to most people's prospect for living what they can identify as a good life" (Gutmann 1994, 5). Gutmann considers "needs" as immutable. Needs, in her view, are not social products; they are not a product of social human activity. Rather, they are social in a naturalistic, reified way: for some or for all communities, a "secured cultural context" is claimed to be a basic right. Multiculturalists ignore the historic-social aspect of the question about culture. Perhaps some persons demand a secure cultural context as a need in order for them to feel free; once such a need is in demand it may be supplied. The magic hand of the liberal market economy is once again at work.

The sociality of need has a different meaning than the one Gutmann suggests. Need is determined by human activity within the limits of technical-cognitive abilities—where such technical-cognitive ability includes conceptual and ideational stockpiling too. Need is not something in itself; no need is essential, and therefore needs are subject to change. Virtually speaking, human needs are infinite; the scope of human needs is much broader than those which can be defined by a person from within a particular socio-historical position. Gutmann's view above conceives the needs of the "minority" culture as limited in time and space. Moreover, it considers need as a homogenising element: members of a particular community, in this view, cannot have a need peculiar to themselves and they cannot determine what "social needs" should be. This resonates with the traditional liberal dualism that contraposes the individual to the social.

Taylor (1994, 26) formulating the theory of political recognition, reveals a similar type of approach to human needs. He states: "Due recognition is not just a courtesy we owe people. It is a vital human need."

What is the content of this "need"? Does recognition mean recognising the rights of the individual such as the right to life, the right to freedom, and to happiness? To fill the content of the political needs of the yet-to-be-recognised people with anything beyond rights of humans, means attributing eternality to a socio-historical situation and dehumanising the yet-to-be-recognised persons by subordinating one's humanity and personality to some particular aspect of one's activity—a particular socio-historical situation, after all, is the outcome of human praxis. In other words, this view ignores the historical limitations and conditions that yield to reification of the products of human activity; it amounts to an uncritical approval of the existing mode of alienation as mere self-realisation, thus proposing it as inevitable and necessary.

Even the "ushering" function of democracy (Taylor 1994, 27) is presented as if it is a *sui generis* process in which humans partake only contingently and mechanically. Thus follows the enigmatic change of politics of equal recognition that "has now returned in the form of demands for equal status of cultures and genders" (Taylor 1994, 27). Reification of culture, in this case, takes place in the form of the personification of culture as an organic unity, a body, which has an existence by itself that transcends the existence and activity of persons that are in fact its producers.

In order to legitimise this stance, Taylor bases his argument on Herder's formulation, which clearly bears the mark of the aforementioned personification of culture. Herder attributes originality not only to individual persons but also to "culture-bearing people," to the Volk (Taylor 1994, 31). A Volk should be true to its own culture. As Sarah Song puts it, Taylor's position conceives culture as an "irreducibly social good." In this view culture is the expression of the authenticity of a Volk (Song 2007, 17). This view amounts to demands for cultural preservation. "A conception of culture as coherent, self-contained, and tightly knitted wholes is at the heart of multiculturalists' case for cultural preservation" (Song 2007, 32).

Taylor is aware that the mind of the human self is not an entity in itself. He writes, "The genesis of human mind is in this sense not monological, not something each person accomplishes on his or her own, but dialogical" (Taylor 1994, 32). Taylor (1994, 32–33) rightly argues that the dialogicality of the mind is not confined to its genesis only but contains its present mode of being as well. However, he does not argue against the idea of a self-contained, inner self. Rather, he argues that this self should be conceived not monologically but dialogically. Yet this dialogicality simply requires reciprocal activity of externally situated and self-contained individuals.

Taylor claims that the whole modern idea of the individual is based on the dialogical relationship among human individuals. However, he takes the individual as an abstract entity, where social relations and the individual's position within the social order have no particular influence on the formation of this person as a specific self. Consequently, Taylor does not fall short in introducing race, ethnicity, gender and religion as aspects of the human self that reside outside the boundaries that are defined by social relations; these factors are added to Taylor's allegedly dialogical relation between individuals from without. Taylor's position on this is reminiscent of Bauer's allegedly Hegelian stance concerning history that Marx criticises:

> Hegel's conception of history presupposes an Abstract or Absolute Spirit which develops in such a way that mankind is a mere mass that bears the Spirit with a varying degree of consciousness or unconsciousness. Within empirical, exoteric history, therefore, Hegel makes a speculative, esoteric history, develop. The history of mankind becomes the history of the Abstract Spirit of mankind, hence a spirit far removed from the real man. (Marx 1975)

Taylor then arrives at the stance associated with the politics of difference. The question he never answers is that of the identification of the uniqueness of the self with that of culture. In his view all cultures are equally valuable. He treats this as a principle that is supposedly an instantiation of the principle of dignity that attributes a universal value to human life.

There are a number of problems which this approach ignores. Firstly, culture, obviously, is not identical to a person or to an amalgamation of persons. Secondly, culture is an artifact. We may attribute value to all the artifacts that humans produce; yet this does not exclude the possibility that some artifacts are "better" than others or that some are dangerous even to the persistence of humankind (e.g., nuclear weapons, Auschwitz). The universality of the values that are attributed to the human being is based on the simple fact of humanity of that particular person—as simple as the fact that he or she is born into human society. This principle may also be extended to embrace the organic life of non-human animals, if one wishes. However, this value cannot be universalised so that it embraces all artifacts and human products—be they physical or ideational. Such transcription is both logically and actually illegitimate. An axe, at a particular moment, may be more valuable than a bow or vice versa. Even when it comes to human personality and consciousness, there may be traits of behaviour that are unacceptable. For instance, the right to life of a convict should be guaranteed; however, this cannot simply be transcribed to the acceptability of the behaviour that has resulted in his or her conviction.

Taylor's associationist conviction that reduces culture to an amalgamation of reified elements becomes more evident when he states: "How we do things covers [only] issues such as right to life and to freedom of speech" (Taylor 1994, 63), and this is how we do things here: If you don't love it, we don't say leave it, but we let you exercise your own "culture" only in your ghettos and among your fellow culture-mates and wallow in your own filth.

Taylor argues that the presumption or the demand for "respecting all cultures" is a logical extension of liberal principle of the "politics of equal respect" (1994, 68). If culture is not considered a thing in itself but a product of human activity, then one cannot make such a demand or presumption based on the aforementioned liberal principle. Humans, supposedly, ought to respect other persons. However, they cannot be expected to respect whatever values a person has or produces. The principle of equal respect also requires us to conceive humans as the authors of the laws and regulations they submit to—of course, this is true only in an ideal world where people enjoy an actual state of equality. This means that humans not only deserve respect, but are also answerable with regard to their activities and to whatever they create and produce. Taylor's demand for unconditional respect for "cultures," notwithstanding the aforementioned logical deficiency, reveals the low-scale racism that is implicit in this approach. It expresses itself in the form of a paternalistic, uncritical approval of the culture of the "other"—e.g., the underprivileged, the subordinated and the immigrant communities.

Taylor and other multiculturalists assume that whatever is produced within a culture is the private property of that culture. Taylor's discussion concerning the school curriculum debates discloses this aspect of his approach. It can be true that the existing curricula have been made by some who may have racial and/or Eurocentric prejudices. However, both sides agree that what the "white" man has written belongs to white men, and what the "coloured" man has written belongs to coloured men. Both sides of the debate assume that the products of a group of people belong to that group or to their alleged genetic successors, and not to humanity. Liberal abstract universalism and multicultural particularism meet at this conjunction. For instance, Saul Bellow demands "other" cultures to bring forth their own Tolstoy if they want their demand to be included in curricula to be met; he obviously defends the idea of supremacy of the so-called liberal West.[1] Multiculturalists, in response, negate this requirement and demand the inclusion of "genuine" artifacts of other forms produced by other cultures into the curricula. Both sides, however, agree that Tolstoy, the modern novel, Beethoven, etc., belong to "white," Western "culture" exclusively.

According to Blum (1998, 75) the "equal worth of cultures" that Taylor proposes is a meaningless notion that should be discarded. Blum's consideration of the cultural recognition of individuals is an attempt to theorise and conceptualise what I identify as the significance of culture fetishism. Answering the question "in what recognition consists with regard to [the] individual," he states: "The obvious feature is according explicit acknowledgement [to] the cultural marker or markers that the individual regards as indicating her distinctive cultural identity (for one this could be language, for [an]other it could be food, music, etc.)" (Blum 1998, 78–79). Blum is aware that no particular aspect or group of aspects can be attributed as the element(s) of defining and determining cultures. However, he chooses to valorise this ambiguity or vagueness by promoting it to a theoretical level.

Blum (1998, 81) also claims:

> [the need for recognition] involves no evaluative judgment at all, nor is it particularly appropriate, or even natural, to engage in assessing the culture of the student or the cultural group, when all that is at stake is recognizing that forms of cultural expression and historical experiences of the group are important to that student, and that in the context of a school, they warrant an institutional acknowledgement.

Blum rightly criticises Taylor for not explaining and justifying the claim that recognition of cultures requires and includes attributing value to that culture. In other words, the passage from respecting the dignity of the individual to respecting culture is illegitimate. Yet Blum ignores that such a demand for valorisation is implicit in the politics of identity. Recognition can simply mean acknowledging the existence of a culture as an artifact and further acknowledging that that artifact has some value for someone. However, for the politics of difference, recognition bears a positive load just as the "right to self-determination" bears a positive load for nationalism. Blum's stance, therefore, appears as a pre-emptive move in order to prevent a "negative" evaluation, that is, any criticism of acknowledged cultures. Consequently, Blum (1998, 83), unwillingly as it may be, arrives at a relativist stance. Ironically, relativism goes hand in hand with the idea that cultures have equal worth. Taylor's point is not that cultures have an equal value with respect to some common measure. Rather, he states that we should not only acknowledge a culture but should also respect the ways of life that are dictated by that culture. This last aspect is identical with the practical outcome of cultural relativism.

Blum's (1998, 85) resolution to the problem of "equal value" of cultures is to relativise and fetishise valorisation. This means, "treating each culture in its own right and admitting that each culture contains *something* of value." Thus, he arrives at the demand for coexistence of cultures, which are neither equal nor unequal. Blum suggests leaving them to exist, as if they are immovable, self-contained architectonics.

The debate about valorisation of culture is in response to the problem of producing demeaning imagery of certain groups. The source of demeaning self-imagery is the automatic attribution of a certain identity to a person. Mostly, the presumed identity is based on stereotypes that yield such demeaning imagery. One should consider the ways in which such an identity and imagery is reflected upon a group of people and thus on the members of that group, as well as the ways in which a particular image of a "culture" is produced. For instance, female genital mutilation is not a component of a culture that determines a group's identity. Rather, it is a practice of certain human beings that should be criticised and banned, as it is part of a misogynist, discriminative human activity. For multiculturalists, such a case would be a deadlock because they do not consider culture a product of human activity. Rather, they assign a *sui generis* existence and an internal worth to cultures. In the absence of a concept of culture as product of human practice, one ends up either approving such a practice or using it as a source for forming demeaning imagery about those particular people. One could also covertly approve this practice by relativising the valorisation of practices. The irony is that both racism and multiculturalism consider the victims of such acts as participants and members of those "cultures," but not as human beings in need of support. This is how multiculturalism contributes to the reproduction of demeaning self-imagery of members of a society.

Guiliana Prato also draws attention to the illegitimacy and political dangers of attributing the rights of the individual to communities or cultures. She states that both Gutmann (1994) and Tamir (1999) are critical of bestowing rights on collectivities or communities, since such attribution of rights to groups forms a threat to individual freedoms. Prato (2009, 16–17) states: "In emphasising group rights multiculturalism presents itself as a form of cultural determinism that curtails citizens' freedom of choice … By celebrating diversity in the form of group membership, multiculturalism does not break down cultural barriers; it reinforces both the barriers and the attendant cultural stereotypes." Multicultural recognition is inherently limited in two other interrelated ways: firstly, an abstract, contentless view of culture, which may be conceived as a reified or fetishist view of culture. Secondly, multiculturalism, which regards culture as immutable.

Habermas formulates the aforementioned problem of the shift from the rights of the individual to "collective" rights as follows: "The basic tension in constitutional democracies is the problem of reconciliation of 'individually designed' laws with the collective demands of recognition and dignity" (Habermas 1994, 107–8). Habermas claims that liberalism and social democracy can overcome this tension, or at least that they suggest an affirmative answer to this tension.

Despite his proper formulation of the question, Habermas falls short in articulating the real reasons behind such a tension. Liberalism, traditionally, attributes rights to the individual because it considers the individual to be a self-contained, autonomous entity. Thus, the duty of the state and of political society, theoretically and ideally speaking, is to protect the rights of the individual. If there is a tension between the social and the individual, it should be resolved to the benefit of the individual. This follows from the traditional liberal stance that contrasts the individual and the social. Society, in this classical picture, is an association of free individuals, just as any meaningful generalisation is an association of atomic impressions and ideas. If this is the case, the rights of the individual cannot coherently be attributed to the social. In order to surmount this difficulty, a naturalistic notion of society is introduced. This follows the culturist view that proposes the one-sided determination of the individual by the social, i.e., social determinism. Yet, the attempts of theorising such determinism will vary from thinker to thinker. Where Taylor formulates the tension between the individual and the social as an opposition between the theory of rights and cultural differences, and then tends to resolve it with reference to the dialogicality of the individual, Habermas proposes that the two are compatible and intends to resolve the aforementioned tension with reference to notions of authorship of the law and inter-subjectivity.

Taylor's conception of cultural rights, according to Habermas, misinterprets the Kantian dictum that "those to whom the law is addressed can acquire autonomy only to the extent that they can understand themselves to be the authors of the laws to which they are subject as private legal persons" (Habermas 1994, 112). There is no blindness to differences, however, on the side of the theory of individual rights because, according to Habermas (1994, 113), individual identity is conceived inter-subjectively: "People become individualised only through a process of socialisation."

Although Habermas tries to show that there is an "internal" link between the social and the individual, his definition of the process of socialisation reveals the atomic-individualist tendencies in his formulation. In the final analysis, the process of socialisation is external to the subject, which implies that the subject is conceived as an entity independent of society and sociality. Thus, the tension between the individual and the social remains unresolved.

Similarly, traits of cultural fetishism are also visible in Habermas's account of identity politics. He states: "Feminism, multiculturalism, nationalism, and the struggle against [the] Eurocentric heritage of colonialism are related phenomena that should not be confused with one another" (Habermas 1994, 116). Although he warns about the conceptual complexities that may result from confusing these phenomena, Habermas treats all of them as if they belong to the same level of abstraction: nation, as well as culture is confined with gender, which is biologically determined. And all these are related to the just cause of struggling against colonialism. Habermas considers nation and culture as *sui generis* entities. This essentialist aspect becomes more evident in Habermas's treatment of self-recognition of women. If a self is a socio-culturally determined entity, where society and culture represent blanket terms that denote phenomena external to the subjectivity of the subject, then how can "women's cultural self-understanding" provide any grounds for criticising the existing social order and cultural context towards the aim of emancipating women?

Will Kymlicka's approach to the questions regarding culture, minorities, ethnicities and nations is another showcase of the multicultural fetishist conception of culture. In his "Reply to Kukathas" (Kymlicka 1992), for instance, he conceives the relation between the so-called culture and the individual so that, firstly, culture one-sidedly and absolutely determines the individual; and secondly, all "members" of the so-called culture are determined by it homogeneously; i.e., whatever this culture is, it is evenly distributed and has evenly determined its alleged members.

It is on the basis of these hidden premises that Kymlicka infers that "[special rights] are indeed required by the view that justice requires removing or compensating for undeserved or 'morally arbitrary' disadvantages, particularly if these are 'profound and pervasive and present from birth'" (Rawls 1971, 96, cited in Kymlicka 1992, 140).

Kukathas (1992, 141) underscores a central flaw in multicultural approaches while pointing to a shortcoming in Kymlicka's theory: not all members of minority cultures suffer the same disadvantages, and not all the disadvantaged are members of minority cultures. To put it more generally, the so-called "cultures" are not isolated wholes; they are interacting with other cultures; moreover, they are the products of human activity and social interaction, and carry the stamp of the time they persist in. Inequalities, therefore, are not a product of cultures and neither are they exclusive to a number of them—say minority cultures. Inequalities, alongside other qualities and social relations, are being continuously produced; cultures are the carriers of inequalities inherited from the past, for example, discrimination against certain communities and their members, and not the demiurges of these inequalities.

Inequality in this view is just a matter of gaining an advantage and not a matter of produced and reproduced social relations. In other words, according to this view, the source of suffering certain inequalities or being discriminated against is not social relations, but is membership of a particular culture and/or community. Thus, it remains an enigma as to how these inequalities can be surmounted at all: why should a culture, say a dominant "white" culture, which enjoys the "advantages" of being dominant over and discriminative of other cultures agree to assume certain measures that benefit the disadvantaged culture and its members? This is why Kukathas states that Kymlicka's suggestion is also unacceptable for liberals (perhaps for the theorists of the dominant, advantaged culture). Does Kymlicka suggest any other solution than reliance on the mercy of the dominant culture? And what is the source of such a mercy if it exists at all? Perhaps it is an implicit aspect of the dominant, white culture; a natural attribute of a certain group of people.

Even if we accept Kymlicka's argument that we can acquire a balance between the liberal notion of individual rights and the special rights of minority cultures, who is to decide how an individual is defined and determined in a particular culture? There is an unresolvable tension at the core of Kymlicka's conceptualisation of individuality and culture. He takes both the individual and culture (interchangeable with community) as *sui generis* entities; he conceives of them from a naturalist-liberalist stance; in other words, he takes the individual, the real human person, as the embodiment and the instantiation of the liberal notion of "individual" on the one hand, and as the instantiation of "culture" on the other hand. It is then implied that the dominant culture that is endowed with liberal values promotes the individuality and independence of persons, that is, the dominant, liberal culture is so structured that it submits to its own instantiation, while, when it comes to the disadvantaged cultures, they are so conceived that they do not attribute independence to the person, which is its instantiation or embodiment. In other words, members of liberal cultures are independent and liberal, while members of disadvantaged cultures or non-liberal cultures are non-liberal and disadvantaged. Notwithstanding the obvious determinism of this account, as a well-intentioned member of liberal culture he assumes the right to first submit the right of the individuals and the cultures to enjoy certain rights and privileges, and second, he assumes the right to decide which element should be preserved in certain cultures with reference to liberal cultural standards.

This tension or shortcoming is also visible in Kymlicka's "Categorizing Groups, Categorizing States" (2009). Criticising/elaborating on Walzer's theory, Kymlicka treats "ethnically divided societies" as given, entities in themselves; in other words, for Kymlicka it is the given ethnicity that brings about ethnic division; the political division is based on some apolitically and a-historically given identity.[2] Hence, his criticism of Walzer for ignoring this "given" diversity (Kymlicka 2009, 372). In this view language, history and culture are treated on the same footing:

1. Kymlicka simply ignores the fact that neither of the aforementioned has any reality or significance independent from social relations.

2. The differences between languages, historiographies and "cultures" are also, in the final analysis, and at a very basic level, consequences of human activity. Moreover, at a more particular level, these differences acquire political significance because they have been made politically, that is, they acquire political significance within the framework of modern capitalist society, for instance, in the process of nation-formation. Kymlicka's stance is just the altruistic expression of "diversity." In this, it turns into the justification of the status-quo. The point, however, is to explain this diversity and differentiation. Kymlicka's stance is like pointing to a social stratification, "identifying" that some are poor and some rich, and then making a virtue (a theory) out of this. The point, however, is to explain the phenomena of poverty and wealth and the reality of this very stratification.

Nancy Fraser's discussion of the politics of recognition reveals the theoretical and political affinities between mainstream and leftist conceptions of culture. According to Fraser (1998, 19), the rise of the politics of recognition is neither a lapse into "false consciousness" nor a redressing of the culture-blindness of socialism. Fraser (1998, 20) intends to develop a "critical theory of recognition" so that only those politics of difference that are coherently compatible with the social politics of equality are defended. Her main thesis is that justice requires both redistribution and recognition.

Instead of providing a holistic monist theory that includes political answers and solutions to certain burning social questions such as national-ethnic and sexual discrimination from within a radical egalitarian perspective, Fraser echoes the traditional left stance that aims to form collations and alliances of the "oppressed." Both the traditional left and Fraser view the social world as fragmented and divided into identities. Political movements, in this view, are the expression of the struggle of identities toward the realisation of their rights, just as for Taylor and liberal multiculturalists, politics is the expression of a culture. Consequently, Fraser aims to provide a theory that functions as a magical agglutinating device.

According to Fraser (1998, 24), recognition promotes the putative specificity of a group, while redistribution is aimed at abolishing the economic base of group specificity. Thus follows the redistribution-recognition dilemma.

Fraser's understanding of class and class relations is the counterpart of the culture-fetishist conception of identity. Class, for Fraser, first and foremost, is but another form of identity, which, due to the goodwill of redistribution politicians, ought to be abolished. Moreover, it is a conglomeration of individual labour-force sellers. This is to view class through an individual bourgeois lens as a fetish that is best expressed in trade unionism. This view does not consider class to be a social relation, but to be a physical-mechanical relation of some end-product, that is, the workers. This fetishist analysis of class, which reduces class to a guild of individual work-force sellers, is visible in Fraser's example of the homosexual worker. She states,

> Sexuality in this conception is a mode of social differentiation whose roots do not lie in political economy, as homosexuals are distributed throughout the entire class structure of capitalist society, occupy no distinctive position in the division of labour and do not constitute an exploited class. (Fraser 1998, 26)

According to this view exploitation takes place in the workshop only. With the same token, a worker is not exploited when he or she is asleep or when she or he is unemployed. Following the same path of reasoning one can say that the human being is not alienated as a result of the existing mode of production, which is a social relation, because human beings are distributed throughout the entire class structure of capitalist society. Fraser's stance is a distortion of Marx's analysis of political economy and the process of production that continuously produces and reproduces capitalist society together with its political economy. This view fails to see that society itself is the very product of relations of production and is thus a social relation. All relations, roles, inequalities and injustices are continuously produced and reproduced within the existing society and are parts of social relations. Certain inequalities, for instance sexual discrimination, may be rooted in and inherited from the past. However, this does not make sexual discrimination an archaic problem; sexual discrimination is produced in the present, under the capitalist mode of production, and thus the struggle against such discrimination is an aspect of class struggle. Interestingly, Fraser's position reminds us of Bauer's position concerning the Jewish Question. As Marx states: "Religious questions of the day have at the present time a *social* significance. It is no longer a question of *religious* interests as *such*. Only the *theologian* can believe it is a question of religion as religion" (Marx 1975, 108).[3] The "cultural-valuational structure of society" that is the root of e.g., discrimination against homosexuals is itself being produced now, at present, under the existing relations of production. Fraser, to the contrary, conceives both class and culture as atomic things in themselves.

In considering gender and race as "bivalent" cases, Fraser fails to see that the identity that is attributed to a specific gender or race is itself the product of the discriminatory dominant ideology. The immediate response to sexual or any other form of discrimination is to abolish discrimination and construe reverse discrimination if necessary. However, abolishing discrimination and imposing reverse discrimination does not have to be transcribed into the recognition of this very identity as something *sui generis*, just as the response to racial apartheid is not a "black apartheid state," and the response to national discrimination is not an automatic affirmation of the right to self-determination or an ethnic federalist state.

Marx's reconstruction of Absolute Critical speculative philosophy sheds light on one of the most important aspects of the culture fetishist point of view. The speculative thinker reduces the real entities into manifestations of an essence, which is arrived at through mere abstraction. Reifying this abstract idea as the substance, the real thing appears as its semblance. The multitude of the real being is explained as the manifestation of the self-movement of the substance—the real becomes a mode of this substance only. This line of reasoning is not limited to speculative "criticism" only. The political-economic view of capital as self-generating wealth and the idea of culture, not as the totality and ever-changing products of human activity, but as a self-contained fetish, are among other examples of such an outlook. If culture determines, in the way multiculturalism claims it does, the being of its members, then how is diversity within one culture to be explained? How come, say, I am different to my fellow culture-mate? The multiculturalist might answer, "due to self-movement of culture." Just as "speculative philosophy has as many incarnations as there are things, just as it has here in every fruit an incarnation of the Substance, of the Absolute Fruit," the multiculturalist has as many incarnations of Culture as there are real human individuals. Nonetheless, what remains is the enigma of why Culture manifests this self-movement in the form of culture, and at other times in the form of the individual person. Perhaps, some Medieval-type theory of emanation is at work.

The political aspect: essentialism

Multiculturalism and cultural relativism also have a number of immediate political consequences. Multiculturalism divides and categorises people illegitimately and unjustifiably. In this view, the idea of the existence of human rights regardless of certain historical and social attributes is not plausible. This is to say that, according to the multiculturalist view humans do not have human identity *per se*, and neither do they have human rights.

Culture as a political phenomenon is the product of culturist movements just as nation is the product of nationalism. Culturism, in most cases, is a covert form of particularist, localist, nationalist, religious or ethnicist politics. Ontologically speaking, culture does not exist independently from human activity. Culture is not a *sui generis* entity. Regardless of this dependency, culture, in the hands of culturist movements, is made into an imaginary self-contained entity that has the ability to mobilise groups of people in the service of certain terrestrial benefits. The alleged essentiality of culture and its appearance on the political scene as a political entity does not make it ontologically self-contained; culture does not become an entity in itself just as nation does not become an entity, and it never loses its socio-historical determinations despite the claims and wishes of the nationalist movements. Attributing essentiality to culture out of goodwill reproduces this reified image of culture as a permanent entity in itself, and consequently, voluntarily or involuntarily, contributes to strengthening of culturist ideology and its political position.

It is interesting to see how liberal thinkers—who criticise Marx for what they call "determinism" in his system that supposedly deprives human beings of their freedom of will and choice—lean toward the crudest types of historical determinism that is expressed in works of

Maoist-inspired authors such as Fanon, and traditional left organisations that formulate this allegedly "Marxist" historical determinism in the form of the "theory of stage." Thus, Taylor, in order to justify the expansion of the traditional liberal conception of rights of the individual so that it covers the realm of cultures, and to legitimise disregarding the contradictions between the liberal conception and the identity-politics approach to the question, refers to Fanon (1994, 66): "The struggle for freedom and equality *must* therefore pass through a revision of these images" [emphasis added].

Attributing an immutable essence to "culture" is another common aspect of multiculturalist (mainstream and left) conceptions of culture. Taylor's elaboration of what he calls the clash between the two modes of liberalism—procedural and substantive—also reveals the essentialism or liberal naturalism inherent in his stance. Evaluating the Quebec problem from within this perspective he writes:

> But both [Quebec and the rest of Canada] perceived each other accurately —and didn't like what they saw. The rest of Canada saw that the distinct society clause legitimated collective goals. And Quebec saw that the move to give the Charter precedence imposed a form of liberal society that was alien to it, and to which Quebec could never accommodate itself without surrendering its identity. (Taylor 1994, 60)

Societies, accordingly, have characters that determine what kind of rights and what type of system of governance should be chosen for them. Notwithstanding that fact, Taylor identifies societies with states, that is, he reduces the so-called "civil society" that is so dear to liberalism to political society or the state.

Taylor's approach to Salman Rushdie's case makes this essentialism even more evident. First, Taylor identifies Islam with the Muslim and whoever is born to a "Muslim" family, society or country. Then he states: "Liberalism is not a possible meeting ground for all cultures, but is the political expression of one range of cultures, and quite incompatible with other ranges" (Taylor 1994, 62). Clearly, Taylor reproduces the aforementioned culturist stance that takes politics to be the reflection of culture. Taylor eventually defends political Islam and its totalitarian politics, because such politics is the political expression of another culture. Liberalism is not the common ground upon which cultures of different ranges can meet; however, this does not exclude the right of these non-liberal cultures to practise their undesirable ways in their own societies. Hence follows the peaceful coexistence of cultures. Furthermore, members of "liberal" cultures should not try to impose their political values onto the politics of a "non-liberal" culture, because it would violate the right of the non-liberal culture to express its values. However, it remains an enigma why Taylor and others do not show the same sensitivity when it comes to the export of ultra-modern weapons, technological equipment, means of communication such as computers and cell phones, automobiles and techniques of interrogation—all of which are products of the "liberal culture"—to these societies.

All in all, in order to justify this implicit defence of political Islam and its totalitarian regimes, which is the inevitable result of viewing politics as nothing but the expression of culture, Taylor claims that liberalism is the product and continuation of Christianity and Christian culture. The picture is complete: Christian religion yields to Christian culture, which finds its expression in liberalism and a half-hearted defence of basic human rights. On the contrary, Islam yields to Islamic culture, the political expression of which is political Islam and its totalitarian regimes. Taylor's position regarding culture is the replica of Herr Bauer's position about religion and Judaism in the "Jewish Question," which is criticised sharply by Marx:

> Herr Bauer, as a genuine, although Critical, theologian or theological Critic, could not get beyond the religious contradiction. In the attitude of the Jews to the Christian world he could see only the attitude of the Jewish religion to the Christian religion ... For the orthodox theologian the whole world is dissolved in "religion and theology" ... Similarly, for the radical, Critical theologian, the ability of the world to achieve freedom, is dissolved in the single abstract ability to criticise "religion and theology" as "religion and theology." The only struggle he knows is the struggle against the religious limitations of self-consciousness, whose Critical "purity" and "infinity" is just as much a theological limitation. (Marx 1975, 110)[4]

Parekh's definition of culture and his approach to the problem of recognition is but another example that reveals the multiculturalist conception of culture as an immutable, self-contained entity. According to Parekh (2005, 13): "Culture refers to a historically inherited system of meaning and significance in terms of which a group of people understand and structure their individual and collective lives." There is no place for productive and reproductive activity in this definition. Culture is a historically given ready-made good. Such depiction is a fetishist conception of culture: in this view culture is independent from humans. People may enter or exit the culture but it continues to exist. Thus Parekh (2005, 14) writes: "Some immigrants do assimilate and others do not. And even in the former case, their children and grandchildren sometimes seek to revive aspects of their ancestral culture." Despite the fact that these "aspects," whatever they are, are revived in the present day, they are said to remain "ancestral" and archaic. This is to view these aspects and cultures in general as meta-historical and non-personal transcendent.

Parekh adopts an apologetic, closet-relativist stance. In his criticism of what he calls the feminist misconception of multiculturalism he states:

> The feminist critique is mistaken [in criticising multiculturalism] because, as we saw, multiculturalism implies no such thing [as unequal treatment of women]. All it requires is that we should first understand other cultures from within before passing judgments and the criteria we employ should be shown to be universally valid. (Parekh 2005, 18)

There is no political and social struggle, and no changes in the structure, system of beliefs or outlook of societies (cultures) in Parekh's view. Thus follows his suggestion that we may criticise, since this view amounts to implicit approval of "cultural" practices. Parekh's position theorises the policy of the European Union with regards to the Islamic Republic of Iran: the EU legitimises its relations with the IRIP under the pretext of "critical dialogue." Parekh makes this affinity evident while criticising feminists:

> A culture might treat women unequally in civil and political matters but give them a superior social and religious status, or treat them as inferior when young and unmarried but revere them when they are old or are grandmothers. (Parekh 2005, 18)

A culture may deprive women of a decent life in this world but reserve the best seats and suites for them in heaven.

Habermas, on the other hand, tries to reconcile the liberal notions of rights and individuality with cultural rights through what he calls "intersubjectivity." This is why he opens his paper with the following: "Modern constitutions owe their existence to a conception found in modern natural law according to which citizens come together to form a legal community of free and equal consociates" (Habermas 1994, 107). However, the Kantian notion of autonomy and the idea of free association of individuals on the basis of natural law to which he appeals are in contrast to his effort. Firstly, this Kantian notion is based on the idea of a finalised, self-contained, autonomous subject, which is an atom-like entity. Secondly, the notion of intersubjectivity that is based on Kantian autonomy presumes that the autonomous subjects—the contract among which amounts to intersubjective relations—are equal, that is, it assumes they represent equal social positions. This latter supposition is empirically falsified. Culture is produced socially, but this does not mean that all the members of that culture have an equal share in producing, appropriating and reproducing that culture. The inherent inequality that is produced and reproduced within society and in ideational realms is thus transferred to the inter-cultural realm. Habermas's view, on the one hand, reproduces the ideological claim of the "culture"—and other totalising ideational entities such as nation—that stamps all its "members" as "we" who are allegedly participants in its production as equal counterparts, while, on the other hand, mystifies the essence of the unequal relation between different societies by depicting cultures as uniform formations—an outlook that amounts to losing the real grounds for a proper analysis of the unequal relations.

The example that Habermas uses and his elaborations on societies, communities and cultures depict his culture-fetishist outlook. He considers societies and cultures as subjects that survive beyond the conflicts they get involved in. In other words, cultures, nations, communities, ethnicities, etc., are considered entities-in-themselves that will later acquire self-recognition through conflicts and become entities-for-themselves. The conflict between cultures, at points, is the inevitable consequence of their existences. Thus, ideologies such as nationalism and ethnicism, for Habermas, are the political expression of self-recognition of nations and ethnic communities. However, a quick look at the history of nations and national states, past or present-day, shows that nations and ethnicities in particular, and identities in general, are products of ideologies such as nationalism, ethnicism and sectarianism. From France in the eighteenth century, to the dissolution of Yugoslavia, Czechoslovakia, the former Soviet Union and Iraq, we witness the process of identity construction by competing political movements, which are the political expression of social movements in class societies. In Habermas's view, even a phenomenon as horrifying as national cleansing is an expression of the existence-in-itself of some nation.[5]

Habermas conceives social, social identity and socialisation as identical to nature, naturality and naturalisation. He states:

> From a normative point of view, the integrity of the individual legal person cannot be guaranteed without protecting the intersubjectively shared experiences and life contexts in which the person has been socialised and has formed his or her identity. (Habermas 1994, 129)

The question is why "socialisation" and "identity formations" have come to an end? If the socialisation that Habermas has in mind is a real dialectical process, the resulting identity of such a process will be subject to perpetual change; that is, such an identity will change to the extent that the context within which the subject acts intersubjectively changes. Habermas's conception, however, is self-undermining in that it contradicts his claim about the intersubjective construction of identity. Moreover, it reveals the essentialist core of Habermas's consideration of the subject—subjects exist prior to intersubjective interaction. Since cultures are totalities that determine the individual that is born into their context once and for all, Habermas's stance requires him to demand the separation and thus coexistence of different cultures.

In response to political aspects of identity politics, Fraser distinguishes between two modes of politics: transformative and affirmative. The former may be considered a counterpart to revolutionary action that is aimed at transforming the substructure of society, whereas the latter is the counterpart to reformism that intends to improve the conditions of life leaving the substructure intact. According to Fraser, the affirmative approach to culture redresses disrespect toward certain groups by demanding respect for them, leaving the content of these cultures intact. Transformation, on the other hand, is related to deconstruction. It redresses disrespect by changing "everyone's sense of belonging, affiliation, and self" (Fraser 1998, 32).

In its most radical form and when taken to its logical extremes, multiculturalism is pushed to challenge and reject all those social values that make the realisation and actualisation of human rights possible. The multiculturalist approach to humans, not as individual persons but as representatives of particular structures, represents a retreat from the notion of citizenship and the rights and the attributes of the citizen. Fraser's elaboration on the deconstructive approach to culture provides a clear instance of such upside-down radicality. In general, according to Fraser, the transformative approach tends to destabilise existing identities so as to make room for future regroupments. What is ironic in this approach is that it considers groupments a deliberative decision of some kind. This is the replica of contract theories that form the basis of the liberalist notion of natural right. Fraser's view ignores the real basis of production and reproduction of ethnic, sexual, national, etc., identities. Even class, in this view, is but another form of groupments, a form of deliberative identity. Thus, Fraser's analogy between mainstream multiculturalism and liberalism, on the one hand, and deconstruction and socialism, on the other, misses the point. Socialism, at least its Marxian form, does not demand abolishing the class as a moral or purely political request (if there is anything such as pure politics). Rather, it states that classes disappear as the money economy, which is the expression of the commodification of labour, is abolished.

There is an inconsistency in Fraser's formulation of the relation between "transformative" and "affirmative" politics. On the one hand, she seems to admit that relations of production are the determining factor that produces and reproduces present-day identities such as race, ethnicity and gender. On the other hand, she states that transformative politics is "far removed from the immediate interests and identities of most people of (colour, different genders, etc.) as these are currently culturally constructed" (Fraser 1998, 39–40). This shows that, for Fraser, "identity" and "culture" denote *sui generis* entities. In other words, race, gender, ethnicity, etc., come into being despite the existing social order and relations of production. In this, they are not social but are cultural. Thus, she ends up attributing eternality and meta-historicalness to culture.

Young's formulation of injustice in a more plural way is but another example of the fetishistic, reified view of culture: she proposes five categories, in contrast to Fraser's two categories, in order to show the channels through which injustice appears in present society (Young 1998, 54). The question, according to Young, is why Fraser reduces these five categories to two? However, we should add, following Young's line of reasoning, why should we not add more categories to the five she suggests?

Young (1998, 56) claims that recognition is a means to economic and social equality and freedom. This political stance revitalises the nationalist forces' claims that tend to subordinate freedom and equality to the formation of nation-state. Young's approach is blind to the political aspect of the ongoing social-political struggles; she buys the claims of identity-politics at face value.

Young, at first sight, seems to articulate a monist theory of culture and economy. She states, "Culture is economic and economy is cultural" (Young 1998, 58). She is aware of the need for a holistic monist materialist theory of social movements. However, her formulation above is far from fulfilling this need. That everything, including culture, is economic, in Marx's sense, means that everything in society, including human identities, is the result of productive and reproductive activity (praxis) of real human beings. Thus, Young's alleged Marxist political economy that reduces economy to its mainstream academic meaning is a misconception of Marx's original formulation.

Young states that because the source of oppression against certain identities and groups and the source of inequality between communities are cultural, the solution should also be cultural. Hence, she arrives at the necessity of the politics of difference (Young 1998, 61). However, she ignores the fact that identity-making is the consequence of such an unequal social order. The imagery that is attributed to certain groups, e.g., women, homosexuals and blacks, is based on stereotyping generalisations, which marks a particular group as "alien," uniform and self-identical. Thus, the only alternative is not adopting a politics of difference; an egalitarian position can also be adopted. The politics of difference reproduces the imagery of the dominant discriminative politics. Young criticises Fraser for polarising political economy and culture. Her own "plural" stance appears as monistic because she eventually reduces political economy to identity—this is an aspect she has in common with Fraser.

Young treats culture as *sui generis*, as an end in itself. She states affirmatively:

> Most African-Americans who support culturally based African-American schools and universities, for example, believe that schools will best enable African-American young people to develop the skills and self-confidence to confront white society, and collectively help transform it to be more hospitable to African-American success. (Young 1998, 63).

According to this passage, society is owned by whites, it is a white society; African-Americans are alien to this society (after all they are called "African"-American); in this view, African-American, whatever this term may denote, is an identity in itself. Moreover, this view simply reproduces the "white" prejudice that treats blacks as "others" and outsiders. This view considers society as a crowd of some people that happen to have certain features such as skin colour, eye colour and hair colour in common. The difference between society, as put forward by this view, and nature is only nominal. Furthermore, the defining elements of this "society" are randomly chosen.

The mechanical understanding of society and economy in this view is evident in Young's defence of "local" modes of production. She advocates protecting indigenous economy as a transformative power confronting capitalism (Young 1998, 63). Capitalism, in Young's view, is identified with large-scale factories and workshops and not with a form of production and relations of production, which, in essence, signifies the relation between the capital and the workforce. Young views both culture and economy through fetishist lenses.

Multiculturalism sanctifies these categories. If this is the case, multiculturalism prevents a critical approach to and criticism against these historico-social phenomena, on the one hand, and legitimises the hegemonic determination of "members" of these groups and categories and the limitations that would possibly be imposed upon people by their so-called culture, tradition, beliefs, etc., on the other. In this way, people are left to the mercy of the arbitrary rules and regulations that are dictated by these structures, which, in turn, means that they are left to the mercy of those who assume higher and more powerful positions within these frames. For instance, multiculturalism ferociously defends the "rights" of Muslim women to be present in political society wearing a headscarf, while it does not mention anything in defence of the rights of girl children that have been born into Muslim families to equal opportunities and education, nor does it defend their basic rights against their parents. Neither is it concerned with the socio-historical roots and political significance of wearing the Islamic veil, etc. It says nothing to prevent Muslim families and communities from imposing the veil upon their children.

The political and social consequences of the politics that Young advocates are indicative of her theoretical stance. Immediately after Young gives the example about Muslims' demand to send their girls to school in headscarves, she states, "people should not suffer material disadvantage and deprivation because they are culturally different" (Young 1998, 64). People, in Young's view are different, but they are not made different. It never occurs to Young that by calling the girls that are born to Muslim families "their girls" she simply deprives these kids from their right to education, protection, etc. Kids, in this view, are the properties of their families, and because these families are culturally determined they have the right to deal with their property in the way they wish, so that they "do not suffer material disadvantage."

Conclusion

The Iraqisation of society is the necessary logical outcome of multiculturalist theses. In other words, what has been realised through the American invasion of Iraq—that is, dividing the Iraqi society into ethnic, sectarian and tribal factions—has in fact happened in concordance with the multiculturalist depiction of every human society. In this picture people are not citizens who have certain equal rights and duties regardless of their sex and race, but are members of this or that ethnicity, religion, sect, tribe, linguistic community, etc. And as it is clear from the example of Iraq, women and children, as the most vulnerable sections of society, are the first-hand, immediate victims of such categorisation. In short, multiculturalism, despite its radical and humanitarian self-depiction, justifies, advocates and actively supports the most reactionary ideologies and activities in the name of defending cultures, traditions and cultural values. This is done at the expense of real, actual humans' lives, rights and liberties. In addition, multiculturalism and cultural relativism function as the ideological apparatus in the hand of the most reactionary regimes around the world and their "progressive" apologists to politically justify their being and their politics as the representation of certain cultural and traditional values that also allegedly determine the being of people. In "The World after September 11," Mansoor Hekmat addresses the ideological aspect of the political—and military—confrontation between the two reactionary poles of state militarism and terrorism led by the United States government and the Islamic terrorism and political Islam. He writes:

> With the intensification of this conflict and particularly with the imminent US and NATO attack on Afghanistan, the "anti-imperialist" defence of Islamic groups and rationalisation of their terrorist actions by reference to Israel and America's crimes and oppressive acts, can once again gain foothold among the people and political parties of the Middle East and also among sections of the traditional radical and intellectual Left of western societies. The main ideological refuge of Islamic gangsterism and Islamic reaction in this power struggle will not be the worn-out and openly anti-human religious and Islamic slogans, but rather the so-called 'anti-imperialism' of the religious-nationalist and petit bourgeois apologists. (Hekmat 2001/2006, 6)

The question is why multiculturalism is preferable as an ideological framework for the bourgeoisie? The answer should be searched for within the present-day needs of capitalism, on the one hand, and on the other, the politico-historical dead-end of capitalism, which is represented in the form of reactionism and reactionary backlashes.

Multiculturalism and cultural relativism should not be considered in relation to immediate economic benefits. As a matter of fact, the relation between the economic substructure and the political and ideological superstructure is not a direct one; politics is the actualised viewpoint of a class that is concretised in the form of a certain horizon and particular demands. As an ideological framework, multiculturalism is in a more immediate relation with the bourgeois political horizon. Multiculturalism serves the bourgeoisie in its attack against certain basic human rights that have been achieved throughout the long and permanent struggles of the working class and different social movements. The real, worldly meaning of this retreat from human identity and such universal notions as human rights or the citizen and citizenship, and the emphasis on the most archaic beliefs and superstitions and their sanctification under the pretext of culture and respecting the other and the culture of the other, and the return to pre-modern, medieval forms of human identification, is depriving humans of their most basic rights, restricting and, at points, annihilating particular social securities and benefits, attacking the ideals of freedom and equality, and reproducing and promoting misogynism and sexism.

Up until the recent past, capitalism could still suggest a model of development for the so-called underdeveloped societies, either in the form of the free market model, or in the form of state capitalism. This meant that capitalism could then provide a relatively more prosperous life for the masses, as the pre-capitalist forms of production would be replaced by the capitalist mode of production. However, as the capitalist transformation of the world has been completed there is no such prospect on the horizon, as far as the quality of the lives of the working masses is at stake. The increase in profitability of capital is in direct contrast to the increase in the quality of the lives of working people; the removal of welfare states from the scene, the economic programs that are dictated by finance capital on a global scale and which are applied by all the states; the impoverishment of people's lives all around the world which is manifest in the form of the rapid increase of the cost of most basic needs such as food—all these are among the empirical facts that justify claims about the incommensurability of profitability of capital and the prosperity of the people. The attack on such notions as universal human rights, humanity and citizenship should be conceived within this global political perspective. Multiculturalism is the ideological framework of the bourgeoisie in the service of this politics in the age of New World Order.

Acknowledgment: This paper was made possible in part by a postdoctoral grant provided by the Scientific and Technological Research Council of Turkey (TÜBİTAK).

CHAPTER FOUR

DEFINING URBAN INTEGRATION THROUGH ACTIVE PARTICIPATION OF RURAL MIGRANTS

Z. EZGI HALILOĞLU KAHRAMAN

Introduction

Urban integration is a broad and complex concept that explains the changing features of and relationships between migrants and the society in which they live. The complexity of the concept stems from its multi-dimensional characteristics. The literature examines urban integration with respect to a wide range of dimensions—economic, political, cultural, etc.—and all these dimensions together are considered to shape the overall process of urban integration.

Definitions of urban integration vary according to the range of features that it is taken to include. This understanding formulates urban integration as a subjective and context-dependent phenomenon. Within this framework, this study aims to define urban integration through the active participation of rural migrants living in a specific rural migrant district in Ankara. To do this, it explores the subjective descriptions and perceptions of urban integration as expressed by rural migrants living in physically different neighbourhoods of the Dikmen district in Ankara. Thus, this study not only reveals rural migrants' definitions of urban integration, but also demonstrates the extent of the diversity of such definitions which can arise even within the same district.

This paper has five main sections. The following section summarises previous studies of integration, focussing on conceptualisations and other related concepts, dimensions and variables of integration. The third section discusses the urban integration process in the Turkish case. This section presents the changes in the lifestyle of rural migrants and the physical transformation of squatter housing districts. The fourth section discusses the methodological framework and the results of the study, concentrating on the study area, the sample, the data collection and analysis procedures and their results. The last part presents a summary and the overall conclusion of the study in relation to the existing literature on integration.

Literature review on integration

Integration is not an end state, but an ongoing process (Penninx 2004). The integration of migrants attracts researchers from various academic disciplines, such as economics, human geography, anthropology, political science, sociology and city planning. Those researches focus on conceptualisations, degrees, dimensions and variables of integration.

The conceptualisation of integration has changed over time as to the scope of what it is taken to include. The previous studies discuss integration within the processes of assimilation, accumulation, unification, acculturation, placement, interaction, identification, adaptation, cultural pluralism and multiculturalism.

The early models of integration conceptualised it as a process that ends with the assimilation of migrants. In Europe, with the rise of nationalism in the late nineteenth and early twentieth century, integration referred to the assimilation of national minorities to create culturally homogenous nations (The European Foundation 2006). According to Patterson (1963), assimilation is a one-sided process in which migrants give up their culture and adapt completely to the values and patterns of the society to which they have migrated. The host society expects them to lose their own traditional characteristics, and to adopt the language, culture and social structure of the receiving society (Gordon 1964; Bookman 1997). Berry (1992) includes integration within the strategies of acculturation. He defines other categories of acculturation strategy as separation/segregation and marginalisation, both of which involve strategies of exclusion, alienation and loss of identity. Sadhu and Chattopadhway (2006) explain integration as the unification of units or parts of a larger thing into a whole. The unification varies according to the social situation as well as the context which creates the situation.

After World War II, the relevance of human rights and the confidence and cultural pride of minorities gained strength as against the extremes of nationalism, fascism, and the suppression and expulsion of minorities. This development framed assimilation as a taboo concept, something which has endured until the present time (The European Foundation 2006). The recent models of integration criticise those early approaches that refer to differential exclusion and assimilation of migrants. Integration has become a concept that carries a more positive and wide meaning.

Some researchers (Heckmann and Schnapper 2003; Esser 2003; The European Foundation 2006) suggest that acculturation, placement, interaction and identification generate the processes of social integration. Acculturation or socialisation is the process by which an individual acquires the knowledge, cultural standards and competencies needed to interact successfully in a society. Placement refers to gaining an educational, economic, professional or social position in society. It also implies the acquisition of rights associated with particular positions and the opportunity to establish social relations and to win cultural, social and economic capital. Therefore, acculturation is a precondition for placement. Interaction is the result of relationships and networks, by individuals who share a mutual orientation. These relationships and networks include friendships, romantic relationships or marriages, or membership of social groups. Identification defines the individual's identification with a social system. With identification, the person sees himself or herself as part of a collective body. Berry (1992) evaluates integration, like adjustment, as a one-way process. The process of adjustment is a process of change which reduces the conflict between the environment and the individual. It brings harmony with the environment in which the non-dominant group preserves its cultural identity and the group becomes an integral part of the larger society.

Some researchers (Patterson 1963; Berry 1992; Bookman 1997; Vermeulen 1999) who accept integration as a positive strategy of acculturation explain integration as a two-way process. They investigate the integration of migrants within the process of adaptation. According to Patterson (1963), integration, understood as referring to cultural pluralism, determines a stage in which the incoming group as a whole through its own organisations adapts itself to permanent membership of the economic and civic life of the host society. Bookman (1997) stresses the positive dimension of integration which highlights common characteristics rather than differences of groups in society. This dimension of integration as a part of the adaptation process establishes peaceful relationships among groups in the society.

Enzigner (2003) states that the growing awareness of cultural identities and ethnic minority identities among migrants has led to ethnic stratification and ethno-cultural conflict in Europe. Therefore, many countries—such as Netherlands, Sweden and Canada—have recorded progress in integration policies. The European Commission (2002) supports the model of multiculturalism for integration of migrants.

Multiculturalism means the public acceptance of immigrant and minority groups as distinct communities which are distinguishable from the majority of the population with regard to language, culture and social behaviour, and which have their own associations and social infrastructure. Bauböck et al. (1996) consider that multiculturalism and its sensitivity to cultural difference is evident in democratic civil societies. Multiculturalism, which recognises cultural difference and takes measures to ensure social equality, has the potential to overcome division and segregation.

Some authors criticise multiculturalism, however, and draw attention to its negative aspects. Berry (1992) proposes that multiculturalism is a process lived between the powerful and powerless group. According to him, multiculturalism is a negative process of integration since it includes power relations. Entzinger (2002) and Rex (2003) argue that multiculturalism hinders integration, reinforces boundaries, and keeps immigrants separate from host populations by encouraging cultural difference.

Another group of integration studies focuses on dimensions of integration. These studies examine various dimensions of integration including the migrants' background, and economic, political, cultural, social, institutional, physical and personal dimensions. Integration at one level may facilitate integration at other level(s), since they are closely related with each other. However, as Göschel (2001) concludes, integration or disintegration in one dimension does not mean exclusion or inclusion with regards any or all other dimensions. Dimensions of integration include a range of variables which help researchers estimate the level of integration; however, there is no set of variables pertaining to integration that is appropriate to all individual cases.

The first dimension of integration is that of 'background,' which encompasses the demographic features of migrants. Additionally, it aims to get some background information about regions in which the integration study takes place or on migrants who have experienced migration. This dimension includes age, gender and household status as the variables of social integration (Cars et al. 1999). The European Commission (2002) defines fertility and mortality rates, life expectancy, and intermarriage as variables of integration. Baldwin-Edward (2005) adds the length of continuous residence of migrants. He observes that when the length of continuous residence increases, the level of integration also increases. Some researchers (Levine 1973; Kongar 1973; Şenyapılı 1978; Kartal 1978; Ersoy 1985; Erman 1998) explain the relationship between the duration of stay and integration through reference to knowledge of the new society and environment. This knowledge helps migrants to think independently and to determine their preferences as related to the place or the class that they belong to in the society. These researchers support the idea that birthplace is an important factor in integration.

Some researchers see education as an important variable of the background dimension. There are many variables in the literature that are associated with education; these include enrolment in education and the education levels of the migrant population (Levine 1973; Kongar 1973; Şenyapılı 1978; Kartal 1978; Ersoy 1985; Car et al. 1999), performance in school (Azevedo and Sannino 1997), and satisfaction with the school experience (Ager and Strang 2004). Coussey and Christensen (1997), Dagevos (1997), Ekholm (1997), The European Commission (2002), Baldwin-Edward (2005), and Spoer et al. (2007) relate educational indicators to labour market measures and social relations. According to them, migrants with lower education levels may possibly face unemployment. Moreover, satisfaction with school and attending school indicate the existence of social relations in school. These researchers show that the higher the level of education, the higher the integration level.

Secondly, the economic dimension refers to economic rights, performances and obligations (Bijl et al. 2005), participation of migrants in working life (Şenyapılı 1979; Göschel 2001), and social-security-based employment (Kongar 1973; Kartal 1978; Şenyapılı 1979; Şenyapılı 1981; Göschel 2001). Cars et al. (1999) specify the economic dimension of integration through variables focusing on access to the labour market including employment, unemployment, sector of economic activity, labour force participation rate, and unemployment by educational level. Working hours and occupation (Dagevos 1997), having a work contract (Dagevos 1997; Spoer et al. 2007), the type of job (Kongar 1973-a; Şenyapılı 1978-b; Ersoy 1985), job satisfaction (Kongar 1973-a; Şenyapılı 1978; Ersoy 1985; Ager and Strang 2004), and self-employment and periods of unemployment (Edwards 2004; Spoer et al. 2007) are other economic variables of integration. These researchers note that unemployment and a low level of participation in the labour force—especially among men—often results in isolation and social exclusion, whereas employment often results in social integration (Coussey and Christensen 1997; Fitzgerald 1997; Werner 1997; Ekholm 1997; Baldwin-Edward 2005; Salzer and Baron 2006).

Some researchers include variables about the income of migrants within the economic dimension of integration. They emphasise that integration is possible when the migrant earns a living without public assistance or support from others (Dagevos 1997; Ekholm 1997; Ager and Strang 2004; Spoer et al. 2007) or when the migrant achieves an adequate level of income (Kongar 1973; Kartal 1978; Şenyapılı 1979; Şenyapılı 1981). Cars et al. (1999) specify the variables of income as average annual earnings, wealth, public assistance and poverty rate. To this, other researchers add social insurance contributions (Edward 2004) and receiving support from others (Edward 2004; Salzer and Baron 2006) in the economic dimension of integration. Additionally, some researchers use having durable goods, home ownership (Şenyapılı 1978-b; Ersoy 1985), eating in restaurants and spending money on entertainment (Kongar 1973; Baum et al. 2000; Edwards 2004) as attributes to understand and measure the level of integration.

The third dimension of integration—that of culture—is not only a process that concerns immigrants and their subsequent generations, but is also an interactive process in which the host society must learn new ways of relating to immigrants and adapting to their needs. It does not necessarily signify that migrant groups must renounce the culture of their home country. The cultural dimension of integration represents the migrant's cognitive, behavioural and attitudinal changes (Heckmann and Schnapper 2003).

Fourthly, the social dimension of integration concerns the formal and informal relations of migrants in the host society. Social integration refers to a change in the social life of migrants. It assists in lessening social differentiation and social distance between groups, and in provoking social cohesion and connection between them (Putnam 1995; Haines 1996; Alba 1999; Pillemer et al. 2000; Gold et al. 2002; Esser 2004). According to Glasgow and Sofranko (1980), as well as Putnam (1995), community or social integration is described by dense networks and strong ties among community members which provide social support. Haines et al. (1996) define these ties by reference to membership in fraternal organisations (family and kinship relations) and community organisations. These ties can provide the support and solidarity of relatives and kin, and help share information and experiences in the migrant society. However, in the long term, such integration may hinder the migrant from creating links with the host (House et al. 1988; Heckmann and Schnapper 2003; Glasgow 2004). There are many variables that directly or indirectly affect social integration. Guest and Stamm (1993) analyse the presence of friendship and kinship networks to understand the informal ties of migrant groups. Levine (1973) considers old culture contacts to be a positive factor in adapting into life in the city. He defines old culture contacts as visits to/from the hometown, receiving letters from home, and having friends from the hometown in the city. Suzuki (1964; 1966), Şenyapılı (1978) and Ersoy (1985) explain the development of social relations and solidarity networks of rural migrants as alternative ways to cope with the city lifestyle and its problems. However, Şenyapılı (1978) supports the view that relations with relatives and the hometown postpone the urban integration of rural migrants. In their integration studies, Baum et al. (2000) discuss visits to friends and neighbours, and involvement in social activity groups, Ager and Strang (2004) examine social contacts with relatives and neighbours, and Ekholm (1997) investigates contacts with others and using mass media. Additionally, some studies use discrimination rates (Fitzgerald 1997) and crime rates (Fitzgerald 1997; The European Commission 2002; Baldwin-Edward 2005) as variables that negatively affect social integration.

Fifthly, the political dimension of integration can be evaluated as an extension of the social dimension. This concerns migrants as full members of the political community (Bijl et al. 2005). Therefore it covers the participation of migrants in democratic forms of political decision-making, self-administration and the exercise of power (Göschel 2001). A group of researchers (Yasa 1970; Kongar 1973; Şenyapılı 1978-b; Ersoy 1985; Guest and Stamm 1993; Baum et al. 2000; Edwards 2004; Salzer and Baron 2006; Spoer et al. 2007) measure civil and political participation via formal ties, where these include participation in associations or member-based activities. The variables within this dimension include formal involvement in neighbourhood groups, religious groups and civil organisations (Guest and Stamm, 1993); participating in social networks, organisations and common activities (Cars et al. 1999); participation in human and civil rights groups, welfare clubs and political parties (Baum et al. 2000; Edwards 2004; Salzer and Baron 2006; Spoer et al. 2007), and participation in voluntary work (Baldwin-Edward 2005). Furthermore, to examine political participation, Coussey and Christensen (1997), Ekholm (1997), The European Commission (2002), Baldwin-Edward (2005) and Salzer and Baron (2006) use voting registration, participation in local and national elections, and participation in key institutions and organisations (trade unions, school boards and work councils) as variables. Şenyapılı (1981-b) takes the political dimension of urban integration to correspond to the hope of holding a position in the city: that is to say, any economic or political position that influences decision-making processes about the future of the city.

The physical dimension constitutes the sixth dimension of integration. It concerns information about the housing and living conditions of migrants, and other aspects of integration that are related to the living standards of migrants. As variables of integration, this dimension covers housing standards (number of rooms, bathrooms and toilets) and expenditures, ownership, tenure and homelessness rate (Cars et al. 1999); housing typology, the number of persons per unit of surface area and services per accommodation (sanitary installations, central heating) (Azevedo and Sannino 1997); housing quality and percentage of income used for housing (Dagevos 1997); satisfaction from housing conditions (Ager and Strang 2004); formation of ghettos and urban segregation, discrimination in the rented housing market (refusal to rent or charging higher rents) (Baldwin-Edward 2005); and living rent-free (Spoer et al. 2007). Coussey and Christensen (1997), Ekholm (1997), The European Commission (2002) and Salzer and Baron (2006) note that low standards of living indicate poverty and social exclusion. Moreover, poor housing conditions in many cases lead to the spatial segregation of migrant groups from the rest of the society, and consequently low levels of integration. On the other hand, Sencer (1979) and Erman (1998) support the positive role of physical improvements in rural settlements in the city as regards integration. They also add living in apartment buildings to the list of physical attributes. Another group of researchers (Şenyapılı 1979; Türksoy 1983; Ersoy 1985) use "having knowledge of urban landmarks" as an integration attribute.

Seventhly, the institutional dimension of integration has both local and national levels. In the institutional integration process, core institutions such as the education system, the labour market, the housing system, the political system and the institutions of law (laws, regulations and unwritten rules and practices), are all expected to serve and be accessible to all citizens equally (Bijl et al. 2005; The European Foundation 2006). The literature discusses certain variables to define this dimension of integration including access to social services (Coussey and Christensen 1997); use of educational services (Yasa 1970; Kıray 1972; Kongar 1973-a,b; Öncü 1976; Karpat 1976; Kartal 1978; Şenyapılı 1978; Şenyapılı 1981-a,b; Eke 1981;Türksoy 1983; Ersoy 1985; Aslanoğlu 1998; Erman 1998); participation in activities such as concerts, sports activities, hobby courses; internet activities in public spaces (café, restaurant, cinema, theatre, party, museum, library, art gallery, park, etc.) (Şenyapılı 1978-b; Baum et al. 2000; Edwards 2004); going to entertainment places (Kongar 1973); receiving health care services (Berkman 1994; Yasa 1970; Kıray 1972; Kongar 1973-a,b; Öncü 1976; Karpat 1976; Şenyapılı 1981-a,b; Eke 1981; Türksoy 1983; Ersoy 1985; Aslanoğlu 1998; Erman 1998; The European Commission 2002; Ager and Strang 2004; Baldwin-Edward 2005; Salzer and Baron 2006); satisfaction from health services (Ager and Strang 2004); participation in leisure time and recreational activities (Salzer and Baron 2006); access to transportation (Edwards

2004; Spoer et al. 2007); using public transportation (Edwards 2004); and information services (Spoer et al. 2007). Türksoy (1983) adds that knowledge of urban services has a critical role in using these services. According to her, people who do not have enough knowledge about services may not be brave enough to use their economic power to access those services.

The last dimension of integration, the personal dimension, is equivalent to identification. It refers to the feeling of belonging to the host society, and thus the inclusion into the new society at a subjective level which develops as a result of participation and acceptance (Kartal 1978; Heckmann and Schnapper 2003). Some Turkish authors (Kongar 1973-a,b; Şenyapılı 1981-b; Ersoy 1985) add to this dimension the positive effect of having future expectations for oneself or one's children regarding the prospects for integration.

Urban integration processes for rural migrants in the Turkish case

In Turkey, the urban integration process started with the process of migration from rural areas to large cities initiated in the late 1940s. The reason behind this migration was the decrease in rural job opportunities due to mechanisation in agriculture. The 'push' effect of rural life together with the 'pulling' forces of the urban in the context of industrialisation accelerated the migration process. The male rural migrants who are responsible for the economic subsistence of the family in traditional societies led this process. After they had established a stable life in the city, their families migrated to join them.

The efforts of rural migrants to find a job in the city constituted their first attempt at urban integration. Since the growing industrial and service sectors needed skilled labour in the cities, rural migrants remained at the margins of the labour force. However, the construction sector, which was the newly flourishing sector in the cities, and the urban commercial markets resulted in a need for cheap labour (Şenyapılı 2004). Through working in low-paid jobs which did not need a trained and skilled labour force, and filling the labour vacancies, migrants started to engage in the labour market of the city.

One of the most important problems for rural migrants concerned housing. The cities were not prepared for the invasion of rural migrants. Additionally, the limited budget of the rural migrants did not permit them to take a house from within the cities' legal housing stocks. Therefore, rural migrants illegally constructed shanties during the course of a single night, using their own labour force, on public land. In time, rural families encouraged their relatives and friends in the country to migrate to the city. Shanties turned into shanty towns inhabited by rural migrants from the same region. They grew vegetables and kept barnyard fowl in the garden of their shanties (Yasa 1970). All of these efforts to seek a spatial order in the city displayed their need for integration into the city physically (Kahraman 2008, 2011).

The growing economic role of rural migrants as a new consumer group in the domestic market and their political role as new voter group for governments prepared the basis for squatter housing acts in Turkey. The first Squatter Act issued in 1966 proposed to bring infrastructure and services to squatter housing settlements which were in relatively good condition, and to clear out the uninhabitable ones. Thus, this Act led to the transformation of low-quality squatter housing settlements into low-density neighbourhoods (Şenyapılı 1982; Erman 2001).

During those years, rural migrants tried to carry their rural lifestyle over to the city and only drew limited benefit from the opportunities of the city itself. Their family sizes, hygiene practices, eating habits, dressing style (Yasa 1970; Ayata 1988) and social relations based on old cultural contacts and para-kinship relations (Suzuki 1964, 1966; Levine 1973) displayed their rural characteristics. On the other hand, they started to use urban services such as educational and medical services when they were available (Eke 1981). However, they had low levels of education, income and participation in mass communications such as through reading newspapers and listening to the radio (Yasa 1970; Kongar 1973; Şenyapılı 1978-b). As a result of differences between modern urbanites and rural migrants, as well as the effects of the Western world and modernisation theory in Turkey, rural migrants were blamed for ruralising the city. This tendency created an expectation of the assimilation of rural migrants into modern urban society (Erman 2001).

In the 1970s, rural migrants were no longer temporary or marginal since they constituted more than the half of the urban population. The ongoing rural migration to the cities led to the decrease in the availability of land for new migrants to construct squatter houses. This development changed the characteristics of such houses. Since new migrant groups rented the houses of the first-comers, squatter houses turned into competitive and profitable commodities (Erman 2001). Additionally, the duration of stay of rural migrants in the city increased, and their use of urban services improved over time (Kartal 1978). However, they still had insufficient knowledge of urban services and urban landmarks such as historical places, shopping districts and recreational areas. Therefore, although the economic system imposed on rural migrants the feeling of being integrated, they did not completely integrate into the urban lifestyle (Şenyapılı 1979).

In the following years, the high level of competition in job opportunities for rural migrants, as well as the economic crisis, resulted in an increase in unemployment rates and poverty in squatter housing settlements (Erman 2001; Kahraman 2008, 2011). On the other hand, squatter housing settlements experienced drastic changes with the introduction of a new group of Amnesty Laws issued in the 1980s. Through improvement plans, these laws legalised the illegally developed housing areas and provided development rights to owners or users of land (Leithmann and Baharoğlu 1999). These laws opened the way to transform squatter houses into high-rise apartment buildings (Kahraman 2008, 2011). Consequently, owners of the squatter land became owners of several apartments or flats in apartment buildings (Erman 2004).

Through improvements in the socio-economic status of rural migrants, they shaped the city by creating their own ways of life and values. Therefore, they were named as a sub-culture within the city culture. This culture, carrying both rural and urban features, had the potential to influence social, political and economic structures of the society through its values, and its social, political and economic relations. According to Gökçe (1993), the sub-culture failed to modernise; therefore, it bears connotations of inferiority, being less than the dominant culture and in a permanent state of in-betweenness.

At the end of the 1980s, a new tool of squatter housing transformation was developed as an alternative to improvement plans. These were called urban transformation projects. Compared to the improvement plans, these projects have proved more sensitive to the urban environment, with more green areas and urban services, the financial resources for multi-storey constructions, and have engaged the former squatter housing inhabitants through public participation (Dündar 1998; Türker-Devecigil 2005). Thus, the physical and economic conditions of rural migrants have improved. In contrast, however, their social relations and traditional lifestyle have been damaged (Kahraman 2011).

In the 1990s, rural migrants with Kurdish origins as ethnic identities migrated to large Turkish cities. Since they were faced with social and political discrimination, they usually settled down in the most disadvantaged locations and created their own communities. The politicisation of ethnic and sectarian identities in the political arena resulted in conflicting groups. These groups were associated with poverty, radical actions directed against the state, violence, criminal activities that disturbed the social order, social fragmentation, and danger to the city, its values and institutions (Erder 1995; Erman 2001 and 2004). Ersoy (1985) mentions that social disorder, disorganisation and alienation in the urban social environment impeded the integration of migrants into the urban life.

In summary, the rural migration process in Turkey has resulted in both social and spatial changes within urban space. Today, rural migrants are living in squatter housing neighbourhoods or former squatter housing neighbourhoods transformed through improvement plans and urban transformation projects. They have constituted demographically, regionally, ethnically, economically, socially and physically heterogeneous groups, and they have created their own lifestyles and values wherever they live and whatever their origins (Kahraman 2011).

Methodology and results

This study attempts to explore the attributes defining urban integration via the subjective descriptions of rural migrants themselves. Unlike the Turkish literature on urban integration, this study does not reflect the understanding of the researcher as regards integration. It intends to extract what urban integration means for rural migrants without any prior limitations on their definitions and perceptions.

This study used qualitative data collection techniques to uncover rural migrants' feelings, judgements and behaviours. It conducted analytical procedures to explore and classify the conceptualisation of the sample as attributes and factors of urban integration. This part discusses the methodological framework of this paper. It covers information about the contextual setting of the study areas, the sample, data collection method and data analysis procedures.

1. Study areas

This study is conducted as a case study in three neighbourhoods in which rural migrants are still living. These neighbourhoods, which are located in one of the oldest rural migrant districts in Ankara, have physically different characteristics. This district, called Dikmen, is located in the southern development zone of the city. The migration of rural origin people to the district started in the 1960s. The squatter housing development process in the district followed this trend. In parallel with the increase in the population of rural migrants, the number of squatter houses rapidly increased. The transformation process of the district started with the implementation of improvement plans at the end of the 1970s. With the guidance of these plans, speculative house builders transformed the squatter houses into apartment buildings (Kahraman 2008, 2011). At the end of the 1980s, the Greater Municipality of Ankara initiated an urban transformation project to transform the district. The project, which aims to transform the valley into a recreational, commercial, cultural and social node within the city, provides housing zones for both the former inhabitants and high-income groups (Metropol İmar 1994; Uzun 2003). It consists of five implementation zones, three of which have been completed by now (The Greater Municipality of Ankara 2011). Today, the Dikmen district is rapidly transforming through different models of squatter housing transformation. Few squatter houses now remain.

The three selected neighbourhoods in the Dikmen district are the Mürsel Uluç–Malazgirt Neighbourhoods, the Sokullu Neighbourhood, and the Dikmen Valley Urban Transformation Project area. These neighbourhoods respectively represent a squatter housing neighbourhood, a former squatter housing neighbourhood transformed through an improvement plan, and a former squatter housing neighbourhood transformed through an urban transformation project. The Mürsel Uluç–Malazgirt Neighbourhoods, which have been in the process of squatter housing transformation through improvement plans since the 1990s, includes fewer than forty low-quality squatter houses. The Sokullu Neighbourhood, which is one of the oldest former squatter housing neighbourhoods in the district, completed its transformation 10–15 years ago. The speculative house builders, small entrepreneurs with limited money, obtained the land of squatter houses by contracting the owners of the squatter houses and transformed squatter houses into four to five storey apartment buildings. These buildings were shared between squatter housing owners and the speculative house builder (Kahraman 2008, 2011). The Dikmen Valley Urban Transformation Project area provides houses for high-income groups and the former squatter housing inhabitants in the project area through a relocation model. The transformation process, which was the responsibility of local governments, included limited participation of former squatter housing inhabitants (Metropol İmar 1994; Uzun 2003; Türker-Devecigil 2003). Today the former squatters live in five to ten storey apartment buildings (Kahraman 2008, 2011).

2. The sample and the data collection process

To collect the raw data to define urban integration through the active participation of rural migrants, the study conducted in-depth interviews. Twenty-five rural migrants were interviewed in each of the three neighbourhoods. The interviews, in which respondents freely expressed their perceptions and definitions of urban integration, took at least two hours for each participant. The data collection process was completed within two months from April to June 2007.

The resulting sample had different living environments, gender, age, birthplace, and backgrounds (see table 4-1). The sample was composed of 84% females and 16% males. In terms of age, 44.3% were between 35 and 50, 33.3% between 20 and 35, and 22.7% between 50 and 60. According to birthplace, the sample had 69.3% from Central Anatolia, 28% from Eastern Anatolia, and 2.7% from the Black Sea region.

In the in-depth interviews, which were designed to reveal the urban integration definitions of rural migrants, two general questions were asked. In these questions, the major aim was to extract subjective descriptions by the sample about urban integration and the social, economic, cultural, political and background characteristics seen as relevant by rural migrants for integrating into the urban lifestyle. The answers to these questions constituted the raw data of this study. The following section discusses the analytical procedures applied to the raw data.

3. Data analysis process and results

The data analysis process employed in this study followed three steps: (i) exploration of perceptual attributes to define urban integration; (ii) classification of perceptual attributes of urban integration; and (iii) statistics on frequency of citation of perceptual attributes.

In the first step, to explore perceptual attributes of urban integration, the list of perceptions of the sample was derived from the raw data obtained from in-depth interviews. The content analysis helped to reveal content categories pertaining to urban integration. It allowed the discovery of the existence and frequency of concepts in the text of in-depth interviews. Tables of information were then created, allowing the visualisation and listing of urban integration topics. Then, similar topics were grouped together and labelled as attributes of urban integration (Kahraman 2008).

Table 4-1: Distribution of the Sample according to the Neighbourhood Lived, Gender, Age, and Birthplace Differences

Properties of The Sample			**Sample in**			**Total**
			Dikmen Valley	Sokullu	Mürsel Uluç/ Malazgirt	
GENDER	Female	Count	20	21	22	63
		% within Neighborh.	80%	84%	88%	**84%**
	Male	Count	5	4	3	12
		% within Neighborh.	20%	16%	12%	**16%**
AGE	Between 20-35	Count	4	10	11	25
		% within Neighborh.	16%	40%	44%	**33.3%**
	Between 35-50	Count	10	12	12	34
		% within Neighborh.	40%	48%	48%	**45.3%**
	Between 50-60	Count	11	3	3	17
		% within Neighborh.	44%	12%	12%	**22.7%**
BIRTH PLACE	Central Anatolia	Count	20	21	11	52
		% within Neighborh.	80%	84%	44%	**69.3%**
	Eastern Anatolia	Count	3	4	14	21
		% within Neighborh.	12%	16%	56%	**28%**
	Black Sea	Count	2	0	0	2
		% within Neighborh.	8%	0	0	**2.7%**

The content analysis uncovered forty-five perceptual attributes of urban integration. These attributes are as follows: being a high school or university graduate; being born in the city; being younger than 50–55 years old; spending at least 5–6 years in the city; working in the city, working as a government employee; the existence of employed women in the family; having social security; having an adequate level of income to live in the city; having durable goods and furniture in the house (such as a buffet, a sofa and a dining table); house and car ownership; eating a meal in a restaurant; shopping from luxury shops; spending money on entertainment (such as going to pubs, cafes and clubs); having expectations from oneself (about good income, occupation, and health), and one's children (about good income, occupation, marriage and happiness); having old friends and/or relatives in the city; establishing friendships with urbanites; being formal in social relations (which refers meeting and sharing less with friends/relatives/neighbours, and spending less time in meetings); living in apartment buildings and specific neighbourhoods (in which rich people live); changing hygiene habits (such as an increase in the frequency of washing clothes and cleaning the house); changing the manner of dressing (which refers to dressing similarly to urbanites and not using headscarves); changing the way of talking (kindness in talking and not using village dialect in conversations); changing eating habits (which means changes in daily diet such as eating less red meat and pulses, and eating more vegetables and fish, and changes in cooking habits such as cooking in small proportions and more frequently); being kind in behaviours (which refers being kind in social life); becoming independent individuals (being independent from the family and relatives); giving up rural habits (such as not making bread, noodle and tomato sauce, not beating or washing carpets and bed woollens, and not hanging clothes on the balcony); going to the cinema, the theatre, and the museum; going to historical areas; going on hobby courses; going for picnics; going on a seaside holiday; going less often to his/her village; reading books and newspapers; being an association member; using health, education, transportation and recreational services; and having knowledge of city landmarks (Kahraman 2008, 2011).

In the second step, since this study extracted a very long list of urban integration attributes and it is difficult to follow and assess these attributes, they were classified under more general categories of urban integration. For this, a factor analysis was conducted. Factor analysis is a statistical technique that reduces the number of perceptual attributes to more generalised meaningful content groups (Hair et al. 1995). Considering the small sample size, the present study followed an exploratory factor analysis process (Norusis 1990) which derived general perceptual attribute groups of urban integration. To create data for the factor analysis, subjective descriptions of the sample were transferred to association matrices, which contained frequency of citations for each perceptual attribute of urban integration. After testing the appropriateness of factor analysis for this study, principal components analysis was used to extract the factor groups of urban integration.[1] Then, a "rotated factor matrix" was produced which showed the estimated correlations between perceptual attributes.[2] The estimated correlations found the attributes included in the same categories of urban integration.

This analysis revealed sixteen factors of urban integration.[3] In this step, the Tabachnick and Fidell (1996) rule was used to group the perceptual attributes that load on each factor.[4] Finally, these factors were labelled as categories of urban integration. These labels were identified according to patterns of similarity between items that load on a factor. This study attempted to use labels that already exist in the literature or create names explaining the conceptual structure of the factor. These categories include social and cultural activities; using urban services; luxury expenses and income; ownership and employment; in-house purchasing; social status; future expectations and age; urban manners; eating and entertainment; knowledge of known places and becoming independent; employment of women and their rural ties; urban holiday activity; education; self-improvement activities; time resided in the city; and social ties and living areas (Kahraman 2008).

Table 4-2 displays the categories and perceptual attributes included under each category of urban integration. According to the table, the first category of urban integration, social and cultural activities, is composed of six perceptual attributes. These are "going to the theatre, the museum and the cinema," "being an association member," "going to historical areas" and "reading newspapers and books." The second category of urban integration, which includes the attributes of "using health, transportation, educational and recreational services," is called using urban services. Factor analysis categorises perceptual attributes related with income and expenditures under three separate categories: luxury expenses and income; ownership and employment; and in-house purchasing. Luxury expenses and income is composed of "shopping from luxury shops," "eating a meal in a restaurant" and "having an adequate level of income to live in the city." Ownership and employment covers five perceptual attributes. These are "car and house ownership," "changing hygiene habits," "working in the city" and "having a social security." In-house purchasing includes "having furniture" and durable goods." The sixth category of integration, social status, is composed of "establishing friendship with urbanites," and "working as a government employee." The seventh, the category of future expectations and age, covers the perceptual attributes of "having expectations about himself and children" and "being younger than 50–55 years old." The eighth category of integration, urban manners, has four perceptual attributes. These are "being kind in behaviours," "changing the way of talking and dressing," and "going on picnics." The ninth category, knowledge of known places and becoming independent individuals, covers "becoming independent individuals" and "having knowledge of known places and urban landmarks." The tenth, eating and entertainment, contains

Table 4-2: Perceptual Attributes and Categories of Urban Integration derived from Content and Factor Analysis

	CATEGORIES OF URBAN INTEGRATION							
	1. Social and Cultural Activities	**2. Using Urban Services**	**3. Luxury Expenses & Income**	**4. Ownership & Employment**	**5. In-House Purchasing**	**6. Social Status**	**7. Future Expectations & Age**	**8. Urban Manners**
PERCEPTUAL ATTRIBUTES	Going to the theatre	Using health services	Shopping from luxury shops	Car ownership	Having furniture	Friendship with urbanites	Having expectation from himself	Being kind in behaviors
	Going to the museum	Using transportation services	Eating a meal in a restaurant	House ownership	Having durable goods	Working as a government employee	Having expectation from children	Changing the way of talking
	Going to the cinema	Using educational services	Having an adequate level of income	Changing hygiene habits			Being relatively young	Going to the picnic
	Going to historical areas	Using recreational areas		Working in the city				Changing the way of dressing
	Being an association member			Having social security				
	Reading books/newspapers							

Table 4-2 (cont.)

	FACTORS OF URBAN INTEGRATION							
	9. Eating & Entertainment	**10. Knowledge on Known Places & Becoming Independent Individuals**	**11. Employment of Women & Her Rural Ties**	**12. Urban Holiday Activity**	**13. Education**	**14. Self-Improvement Activities**	**15. Time Resided in The City**	**16. Social Ties & Living Areas**
PERCEPTUAL ATTRIBUTES	Changing eating habits	Having knowledge on urban landmarks	Existence of employed woman in family	Going to a seaside holiday	Being a high school/ university graduate	Going to hobby courses	Spending at least 5-6 years in the city	Living in specific neighbourh.
	Spending money on entertainment	Becoming independent individuals	Having old friends/relatives in the city			Going less to his village	Being born in the city	Being formal in social relations
			Giving up rural habits					Living in apartment buildings

contains "changing eating habits" and "spending money on entertainment." The eleventh category of urban integration, employment of women and their rural ties, is composed of "the existence of an employed woman in the family," "having old friends and relatives in the city" and "giving up rural ties." The next two categories, urban holiday activity and education, include the attributes of "going to a seaside holiday" and "being a high school or university graduate." The fourteenth category of urban integration, self-improvement activities, covers "going on hobby courses" and "going less often to his/her village." Time resided in the city, as another category, has two perceived attributes: these are "spending at least 5–6 years in the city" and "being born in the city." The last category of urban integration, social ties and living areas, contains "living in specific neighbourhoods and apartment buildings" and "being formal in social relations" (Kahraman 2008).

The last phase of the data analysis process examined the frequency of citation of each perceptual attribute and the neighbourhood differences in terms of these frequencies. To do this, this study employed descriptive statistics. To prepare the data for this analysis, the association matrix of perceptual attributes for each neighbourhood and the total sample was used. Dummy coding helped explore the perception of each attribute for each respondent of the sample in total and in each neighbourhood. When the sample cited the perceptual attribute, the score of that attribute was coded as "1," on the contrary, when the sample did not cite that attribute, it was coded as "0."

Table 4-3 displays the most and the least frequently cited perceptual attributes. In the total sample, the most frequently cited attributes were "changing the way of dressing" (76%), "changing the way of talking" (60%), and "being a high school or university graduate" (57.3%). Whereas the least frequently cited attributes were "going on hobby courses" (3%), "having old friends and relatives in the city" (3%), and "going less often to his/her village" (4%).

Table 4-3: The Most and Least Frequently cited Attributes of Urban Integration within Samples in each Neighbourhood and in the Total Sample

	Attributes	**Within Neighborhood**			**Total**
		Dikmen Valley	Sokullu	Mürsel Uluç/ Malazgirt	
The Most Frequently Cited Attributes	Changing the way of dressing	76%	76%	76%	**76%**
	Changing the way of talking	60%	64%	56%	**60%**
	Being a high school/university grad.	32%	76%	64%	**57.3%**
	Being kind in social relations	52%	40%	56%	**49%**
	Using educational services	32%	52%	52%	**45.3%**
	Having an adequate level of income	44%	52%	40%	**45.3%**
The Least Frequently Cited Attributes	Going to hobby courses	8%	0	0	**3%**
	Having old friends/ relatives in city	4%	0	4%	**3%**
	Going less to his/her village	8%	4%	0	**4%**
	Going to historical areas	12%	0	8%	**6.7%**
	Having durable goods	8%	0	12%	**6.7%**

According to the frequency of citation of perceptual attributes, each neighbourhood differed from the others. In the Dikmen Valley, the most frequently cited perceptual attributes were "changing the way of dressing" (76%), and "changing the way of talking" (60%); whereas the least frequently cited attribute was "having old friends and relatives in the city" (4%). In the Sokullu Neighbourhood, the most frequently cited perceptual attributes were "being a high school or university graduate" (76%) and "changing the way of dressing" (76%). In this neighbourhood, to explain urban integration, nobody cited "giving up rural habits," "having expectations from his/her children," "having expectations from himself," "having durable goods," "going to historical areas," "going on hobby courses," and "having old friends/relatives in the city." In Mürsel Uluç–Malazgirt Neighbourhoods, the most frequently cited perceptual attributes were "changing the way of dressing" (76%), "being a high school or university graduate" (64%), and "changing the way of talking" (60%). In this neighbourhood, nobody cited "going to the museum," "going less often to his/her village," "having expectations from his/her children," and "going on hobby courses" to define urban integration (Kahraman 2008).

Conclusion

This paper, in general, attempted to define urban integration through the descriptions of rural migrants who are at the centre of this ongoing process. Specifically, it aimed to reveal the perceptual attributes and categories of urban integration. Additionally, it intended to examine differences in urban integration perceptions of rural migrants who are living in physically different neighbourhoods within the same district.

Since urban integration is a context-dependent process, this paper employed a case-study methodology to achieve its goals. The case study of this research was applied in one of the oldest rural migrant settlements, the Dikmen district, in Ankara. In-depth interviews with 75 rural migrants constituted the raw data of the study. Subjective descriptions of rural migrants about urban integration with the help of the content analysis revealed the perceptual attributes of urban integration. As the number of these attributes reached 45, these attributes needed to be systematised as more generalised and readable data. The factor analysis categorised these attributes under 16 meaningful categories. To display the perceptual differences and similarities within the same district, the case study in this research included sub-studies conducted in three physically different neighbourhoods of the Dikmen district. Finally, descriptive statistics examined variations in the frequency of citations of urban integration attributes in different neighbourhoods.

Unlike previous studies which have reflected the author's own evaluation of the integration of rural migrants, this study reflected the perceptions of rural migrants about the process without any manipulation. Therefore, this study shows that it is possible to define urban integration through the active participation and contributions of rural migrants. Moreover, the findings of the study show that urban integration is a multidimensional concept including categories related to background, social, economic, physical, individual, cultural, organisational and institutional dimensions.

Some attributes revealed in this study are consistent with previous studies about integration, whereas some are new for the integration literature. The common attributes extracted in the present study and previous studies are having social security (Kongar 1973-a; Kartal 1978; Şenyapılı 1979, 1981; Göschel 2001); having an adequate level of income (Kongar 1973; Kartal 1978; Şenyapılı 1979, 1981); having durable goods; home ownership (Şenyapılı 1978-b; Ersoy 1985); eating a meal in a restaurant and spending money on entertainment (Kongar 1973-b; Baum et al. 2000; Edwards 2004); having expectations from oneself and one's children (Kongar 1973-b; Şenyapılı 1981; Ersoy 1985); living in apartment buildings (Sencer 1979; Erman 1998); having knowledge of urban landmarks (Şenyapılı 1979; Türksoy 1983; Ersoy 1985); having relatives in the city (Suzuki 1964, 1966; Levine 1973; Şenyapılı 1978; Ersoy 1985); being an association member (Yasa 1970; Kongar 1973-b; Şenyapılı 1978-b; Ersoy 1985; Guest and Stamm 1993; Baum et al. 2000; Edwards 2004; Salzer and Baron 2006; Spoer et al. 2007); using health, recreational, and educational services (Kıray 1972; Öncü 1976; Şenyapılı 1978; Kartal 1978; Eke 1981; Türksoy 1983; The European Commission 2002; Ager and Strang 2004; Baldwin-Edward 2005; Salzer and Baron 2006); going to the cinema and theatre (Şenyapılı 1978-b; Baum et al. 2000); reading newspapers (Yasa 1970; Kongar 1973-a; Şenyapılı 1978-b); changing hygiene habits (Yasa 1970); and changing the way of dressing (Yasa 1970; Ayata 1988). Some attributes of the present study are associated with attributes already existing in the literature. Levine (1973), Kongar (1973-a,b), Şenyapılı (1978), Kartal (1978), Ersoy (1985), Coussey and Christensen (1997), Azevedo Sannino (1997), Erman (1998), Cars et al (1999) and The European Commission (2002) used education level as an attribute of integration. They supported the proposal that the higher the education level, the more migrants feel integrated. This bears a similar meaning as the perceptual attribute of "being a high school or university graduate" in the present study. Birthplace and time spent in the city (Levine 1973; Kongar 1973; Şenyapılı 1978; Kartal 1978; Ersoy 1985; Erman 1998) have, respectively, similar meanings as "being born in the city" and "spending at least 5–6 years in the city" in this study. The type of job (Kongar 1973; Şenyapılı 1978-b; Ersoy 1985) and job satisfaction (Kongar 1973-a; Şenyapılı 1978-b; Ersoy 1985; Ager and Strang 2004) are associated with "working in the city" in this study. The equivalent of going to places of entertainment (Kongar 1973; Baum et al. 2000; Edwards 2004) in previous studies is "spending money on entertainment" in the present study. The content of some previously used attributes such as contacts with others (Ekholm 1997), participation in hobby activities (Baum et al. 2000), and sustaining rural ties (Suzuki 1964 and 1966; Levine 1973; Şenyapılı 1978-b; Ersoy 1985) were addressed in this study as, respectively, "establishing friendships with urbanites," "going on hobby courses," and "going less often to his/her village." Finally, using public transportation (Edwards 2004), which is another urban integration attribute used in previous studies, has a similar meaning to "using transportation services" in this study.

This study contributed to integration literature by extracting new attributes of urban integration. These are "working as a government employee," "existence of an employed woman in the family," "car ownership," "shopping from luxury shops," "being formal in social relations," "living in specific neighbourhoods," "changing the way of talking," "changing eating habits," "being kind in behaviours," "becoming independent individuals," "giving up rural habits," "going to historical areas," and "going on a seaside holiday."

This study found that the frequency of citation of each perceptual attribute varies within the total sample and in the neighbourhood samples. "Changing the way of dressing," "changing the way of talking" and "being a high school or university graduate" are the most frequently cited attributes to explain urban integration. These perceptual attributes show the importance of the social and educational dimensions of urban integration. Although the differences in lifestyles and physical condition of rural migrants living in physically different neighbourhoods affected their perceptions, there were no significant differences in the most frequently cited attributes in different neighbourhoods. In the Dikmen Valley, "changing the way of dressing and changing the way of talking"; in the Sokullu Neighbourhood, "being a high school or university graduate" and "changing the way of dressing"; and in the Mürsel Uluç–Malazgirt Neighbourhoods, "changing the way of dressing," and "being a high school or university graduate" are the most frequently cited perceptual features of urban integration.

To conclude, this study proved that urban integration is a multidimensional phenomenon in which the definition changes subject to the perceptions of inhabitants. The social, cultural, physical and economic structures and backgrounds of inhabitants may affect these perceptions. Therefore, further research may reveal the urban integration perceptions of rural migrants who are living in different parts of the city, or in different cities, or who have different backgrounds such as age, gender, education, and income.

CHAPTER FIVE

TERRITORIALISING SPIRITUAL VALUES: NOTIONS OF "BELONGING" AND "POSSESSING" IN THE CONTEXT OF THE CONTROVERSY OVER MAX BROD'S LEGACY

MARKÉTA P. RUBEŠOVÁ

The essential role of space in man's life has long been acknowledged in the human and social sciences. It was only a matter of time before scholars from diverse disciplines placed this topic at the centre of their own academic research, and in parallel, interlinked it with other research themes. The 1960s and 1970s may be viewed in this respect as a turning point. The notable rise of interest among sociologists, geographers, anthropologists, philosophers and historians in the unceasing interaction between human beings and the space around them retroactively engendered the label the *spatial turn* (for a detailed discussion, see especially Döring and Thielmann 2009). This phenomenon opened new possibilities for interpreting the world around us and man's place in it from a spatiotemporal perspective, in all the above-mentioned disciplines. Along with the shift in perceptions of space, but not necessarily in direct relation to it, there emerged a vast amount of academic literature dedicated to the problem of identity. This research theme encompasses large agendas of what can be understood under the rubric of identity and cognate terms such as belonging, identification, consciousness, awareness, loyalty, etc. Identity can be a quality of personal character, but almost every individual embraces in the course of his life various collective identities beyond his own proper identity. It is important to stress that identity is not primordial or given. It undergoes a process of formation, being shaped by multiple external and internal factors, it is further transformed, challenged, competed with and sometimes even abandoned. The social web is thus all the time in motion, strongly marked by strategies of inclusion and exclusion. An interesting moment can be observed when a person is understood to belong to some group of individuals. At that point, the person not only belongs to the group, but he is, so to speak, possessed by this group including with respect to the things he produces (be this output of a material or spiritual character). At some point, the collective claims a right of possession regardless of the person's opinions and feelings. When an individual is desired for the reproduction of the self-image of the collective, his consent to identify himself with the group is no more relevant. He might be "possessed" by a given imagined community even without his knowledge or against his will. In some cases, as we shall see, one person may raise interest in a number of collectives that then find themselves in a silent or open conflict.

In almost any tested terrain, the research fields of identity and space are intertwined with the topics of frontiers and alterity. The study of their reciprocal relations may help us understand the human condition in a given social or historical situation. As was highlighted in the introduction to this volume, the examination of space and boundaries is not restricted to their physical or real, visible manifestation. The authors are cognisant of their existence at the metaphoric or symbolic level. This conceptual statement serves as a cornerstone for the present paper. Admittedly, the author did not execute an exhaustive analysis of all available sources, nor does this paper offers exact statistical data. It wishes above all to test some of the suggested theories via a concrete historical case, along with some suggestions for further deeper exploration of the topic.

The concepts of identities, their frontiers, and the dynamics between belonging and possessing will be used in order to decode the rhetoric used by competing sides involved in a legal controversy that arose over the literary legacy of the writer and philosopher Max Brod (1884–1968), a few years ago. After Brod's former secretary, Ilse Esther Hoffe (1906–2007), passed away in September 2007, the legal rights of her heirs to inherit the manuscripts and correspondence of Brod and Franz Kafka (1883–1924) were called into question by the National Library of Israel (previously the Jewish National and University Library). The case drew the attention of the Marbach Literary Archive in Germany, as they would have liked to purchase some of the subjects of inheritance. This controversy is not the first encounter between Marbach's and Kafka's legacies. Via a private book dealer at Sotheby's auction house in London, Ilse Ester Hoffe had sold Franz Kafka's handwritten manuscript of his novel "The Trial" to the German Literary Archive in Marbach.[1] It should be said that M. Brod bestowed Kafka's and his own writings to I. E. Hoffe. It is only natural that part of Brod's legacy, consisting of writings and documents created by or related to Franz Kafka, proved to be at the heart of the conflict. Max Brod had remained largely in the shade of Kafka, as he had also been during his own lifetime. Therefore, greater attention in the textual analysis of newspaper articles and encyclopedic entries is paid to Kafka than to Brod.

Lack of space prevents a detailed description of the way the collection was managed and cared for by Hoffe. Nor do we wish here to evaluate the legal aspects of the case.[2] We are interested in public reactions on the part of the litigants and their supporters, and also in the silence on the part of those we might have expected to raise a hand and express their claims. The survey shows how diverse attitudes can be to spiritual or literary values created by cultural agents.

Reflection on the notion of identity and an analysis of the public use of identities (collective, individual) and belonging (to a given larger group of individuals) as supportive arguments is herein based on primary sources originating chiefly in Germany, Israel and the Czech Republic. Their connection to the spatial dimension of various sizes and characters remains in the foreground throughout the survey. The first group of primary sources comprises encyclopedias and dictionaries. Newspaper articles make up another type of sources. The focus will be on that part of the public discourse that makes conscious or unconscious use of national, cultural and political rhetoric in order to justify their claims.

Encyclopedias and dictionaries on Franz Kafka

Let me start with a preview of lexical and encyclopedic entries on Franz Kafka. It is usually the first few lines of such entries that strive for the clearest allocation of a person to a time, space, sphere of activity, and national belonging (see table 5-1). While the first two notions are mostly non-problematic and the third only rarely presents problems, the fourth part of the definition is simply a trap, as the meaning of "nationality" or, more precisely, the meaning of the adjectives traditionally attributed to a nation (such as English, German, Czech, Chinese), is complex and depends on the cultural, historical and political setting. It is not surprising, then, that in one place we read that Kafka was a "German writer living mainly in Prague," while in another he is described as "Jewish-Czech writer born in Prague, one of the greatest writers in the German language," and that in one distinguished encyclopedia we read he was an "Austrian writer." To be sure, Kafka is very often connected in the first instance not to some group of individuals (such as a nation), but to a place: "Prague

Table 5-1: Selected Encyclopedic and Dictionary Entries on Franz Kafka

Source (Country, Year of publishing)	Definition
The Blackwell Companion to Jewish Culture (UK 1989)	"AUSTRIAN NOVELIST. BORN INTO A JEWISH FAMILY LARGELY ASSIMILATED TO THE GERMAN-SPEAKING COMMUNITY IN PRAGUE"
Encyclopedia of Modern Jewish Culture (UK 2005)	„CZECH NOVELIST. BORN INTO A JEWISH FAMILY LARGELY ASSIMILATED TO THE GERMAN-SPEAKING COMMUNITY IN PRAGUE“
Diderot (Czech Republic 1997)	„GERMAN WRITER OF JEWISH ORIGIN. HE WAS BORN IN PRAGUE AND LIVED THERE…“
Illustrated Encyclopedical Dictionary (Czech Republic, 1980-82)	„PRAGUE GERMAN WRITER OF JEWISH ORIGIN“
Der Grosse Bertelsmann Lexikothek (Germany 1982)	„WRITER (…) FROM JEWISH (…) FAMILY…, LIVING IN PRAGUE“
Österreich Lexikon (Austria 1995)	„FICTION AUTHOR WRITING IN GERMAN“
THE 4TH ED. CAMBRIDGE ENCYCLOPEDIA (UK 2000)	"novelist, b. in Prague, Czechoslovakia, of German-Jewish parents"
Encyclopedia Britannica (UK 1992)	"Czech-born German writer"
Biograpisches Lexikon zur Geschichte der Böhmischen Länder (Germany-Austria 1979)	„POET… THE SON OF PRAGUE JEWISH BUSSINESS MAN“
Czech Biographical Dictionary of XX. Century (Czech Rep. 1999)	„PRAGUE WRITER IN THE GERMAN LANGUAGE, OF JEWISH ORIGIN“
GENERAL, JEWISH AND ISRAELI HEBREW ENCYCLOPEDIA (ISRAEL 1967)	„JEWISH-AUSTRIAN WRITER…“
General Israeli Encyclopedia (Israel 1989)	„JEWISH-CZECH WRITER BORN IN PRAGUE, ONE OF THE GREATEST WRITERS IN THE GERMAN LANGUAGE.“
Encyclopaedia Judaica (Israel 1971)	"Czech-born German novelist"
Brockhaus Enzyklopädie (Germany, 1990)	„AUSTRIAN WRITER“
Reference Instructive Dictionary (Czech Rep. 1963)	„A GERMAN WRITER LIVING MAINLY IN PRAGUE“

writer in the German language, of Jewish origin." Some works prefer to avoid these attributes altogether, such as *Austrian Lexikon* with its laconic: "Fiction author writing in German." Where does this variety of definitions stem from? What are key factors affecting the multiplicity of Kafka's portrayals? It is now obvious that the ways in which Franz Kafka is presented in Czech, German, Israeli and other media (United Kingdom, Austria, the United States) is not at all accidental, but rather mirrors the image of the writer in the academic, public and popular discourse of a given "national" provenance.

In order to understand the emergence of these images, one has to consider historical developments as well as current cultural, economic and national issues in the countries in question. Before I do that, let me mention some useful analytical tools and concepts, the combination of which will help us to decode the analysed texts.

I would like to refer first to the notion of belonging as a means of identification with some collective identity. When a person feels himself to belong to some specific group, he usually strives to embrace shared views, opinions, character and behaviour. By every individual doing this, the group in the end comes to form a body that shares certain modes of identifications. At the same time, this group of people delineates the boundary between them and the "others," i.e., people outside the group—those who don't fit the predefined criteria or who for some reason fail to be understood as members.

An identity shared by a number of individuals is not a rigid and given quality, but rather an ongoing process of forming, re-shaping, questioning and re-confirming the values and qualities that are expected to be shared and practised by the collective. An essential part of such collective identity-building—and especially when we talk about a nation—is the notion of collective memory. There are two essential elements that we need in order to foster and promote this national memory: its contents, and ways of remembering. As for the contents, the concept of "national, cultural heritage" is useful. Like identities, it is neither self-evident nor an automatic result of collective memory, but rather a social construction (Lowenthal 1998). An important observation has been made that heritage is as much about remembering as about forgetting. Cultural geographers see heritage as "place-based" or a spatial phenomenon: located in or distributed across space (Graham, Ashworth and Tunbridge 2000). This idea was neatly expressed by Nora (1989) as "realms of memory." These can be places, sites, causes or anything else that bears material, symbolic or functional meaning. In our case, the realm of memory can be not only a literary archive or national library, but the literary legacy proper. The realms of memory play an important role in collective identity-building, because they strive to fix the historical memory, which is disappearing. Had there been a spontaneous memory, such realms would not have been created. Powerful groups show a great tendency towards the control of heritage and the realms of memory. I will call these attempts at control and influence in space "territorialisation." Originally, this concept relates to "the control of an area." The process of territorialising one's identity and "cultural legacy" would then mean to exercise power over it. This idea is valid also for the archives and national institutions. Once archival materials bear some spiritual value for the controlling group and are gathered in one place, a connection is created between the materials, their authors, and the controlling group. For the target group of such a strategy (e.g., a nation) there emerges a range of imagined commonalities, such as cultural identity, territorial belonging, shared cultural heritage, etc.

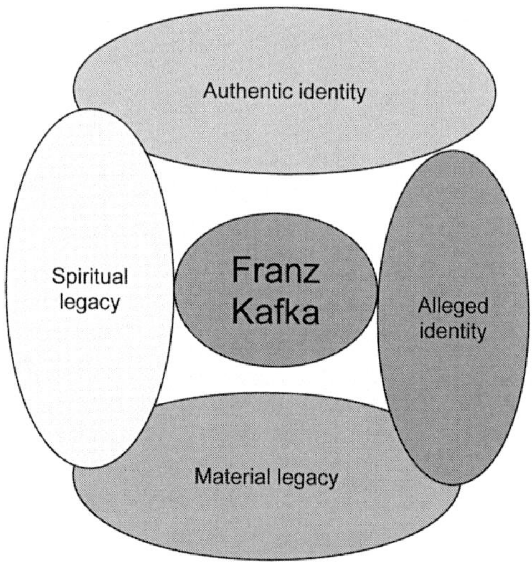

Figure 5-1. *Between Franz Kafka's identity and legacy.*

The case of the diverse interpretations of Kafka's personality and legacy constitutes an interesting meeting point of notions of individual and collective identities. When the media talk about Kafka's identity, this is obviously an image of Kafka's real personal identity rather than the authentic one. In fact, we can view this as a cycle of interconnected "identities" and "images of identities" (see fig. 5-1). First, we have Kafka's own modes of identifications, which will never be fully known to us (Kafka's authentic identity). Kafka left behind him a certain amount of writings, sketches and other materials, which together form the physical/material legacy of tangible character—the object of the lawsuit. On the other hand, the discourse about Kafka and his literary legacy is pursued from the standpoint of the interpreters. It tells us a lot about the perceptions of Kafka and about the intangible value of his spiritual legacy among the large public of readers and non-readers alike. Anyone who writes about Franz Kafka attaches to him various identities, based on their knowledge about the author and their emotional engagement in the matter. This may be called "alleged identity," and precisely this is the source of disagreement in definitions in our sources.

Franz Kafka's history in three countries

What is the position of Kafka in the Czech Republic, i.e., the former Czechoslovakia, and—before 1918—part of Austro-Hungarian Empire? Franz Kafka was born in Austria-Hungaria, but lived to experience the first years of its successor state Czechoslovakia. He lived in times of Czech-German national antagonism and as a Jew was in a complicated situation. The process of Jewish emancipation also brought a dilemma of national identity, which appears to have been the key mode of identification in the nineteenth century. Some Jews saw the only plausible way forward as complete assimilation to a host nation. In the Czech Lands, however, there were two competing national movements—the Czech and the German. Language played a crucial role in shaping national collective identity. For obvious reasons, literature acted as an indicator of national "maturity" and language was seen as an indicator of national belonging. In the growing Czech cultural milieu it was unthinkable for a Czech writer to create in the German language. That is why writers in the German language in the independent Czechoslovak state after 1918 posed a subtle problem. By comparison, František Langer (1888–1965) is perceived as a Czech writer and unarguably belongs to the Czech literature. He was Jewish and wrote in Czech. Kafka and many others, on the other hand, wrote in German. Their more-or-less manifest Jewishness did not deprive them of the title "Czech author"—but the language did. For these writers, some of whom were Jewish, but some—like Gustav Meyrink (1868–1932) or Rainer Maria Rilke (1875–1926)—were non-Jews, the term the "Prague circle" was established, coined by Max Brod and adopted with relief by an academic and literary world which stood puzzled before the group of nationally unclassifiable authors. The situation becomes more complicated when we realise that Prague German Literature also includes many writers who came from other places, mainly Moravia. To name just few of them:

Ernst Sommer (1888–1955), Ernst Weiss (1882–1940), Hermann Ungar (1893–1929), and Ludwig Winder (1889–1946).[3]

After 1948, under the communist regime, the attitude to Kafka was even more complicated. He was officially ignored. Only in the 1960s, with the general wave of loosening, did Czech scholars dare to deal with Kafka, and even organised an international conference with the title "Kafka from the Prague perspective" (Goldstücker, Kautmann and Reiman 1965). Kafka was presented as a Prague writer and the contributors hoped for Kafka's "return to Prague," where he reportedly belonged. Two years later another conference under the title "Weltfreunde. Konferenz über die Prager deutsche Literatur" (Friends of the world: Conference on Prague German literature)[4] was held at the same place, with a broadened conceptual framework. Eduard Goldstücker (1913–2000), a significant scholar of German language and literature and diplomat, was asked what was meant by the "German" in the title. He answered by the way of a story which appeared in one of Kafka's letters to Max Brod (10.4.1920). There, he recalls the experience of meeting a German officer at a place abroad where he had just found accommodation: upon hearing he was from Prague, the officer was sure he was a "Czech." After being assured he was not, the officer became only partially comforted when he learned Kafka was a Jew. In any case, he wondered why he spoke such fluent German, given that he lived in the nest of Czech nationalists.

According to Goldstücker (1967, 22), the realm of the German language does not include Czechoslovakia, as can be understood from the following words: "Probably everyone would agree that the Prague German literature represents the most important complex of literary works in German language, which was created outside the closed German language territory."[5] The problem of the national belonging of these authors is strongly present. Eduard Goldstücker concludes that at some point most of them probably cross regional and even national frontiers. Therefore, they form an "independent chapter in the framework of any national or transnational ('übernationale') history of literature, in which it will be at that point classified" (Goldstücker 1967, 25–26).

Real and uncensored research and popular interest could flourish only after the fall of communism in 1989, and by 1990 the Franz Kafka Society had been established in Prague with the goal of reviving the traditions that surrounded "Prague German literature" and to "make Kafka's heritage a natural component of the Czech cultural context."[6] Apart from the academic preoccupations with Kafka, a huge tourist industry evolved in Prague around the writer, turning him into a profitable economic commodity and leading to massive consumption of history.

On the Czech side, the identification of Franz Kafka with a town (Prague) might be interpreted as an unwillingness or a dilemma: How should this person be presented from the viewpoint of collective identity? The practice of using the name of the town where the individual was born, was active, or where he lived for some period of time, is not confined to Franz Kafka or the "Prague circle"; the strategy is also familiar to German journalists. In an article about the Marbach Literary Archive, for example, the artist Lutz Rathenow (b. 1952) is seen as "Berliner writer" (*Marbach* 2010).

Let us now follow Franz Kafka to Israel. How did he get there? A cynic would say: in Brod's suitcase. The literary legacy of Kafka was brought to Israel by Max Brod, Kafka's close friend, who escaped Czechoslovakia at the last minute in 1939. What did this migration mean for Brod and the many other Jews who made their way to this Mediterranean land? Moving from one country to another, be it a free choice or a consequence of political, religious or ethnic pressure, shows signs of a break, but it also contains signs of continuity. Migration is a staged social change (see Seweryn 2007 for detailed elaboration of the process of migration and identity). An individual experiences moments of detachment from the original place of living, and passes through a liminal phase of loosening his previous social and cultural ties in order to re-incorporate himself into the new environments. The migration to the Land of Israel, the land of the Biblical ancestors, was understood by the Jewish migrants unequivocally as a "return" to Zion. This had its repercussions also in a vehement denial of the Diaspora as a whole, especially after the disaster of the Holocaust. Yet, the specifics of the situation do not dismiss the above-mentioned idea of migration as a process of identity transformation, in which the land, the territory, plays a crucial role. Despite the fact that many scholars called the diaspora Jewry the de-territorialised people, the symbolic and abstract meaning of the Land of Israel had had such a weight throughout history as a physical migrants' destination that the arrival in the dreamed-of "national territory" meant a principal change in the understanding of the Self vis-à-vis the spatial dimension of identity. Whether we call it the territorialisation or the spatialisation of the Jewish identity, this concept refers to the same idea of turning the Jewish identity (as if deprived of the "national" territory) into a newly formed Israeli identity. As Boyarin (1997, 218) puts it: "The territorialisation of identity is a key strategy in the attempt to turn Jews into Israelis." In the circles of secular Israelis, whose cultural hegemony was felt strongly in the politics of mandate Palestine and the young State of Israel, Jewish diaspora identity equalled rigid religion and old times.

They strived to uproot themselves from their own past. However, this strategy proved to be a mission impossible, and both on the personal and collective level the diasporic past had been periodically breaking out. This only verified the assertion that no matter how ambiguous the relationship between the Jewish and Israeli identities was, it was always very tight, and mostly unconscious.

Usually, by migration we understand a physical move that brings individuals and groups from one place to another; but we can also talk about the migration of spiritual values and heritages. Consider our case: we are dealing with a bunch of manuscripts. They represent the physical part of the legacy. Beyond that, however, stands the key idea of representation. Writings have a metaphorical and spiritual meaning in addition to a material value. Thus, carrying in a suitcase pieces of paper with some written contents that together form a valuable object for one or more groups of individuals, is a migration of the whole system of meanings. When Brod "brought" Kafka in this manner, for many he was bringing him "home," into a metaphorical sort of space. This assumption can be supported by a few examples drawn from the terrain. In its biographical sketch of Kafka, the prominent *Encyclopaedia Judaica* highlights the moment of his Zionist metamorphosis, stating that he had studied Hebrew and expressed the wish to move to Israel in his personal documents. But another example shows a certain hesitation as to Kafka's belonging to Israel and balances the picture a little—there was a discussion over naming one of the streets in Jerusalem after him, and the suggestion was declined at an early stage by the Committee for Street Names, which argued that he had no special connection to the city. In this incident we can see the extent to which questions of one's identity and one's inclusion into an official heritage are related to local and regional politics.

In several places Franz Kafka is described as a "German writer." This is, for example, the formulation adopted by *Encyclopaedia Judaica* ("Czech-born German novelist"), *Encyclopaedia Britannica* ("Czech-born German writer") and the Czech lexicon *Diderot* ("German writer of Jewish origin"). What lies behind the attribute "German"? Can it be understood as a semantic equivalent of the adjectives "Czech," "English," "Austrian"? Does it relate to a national belonging, a citizenship, or an adherence to cultural milieu or a language identity? In fact, all options are plausible and realised, but not all at the same moment. The precise meaning depends on the reader—and this is precisely the source of misunderstandings. In all the aforementioned quotations, the term "German" cannot mean citizenship, as Kafka was first an Austrian, and later a Czechoslovak citizen. We cannot, however, make such clear judgements about the other possibilities: national, cultural or linguistic identity. When, for instance, the *Encyclopaedia Britannica* states that Kafka was a "Czech-born German writer," we may be confused. I suggest understanding the term "Czech" here as an expression of the territorial belonging to the Czech lands, to Bohemia, which does not involve, however, a belonging to the Czech nation. As to the attribute "German" we have a sense of an unclear border between the national belonging (i.e., to Germans living in Bohemia) and adherence to the German cultural milieu. It can also simply mean that he wrote in the German language: and indeed some works do cautiously make this distinction: "Jewish-Czech writer born in Prague, one of the greatest writers in the German language" (*General Israeli Encyclopaedia*).

The director of the Manuscript department of the Literary Archive in Marbach, Ulrich von Bülow, says: "it was always a great ambition of the German literary archive to bring the emigrants back to the country, be it in form of *their documents* or also in form of their person proper" (*Hoffnung* 2008; emphasis mine). There are two important messages in this statement: First, the spatial language (coming back to the country) is used to express the movement of both living creatures (people) and the products of their activities (documents). Secondly, Franz Kafka is included in the group of artists who are invited *back*, implying there is a time in the past when they belonged to that place.

Our main question in this section concerns how Kafka is perceived in Germany. First of all, there is a great tradition of research interest in the German-medium writers living in the Czech lands, including Kafka. It should also be noted that most of Kafka's works published posthumously in Brod's editions were printed in Germany. A glimpse into a German encyclopedia reveals some distance, however: according to *Brockhaus Enzyklopedie* he was an "Austrian writer," while for *Der Grosse Bertelsmann Lexikothek* he was simply a "Writer … from a Jewish … family … , living in Prague." The first definition relates to the citizenship that Kafka held for the major part of his life, while the other doesn't use the language of national belonging at all. It seems that in Germany, the term "German" is used as a combination of cultural identity, expressed in spatial terms, and the language. Very often we read about the "German language realm" (*Sprachraum*) or "German cultural realm" (*Kulturraum*; see Joachimsthaler 2002 for a detailed elaboration of the concept of "culture space" (*Kulturraum*) in German academic discourse), which serve as a key method of classification of important figures of European history. This logic stands behind the classical project of "Neue Deutsche

Biographie" (New German Biography), or the recent one with the title "Jewish Communities in the German Language Realm." It is a cultural concept that crosses national and state borders. When conceptualising the project in such a way, one avoids a problem of definition in the entries—Kafka can be defined baldly as an "author" because the decision to insert an entry about him already makes a statement regarding his alleged belonging.

Interestingly enough, the idea of the existence of a space that can be researched coherently because of its belonging to the German cultural/language realm is reflected also in Israeli academia. Take for example the project "Gesharim" ("Bridges: Studies in the History of Central European Jewry"). The authors of this project wish to publish a series of monographs on the history of the Jews in Central Europe. For many decades there has been an ongoing debate on what exactly Central Europe is, how long this term has been used in scholarly and lay discourse, where its borders are and what is to be found beyond its limits. Notably, there is an unspoken agreement about the answers to these questions in the circle of scholars of Jewish studies. The space denoted to Central Europe is usually perceived as corresponding to the realm of Ashkenazic Jewry, thus including Germany (until 1806 the Holy Roman Empire of the German Nation, between 1815 and 1866 the German Confederation, and from 1871 until 1918 the German Empire), the Czech lands, Poland, Austria and Hungary.[7] Besides the political factor (since large territories dealt with in these books were in some way bound, whether more tightly or in a very loose way, to the Holy Roman Empire), the parameter of language plays an important role: the project "Gesharim" focuses on the social, religious and cultural life of the *German speaking Jews*. This denotation includes Poland and the Czech lands, where the Jews spoke variants of Yiddish and probably also the local language. By "German-Jewish authors" one means in academic work Jews who, according to the author, used German as the language of daily communication. Yet on the contrary, scholars from Central Europe proper seem to reject the concept of the German cultural realm as one bringing together Germany and the countries eastwards from it.[8]

Franz Kafka in the media

We will now examine the arguments used in relevant newspaper articles in the three countries. One can find only short factual reports on the ongoing law suit concerning Brod's legacy within these publications. The overall silence that governs Czech newspapers is striking, and was itself the subject of an examination on the part of one journalist.[9] Franz Kafka is herein denoted mostly as a "Prague Jewish writer" (*Dopisy Franze Kafky se* 2011; *Dopisy Franze Kafky mají být prodány* 2011), sometimes with a remark about the language in which he created. It seems that some of the Czech articles were based on information acquired from international press agencies, and in these cases it is interesting to see that while almost all the text has undergone nearly word-to-word translation, in some cases the attributes used for Kafka are slightly different. In the article published in *Hospodářské noviny*, as quoted above, Kafka is viewed as a Prague Jewish author, while according to *Die Welt* only as a "Prague author" (*Marbach und Oxford* 2011). This detail informs us about the importance of paying attention to the diverse ways of cultural translations. One article calls Kafka a "significant Prague German-writing writer of the 20th century" (*Spor* 2009). In other place we find a very similar denotation: "significant Prague author, writing in German" (*Německo* 2009). An article announcing a new book by Johannes Urzidil (1896–1970) calls Kafka a "Prague-native," while in his memoirs Urzidil talks of him as his companion from the "range of authors writing in German" (*Vzpomínky* 2011). In these memoirs Urzidil highlighted Kafka's Czech accent, his sense of humour and his helpless smile. Also, he says, he didn't interpret his efforts to learn Hebrew as a sign of Zionism.

We have already mentioned that Brod, a great propagator of Czech literature beyond the borders of Czechoslovakia, always remained in the shade of Kafka. In one place Franz Kafka is described as a "Prague Jewish author writing in German," while no such attributes are used for Brod. Brod's identity here has no absolute value—it is only relative to the person of Kafka ("his best friend"— *Dostane literární svět neznámou Kafkovu povídku?* 2010). Kafka is presented very similarly by a different journalist in the same newspaper. While Brod remains only Kafka's "best friend," Kafka himself is a "German-writing Jewish author" (*Franz Kafka má v Izraeli svůj novodobý "proces"* 2011).

In other articles Brod and Kafka appear with no further alleged identity indicators. The journalists present the demands of all interested parts, but without exception they do not raise any claim on the part of the Czech Republic. It is only when we look at popular voices—that is, the comments made by readers in the internet editions of the journals—that we find statements using the language of belonging. One of the reactions labels Brod's action a "theft" and demands that the UK, Germany and Israel return the manuscripts. The Czech Republic is not explicitly mentioned; the author of the comment takes it for granted that this is where the manuscripts belong. The question is clear: If the National

Library in Jerusalem and the National Archive of German Literature in Marbach can pursue their claims, where are the Czech national institutions? What about the Museum of Czech Literature in Prague? This state institution already has part of Kafka's legacy, and recently has undertaken a project named "Germanicum," a complete register of documents written in German from the holdings of the museum. Kafka's image appears right next to the main information about the project, followed by J. W. Goethe (1749–1832) and Heinrich Mann (1871–1950). According to the authors of the project, an ongoing process of mingling of "German influences and the Czech national element" has been proceeding without a break over the past few centuries.[10] However, the word "Germanicum" does not reflect the complexity of all the possible manifestations of "German-ness" in the Czech lands. The authors confined themselves to the linguistic criteria. The project thus maps documents written in the German language regardless of the national belonging of their authors. The description of the register makes it clear that there is a strict border between the authors of "Czech nationality" on the one hand, and those of "different nationalities" in relation to the Czech environment on the other. The German language authors "living in the Czech lands" are mentioned as a separate category. Their belonging is purely spatial (to the land), not personal (to some group of people, like the Czechs). And this is the key to the answer—the Czech milieu is not yet ready to fully recognise writers in the German language in the Czech lands as Czech writers, because the attribute "Czech" means here both and simultaneously the national and linguistic identity.

There are only few innovative and daring voices in the Czech media. In an annotation on new books published on Franz Kafka, Kafka's biography, written by Czech Bohemist and Germanist Josef Čermák (b. 1928), is praised for filling the gap that "Czech literary history" contains in regard to "the most famous Prague writer" (*Zápas* 2010). The author tries to explain the lack of interest in Kafka on the Czech side, naming three factors: forty years of forcibly imposed silence; "anti-German nationalism and antisemitism"; and the fact that the Czechs have not, to this day, been able to integrate "German-Jewish literature of Prague and beyond." This author suggests that Kafka belongs to the Czechs as well.

In comparison to the scarce reactions in the Czech Republic, the situation in Israel can be described as a verbal tornado. The principal element that drives the public discourse are emotions and a strong sense of national and territorial belonging. The lawsuit became a symbolic drama. Here the journalists do not have any problem denoting both writers as "Czech," because the deemed decisive component of their identity is their

Jewishness. In some articles published in Israeli newspapers, our author is described as a "Czech writer" (*111 mikhtavim* 2011; *Kafka baderekh* 2011),[11] with no allusion to his Jewishness. This might be explained either it being a well and widely known fact, or by the journalist's wish to highlight Kafka's Czech origins in order to outweigh his alleged Germanness. However, in some articles his Jewish identity was included (*Nish'arim babayit* 2011).[12] In an article announcing a seminar organised by the National Library in Jerusalem and dedicated to Max Brod, neither the name Franz Kafka nor that of Max Brod are accompanied by any qualifying attribute (*Hitgalu kitvei yad* 2010). In other Israeli articles they are both described as "important writers" (*Hadoch* 2011). Anat Peri, quoted in one of the articles reporting on the court sessions over Brod's legacy, thinks that the manuscripts of "this great Czech writer" (referring to Franz Kafka) belong to his lawful inheritors (*Boker* 2011). Kafka and Brod are understood as part of the "culture of the People" as well as "the culture of the country." In this way, Kafka's writings are transformed into realms of memory, which should educate the nation and help to re-affirm the nature of collective national identity. From this point of view, the only logical place to keep these writings is in some state-national institutions, which are realms of memory in themselves. For example, the mission of the National Archives of the Jewish people in Jerusalem is "the unity of the Jewish people and the unity of Jewish history," and to ensure access to it in one central location (Kuperminc and Arditti 1999, 224). In other words, locating historical documents pertaining to all Jewish communities all over the world in one place, with controlled access, turns this place into a territory which also forms the symbolic, imagined unity of the Jewish communities and their members throughout the world and along the historical axis. This mechanism has a reciprocal effect. The fact of possessing the literary legacy in effect confirms the alleged identity of a person, and on the other hand the fact of attaching to someone a certain identity in effect gives a moral right to possess his physical legacy, on the ground that he "belongs to us, here" (where the language of belonging is both spatial and personal). The notions of belonging go hand in hand with the notions of possession and power. The proponents of national collective identity see Brod and Kafka as an important part of the national cultural heritage and see in their "removal" from Israel an unjust cultural appropriation on the part of the other side. The sentiments become the more negative, the stronger the link that is made by the journalists between Germany today and Germany in the past (namely, the Nazi period).

This leads us to the third component of our analysis—the German press. Here we find that the legal case is fully covered, and for obvious reasons—the National Archive for German Literature in Marbach hosts the manuscript of Kafka's famous novel, sold to Marbach by Mrs. Hoffe. The articles in the newspapers share one remarkable component: they do not use the language of national belonging to justify the possession of Kafka's legacy. He is denoted as a "Jewish Prague author" (*Streit um Kafka* 2009), while another source states that he "grew up in Prague, came from the Jewish family and wrote in German" (*Streit um Prozess-Handschrift* 2009). In arguing that Germany has the right to keep Kafka's manuscript, the authors deploy the above-mentioned notion of the "German cultural realm," while also citing the advantages of the high technical standards of Marbach archive.

> There is [in Israel] a lack of people with required knowledge in the language and milieu of these texts written in German in the former cultural realm between Vienna, Prague and Berlin. (*Kafkas letztes Geheimnis* 2010)

Retaining is seen as an "ideal option" because the Marbach has "modern devices for conservation and its technical background" (*Tauziehen* 2010).

The literary archive in Marbach is presented as an institution with many years' experience with preserving "German-Jewish literary legacies" (*Der Prozess* 2010).[13] Kafka researcher Reiner Stach also denies the prospective claims of "Prague" over the manuscripts. Even though his assertion that the placement of the legacy cannot be decided purely on a judicial or national basis, his arguments as to why Kafka does not belong to Prague are also related to his "national" identity ("German-Jewish Czech," "German-Bohemian Jew"—*Der Prozess* 2010).[14] In the end, Prague has no right to possess the manuscripts, as they have to be handled as "world heritage" (*Der Prozess* 2010). When the author mentions Esther Hoffe, he talks of her as a "German-Jewish" emigrant, even though she was born in Opava in Silessia (within the state borders of interwar Czechoslovakia, today in Czech Republic). One of the readers' comments cites yet another reason for not sending the legacy to Prague: according to this view, "had Kafka survived the Nazi persecution, he would have been expelled or murdered as a Sudetes-German by Czech nationalists" (*Der Prozess* 2010). From this hypothetical scenario, it emerges that the commentator views the Czechs as people who would class Kafka with the Germans (more precisely Germans from the Sudetes).

"Kafka belongs to the whole world" is the title of a recent article published in *Die Welt* (*Kafka gehört der Welt* 2011). This article announces the joint purchase, by the Marbach Literary Archive and the Bodleian Library of Oxford, of Kafka's letters to his sister Ottla (1892–1943).

During the period preceding the auction at the Stargardt auction house in Berlin, various culture institutions in Germany and worldwide suspected that the correspondence would end up in the hands of some private collector, which would probably lead to these important sources being withheld from the experts on literary history and Kafka.

According to the head of the Marbach Literary Archive, the transnational purchase of the manuscripts sets a precedent: in future, libraries and archives will no longer compete with each other. Even though they "will purchase some item, they won't own it. It will belong to the whole world" (*Kafka gehört der Welt* 2011).

Academic research might be seen as another vehicle of public opinion, although more regulated and constrained, because, at least officially, it is concerned with the search for neutrality and objectivity. Not surprisingly, there are dozens of conferences, seminars, lectures and other academic activities held each year all over the world on the theme of Franz Kafka, or on some broader topic to which he can be related. Some of them directly address the problem of the literary legacy as torn between the realms of spiritual and material values. In the framework of one conference held by Zürcher Eidgenössischen Technischen Hochschule, the author Peter Stamm asked a crucial question: "By the virtue of which right do the spiritual estates forfeit after seventy years, but the material estates do not?" (*Kafka im Banktresor* 2011). In other words, it seems that the spiritual wealth of each country (in this case Germany) grows thanks to posthumous expropriation of its artists (*Kafka im Banktresor* 2011). At the same conference the professor of literary history Andreas Kilcher chose the litigation conducted between the National Library in Jerusalem and the Hoffe sisters as a case study displaying the legal and administrative aspects of legacies (Kilcher 2011).

To sum up, we can say that the analysis of the current rhetoric around Franz Kafka, Max Brod, and their literary legacies proves the notions of belonging to be powerful and important elements of self-perception of individuals and groups. This can be on the level of a nation (Jewish people), cultural or language space (Germany, German cultural/language realm), transnational belonging (European heritage, world heritage), or a part of local heritage (Prague). National institutions, no matter how internationally directed and open to transnational projects, continue to be the realms of the memory of nations, or alternatively of "Europeans"—as the contemporary popular form of identification would have it. They aim at territorialising the cultural heritage produced and fostered by the powerful agents of cultural and economic politics. When employing this approach, the case will have its winners and losers. The real loser, however, will be the legacy proper, possessed by one of the contesting groups, and thus inevitably excluding any other group in taking hold of it, even if only at the ideological level. The question is whether introducing the concept of "multicultural heritage" can plausibly challenge the partiality of national heritages (this view of cultural heritage in theory and practices is examined, for example, by Graham 2002). Would such transnational cultural heritage be no more a social construct? The answer is no. But a more sophisticated reading of the historical legacy would do real justice to the objects that became part of contemporary use of the past. Moreover, the growing scepticism towards official "heritages" promises interesting developments in the future in this field.

CHAPTER SIX

SCIENCE AND SOCIETY IN A UTOPIAN MAP

MARIANNA FORLEO

Science and Humanities

In recent centuries the relationship between science and literature has had numerous manifestations. One of the most interesting aspects of these is the use of scientific language in utopian texts.

Utopia is a metaphor of a renewal of society, an indication of the need to escape from actual realities in order to organise perfect societies. Utopia is not a place, it is a hypothesis, a projection, and the condition for its existence is its non-existence (*ou-topos*), which defines it as an unattainable and indefinable idea. Literature describes imaginary places (see, among others, Trousson 1992; Baccolini, Fortunati and Minerva 1996; Fortunati and Trousson 2000; Backzo 1989; Matteucci 1982), places outside of geography and history, fantastic lands with imaginative and metaphorical names. These places set the individual free from the known world, in order to place him in an ideal city, in the unknown dimension of the impossible. Utopia is almost a geography of the text, dealing with happy islands without spatial or temporal coordinates, where community life takes place in a long-lasting chronological dimension.

Utopian texts are an exercise of social imagination as well as a project of legislation, and such an ideal city is always framed via the expedient of a detailed legislation, according to the code of reason or nature, whose beneficial effects are highlighted by the description of the ordinary life of the community. In many utopian texts a radical egalitarianism is outlined: the citizens' education takes paramount importance, and social and political institutions are immutable, influencing citizens' lives in a very strong way. The geometrisation of urban space, with a specific obsession with symmetry, characterises the classical model of utopia.

The utopian genre, according to the schema defined in Thomas More's *Utopia* (1516), describes a politically perfect society, twisting the seriousness of moral and social criticism into an intellectual game.

Literature, by its very nature, is an important instrument for addressing political issues, especially when confronted with processes revolutionising the whole society, and indeed is often the only real authentic "source" of their evolution. The description of the utopian world is not always presented in terms of ethics because such criticism is only possible if the political expressions are based on metaphors (Baczko 1979, 3–62), so a scientific approach guarantees a coherent and rational process directed towards a transparent, clear and light result, making the text available to a wider and diverse audience.

In the description of utopian cities, literature uses science as a technical tool for the explanation of the world. Science becomes a clear metaphor for rational organisations and a strategic element for spreading "subliminal" messages. The combination of utopia and science can seem an exclusively theoretical and philosophical relationship, but in reality it is only a way to approach the utopian practice. The main feature of utopian texts is indeed their criticism of society, which is made possible only if it is hidden in metaphorical terms. Mathematical utopias present themselves as multidimensional texts, and the use of geometric structures, in describing utopian spaces, provides for several interpretations. Despite this, science and literature converge throughout the text, yet their different features remain clearly marked. They intersect throughout the text, thus maintaining their own autonomy from which a few epistemological implications can be derived.

Utopias and scientific metaphors

The connection between literature and science is thus not unusual, but in the literature science is hidden, often just used as reference or citation, whereas the scientific disciplines in the utopian texts are not a complement, enriching it through nuances and the instruments necessary for a utopian message.

The scientific method as epistemological model made headway in the nineteenth century, in a period in which the scientific/philosophical debate was at its height and science became a topic of wide dissemination. At the end of the century, as a consequence of Charles Darwin's scientific speculation which culminated in *The Origin of Species*, a new literature spread, often presented as a tale, and made up by scientific fantasies, in order to disclose the importance of the new scientific discoveries.

Several writers have been interested in such a theme and one of the most representative texts regarding this issue is *Flatland, a Romance of Many Dimensions*, by Edwin Abbott (Abbott 1884; Abbott, Lindgren and Banchoff 2010).

Written in 1884, it is a romance, a positive utopia and a mathematical game, a metaphor of the social and scientific requirements of the end of the eighteenth century. The use of scientific language in such a literary piece is strongly evocative value and chimes with the philosophical/scientific debate on the concept of dimensionality. The text has many levels dealing with the complicated message of the romance; the first and most evident of these levels is the description of the geometrical world juxtaposed with the flat.

The little attention the critics paid to the geometrical romance is undoubtedly due to the immaturity of the time, making it incapable of grasping such a complex work in every detail and implicit meaning; thus the paradigm of complexity and the new view of the world are hidden in a very simple metaphor that deceives those who do not pay enough attention to what they are reading.

In *Flatland* geometrical figures whose limits are marked by a bright light lie on a Cartesian plane; the narrator, a square, named *A. Square*, describes the society in Flatland during the life imprisonment he was sentenced to because he dared to challenge the rules of the Plane, the lot that here, as elsewhere, falls to heretics and prophets.

In *Flatland* the sign of a rational mind is defined by the angle of the figures, a purely male inheritance. Indeed, the social pyramid is governed by the complex arrangement of people on the plane: the Female Population lies at the bottom and on the borders of the society as women are completely lacking in angles; Isosceles Triangles, having an acute and dangerous angle, gain one step; then we find the Equilateral Triangles, the middle class; Squares, the bourgeoisie; and finally Regular Polygons, the aristocracy, whose authority increases proportionally to the increase in the number of their sides, and are therefore placed almost at the top of the social ladder.

Circles, the High Priests and organisers of all Arts and Sciences, are at the top of the social organisation in Flatland. They hold power and enforce very strong and irrevocable laws in order to guarantee an oligarchy and reduce the society to a state of political ultra-conservatism. Flatland society, composed of castes, disowns faulty figures. Irregular figures are outsiders; their irrationality in shape and behaviour makes them unforeseeable, imaginative and anarchic, and puts them on the borders of the society.

It is not possible to refer to the category of height on the plane of Flatland, and there is only a gravitational force coming from the south, set as the conventional, fundamental cardinal point. "Upwards, not Northwards": in such a sentence there is a substantial difference intimated between the north and height, a notion that the figures on the plane cannot grasp because they lack the mental categories to understand the third dimension.

Indeed, identification of the different figures occurs only by the sense of touch; their insistence on the assumption that "Feeling is believing" is to relate women and lower classes to a notion of empirical knowledge which is absolute, narrow-minded and limited to sensory perception. On the contrary, the "Art of Sight Recognition," whose induction and deduction processes are reserved for the upper classes and for the teachers of the best universities, represents an intellectual progress compared to touching, but in any case the limit shown by this process is found in the implicit assumption that only what is seen can define the limits of truth.

The Victorian age is presented through several allusions in the text, which reflects the society of the time and outlines the most significant aspects through a geometrical metaphor. British society emerges in a number of textual references, and one of the most representative ones is the political dimension of Flatland, structured as an oligarchy which defines the roles of figures.

Metaphors of Victorian society in a scientific utopia

Angularity as social destiny and geometrical configuration accepted as a natural and moral rule is a mirror of British society, at that time absolutist and self-commemorative (celebrative). The conformity and severity of British society is also reflected in the text in the refusal to recognise the sociological reasons for the moral behaviour of the figures.

In Flatland, status and intelligence are intimately connected, and intelligence can be measured directly in terms of physical attributes such as the size of the angle of the figures. This is a clear reference to the assumption of Victorianists who believed in the intellectual superiority of the upper class, exemplified by the common and shared belief that superior intelligence was embedded in people with big heads.

England was a stratified society, in which social status, as well as the definition of individual identity, was continuously measured and checked, determined and recognised by the slightest detail in language, conduct and appearance.

Biologically the geometric line of Flatland is subject to a peculiar type of evolution. Regular figures go up one rung on the social ladder every generation, so enhancing their "status"; and this evolutionary process allows each son to gain a geometric side in relation to the configuration of his father, thus tending more and more towards the noble polygonal configuration.

This is actually positive progress, but possible only for figures of a high rank. Besides, in Flatland the number of children is inversely proportional to the number of sides of the figures, and such an evolutionistic rule is also supported by the almost complete sterility of the Circles, which foresees an end to Flatland.

This social pattern refers to the criteria set out in the evolutionary theories of Darwin and Spencer, which had a remarkable influence on British society. According to these rules, society is indeed a living organism and as such is the result of an evolutionary process. In this direction the progressive increase in the number of sides from father to son can be understood and makes sense.

In a utopian framework, such as *Flatland*'s, it is attractive that the Darwinian theories are driven to their logical extreme: the rules imposed by such a geometrical society establish a framework of severity and death; and the absolute perfection of the Circles leads at last to the extinction of the line. The law of evolution set out in *Flatland* thus corresponds to the contemporary theory set out by Jean-Baptiste Lamark (now discredited), who considered evolution to be a natural process of increasing complexity in each following generation, always tending to perfection.

In fact *Flatland* does not deal strictly with the theory of natural selection, nor with a simplification of the theory of survival of the fittest—but with the shared, although misleading, Victorian theory which considered evolution to be the main element in a positive process, which always progresses towards a higher level. This interpretation was very attractive for Abbott's contemporaries because it provided a biological justification for the injustices of the society of the time. The biological theory is shifted into the Victorian social setting and thus changes the subject with which it is concerned; in this case it is likely to ensure the survival of the fittest, or of the most suitable; thus economic and social resources are now the focus of the theory, and not the living resources as in Darwin's original biological theory.

To equate natural evolution to social evolution conferred legitimacy and unlimited freedom onto those who are strongest (broadly speaking), as well as an unquestioned acceptance of social inequality. The assumption that cruel competition is useful for improving the human race made it desirable to deny welfare and support to the poor, the new characters of evolutionary theory. Concerning this, Spencer had stated that taking care of social ills, such as poverty, could have prevented the progress which would inevitably result from non-controlled social evolution. He railed against those philanthropists who aimed to prevent misery today at the expense of the evolutionary cleansing process, in this way causing misery and suffering to future generations (Spencer 1851).

Abbott's position regarding this was not to reject the philanthropy which so concerned Spencer; on the contrary, he preached that acts of charity should be replaced by a strategy of social assistance that would include the allocation of decent housing for the poor, as well as respect, the promotion of recreational and leisure spaces, and a systematic system of education which, if well done, would be likely to encourage respect for ourselves, as well as intelligence, diligence and hard work.

In the second part of the tale, A. Square unexpectedly meets a Sphere, who intersects the plane, detaches the square from the plane and lifts it in [the] Space, giving A. Square the opportunity to see his plane world from above and to get perceptible proof of the existence of height. Going back to the plane, A. Square tries to explain his perception but, regarded as a heretic—owing to his three-dimensional experience, which is impossible to prove—he is put in prison for the rest of his days. A. Square, puzzled, infers that via a similar mental process it is possible to prove the existence of n-dimensional worlds; but such a plausible but at the same time insolent hypothesis peeves the Sphere, who drops A. Square back on the Plane.

Abbott's contemporaries perhaps attached slight importance to the geometrical utopia; but, by a kind of irony that history sometimes sets aside for the destiny of literary production, *Flatland* has handed down Abbott's renown to posterity. Even in the panorama of Victorian England, where opportunities of utopian escape in the field of literary production were not so rare, we find talk about the absolute "typical aspect" of a seemingly uncommon work such as *Flatland*. At that time scientific turmoil proceeded right alongside the sluggish peacefulness of middle-class, puritanical society.

This "typical aspect" should not distract attention from its proper literary aspect. Even considering the various levels at which it can be read and the wide variety of references to which it appeals, this work unquestionably presents a clear point of view, making it available to a wide and diverse audience (Calvino 1988, 27).[1]

The complex message of utopia is dealt with at many different levels of the text. Paraphrasing its subtitle, it is really made up of "many dimensions." The first and most evident of these levels is the description of the geometrical world juxtaposed with the flat one. It is essential to observe that A. Square hides in its name a plurality of levels, making the work extremely complex. Edwin Abbott is actually himself a kind of square (Rucker 1984, 27–28). Abbott and the identification between author and narrator displace the utopia from a purely fantastic level to that of an autobiographical narration (Lejeune 1975, 11–50).

Here geometry merges with utopian representation but is not confused with it, gaining an individual, complete autonomy; the first and most obvious of the reading levels, the one on which other levels are based and from which any other reading takes shape, is given by the description of the geometrical world of the Plane. Scientific disciplines are not of minor importance in utopian speeches; on the contrary they are integrated into the literary text, thus improving it by means of the nuances and instruments necessary to define the utopian message. The scientific approach vouches for a rational, consistent but above all verifiable process, which on the one hand makes the text clear and on the other gives rise to a hypertext and to many reading levels (Baldini 1974, and Piattelli Palmarini 2003).

Published anonymously in 1882, *Flatland* was a failure, with reviewers considering the work to be "mortally tedious" and "incomprehensible"; they actually wrote that "the book seems to have a purpose, but what that may be it is hard to discover"; the total lack of height in the *Flatland* figures was thought to be impossible. The history of the critical success of the tale when it was published is widely dealt with in the introduction by David W. Davies to the edition of the work published in Pasadena by Grant Dahlstrom in 1978; reviews show how the work was poorly understood, in particular the fact that the great geometrical precision and the individuality of the figures were accomplished simultaneously was not perceived.

The New York Times added that "it is a very puzzling book and a very distressing one … Some little sense is apparent in an appeal for the education of women"; and it hypothesised that "seven persons in the whole of the United States and Canada" found it agreeable (among a lot of slating criticism only the *Boston Advertiser* critic showed his approval, judging the work positively). Only in 1920 was *Flatland* recommended to a wide audience, by an anonymous letter published in the scientific review *Nature* (Banchoff 1990, 364–72). Below is the text of the letter:

> Some thirty years ago, a little jeu d'esprit was written by Dr. Edwin Abbott, entitled "Flatland." At the time of its publication it did not attract as much attention as it deserved. Dr. Abbott pictures intelligent beings whose whole experience is confined to a plane, or other space of two

> dimensions, which have no faculties by which they can become conscious of anything outside that space and no means of moving off the surface on which they live. He then asks the reader, who has the consciousness of the third dimension, to imagine a sphere descending upon the plane of Flatland and passing through it. How will the inhabitants regard this phenomenon? They will not see the approaching sphere and will have no conception of its solidity. They will only be conscious of the circle in which it cuts their plane. This circle, at first a point, will gradually increase in diameter, driving the inhabitants of Flatlands outwards from its circumference, and this will go on until half the sphere has passed through the plane, when the circle will gradually contract to a point and then vanish, leaving the Flatlanders in undisturbed possession of their country … Their experience will be that of a circular obstacle gradually expanding or growing, and then contracting, and they will attribute to growth in time what the external observer in three dimensions assigns to motion in the third dimension. Transfer this analogy to a movement of the fourth dimension through three-dimensional space. Assume the past and future of the universe to be all depicted in four-dimensional space and visible to any being that has consciousness of the fourth dimension. If there is motion of our three dimensional space relative to the fourth dimension, all the changes we experience and assign to the flow of time will be due simply to this movement, the whole of the future as well as the past always existing in the fourth dimension.[2]

If Abbott cannot be considered a forerunner of physical or mathematical theories, his geometrical utopia certainly gave a series of cues for the scientific debate of that time. In 1920 Arthur Eddington, in his work, *Space, Time, and Gravitation: An Outline of the General Relativity Theory* (Eddington 1987) considered the description concerning the meeting of the Sphere and A. Square as the best popular presentation of the idea according to which a body, even though it stays unchanged, moves in space and gives rise to sections with the inferior dimensions, where only those who live in upper dimensional worlds can feel these transformations. Actually, the revelation of the idea of space in a two-dimensional world as an opportunity for new worlds and thoughts can be considered as a metaphor of the acceptance of a new geometry, the non-Euclidean geometry, an issue much discussed in England at the time when Abbott wrote *Flatland*.

Dimensions

Between 1830 and 1850 Nikolaj Lobacevskij and Yànos Bolyai gave birth to a new geometry, nowadays called "Hyperbolic geometry," which even though it clearly runs counter to the intuitions of Euclidean space, did not involve logical contradictions, thus giving rise to the first systems of non-Euclidean geometry. Lobacevskij would refer to his geometry as "imaginary" because it disagreed with both common sense and Euclidean geometry. Nevertheless, their theories remained on the borders of orthodox geometry, as being a curiosity rather than a real scientific revolution (Cellucci 2002; Russell 1970).

In the history of physics, from Galileo to Descartes, Bacon and Newton, everything was measured, quantifiable and subdivided according to the idea of orientation, an idea typical of those who lived at a time of consciousness and control. In the physical and mathematical sciences a great and satisfying feeling of balance was widespread and it seemed that they were very close to the "real and unique" description, explanation and representation of the world.

Nevertheless, the perception of the world, characterised until then by this potentially static nature, gained dynamism only by accepting new, destabilizing paradigms; Heraclitus defeated Parmenides and reintroduced in physics the irreversible "time indicator," which scientists had tried for ages to get rid of. Accepting non-Euclidean geometry, which differs from Euclidean geometry because it lacks the fifth postulate (roughly speaking, that parallel lines shall not meet no matter how far extended), meant a new attitude to Euclidean geometry. The latter was not completely cancelled; it was still perfectly valid but only under special circumstances; Riemann himself in 1859 in his work, *On the hypotheses which lie at the foundation of geometry* (Riemann 1994) asserted that Euclidean and non-Euclidean geometry are two different branches of mathematics, thus drawing attention for the first time to an overall view of geometry as the study of any kind of size in any kind of space. Then Einstein himself demonstrated that the world geometry is non-Euclidean, and seems to be Euclidean only when the area in question is small, and that the Earth's surface seems to be flat in a limited space, thus demonstrating that the fifth postulate of Euclid is null when the surface is curved. The fact that these two aspects can live together means that pure mathematics is no longer the core example of absolute truth grasped by the human mind, as had largely been thought until then, so the new relativistic perspective contributes in a fundamental way to erode the trust in the absolute truth and nature of human knowledge, showing new possible points of view that Euclidean geometry had hidden up to then (Emmer 2004; Popper 1969).

Assuming a dimensional passage and accepting non-Euclidean geometry represented one of the most significant upsets in the history of human thought, involving drastic changes in the way in which the real nature of things was perceived by Euclidean rationality.

The fourth variable referred to by Abbott is a quantity or quality (Jann 1985) that can be represented geometrically or spatially. He does not consider time as "the" fourth dimension but thinks it is "a" fourth dimension. Nevertheless, even considering that such a variable may be physically perceived only in Thoughtland, the hypothetical Kingdom of Thought, this does not make it less true for the Square, who teaches us that invisible worlds have the same chance of life as the visible ones and that there are different levels of reality and complexity. Indeed, literature's proper task is to elaborate and divulgate the new scientific concepts, usually explaining the fourth dimension as a spatial or geometric variable.

Going back to *Flatland*, the sudden rushes of A. Square into other worlds are visions, and "dimensional diseases" between the lines of unexplored worlds open the second part of the book. The geometrical kingdoms found by A. Square lie in his mind: Pointland and Linealand, the kingdoms of Point and Line, are included in the Plan of Flatland and are also part of a dimensional jump, but the real change is the third one, that is the transfer into the Space, an absolute, inescapable journey from which there is no turning back.

From that moment on, the book branches off and there are two parallel planes which follow two complementary lines: on the one hand there is the level of the two-dimensional world, that is the certainty, induction, and location of the Kingdom of Plane; on the other a new three-dimensional structure of text and thought that involves the reader according to a logic of complexity, deduction, globalisation and complementarity (Forleo 2004; 2008). The description of an unknown three-dimensional world, which embraces values that are different from the prevailing ones, assumes the form of a narrative method that adopts mathematical rules; resorting to contrast or to the method of *reductio ad absurdum* means a forced confusion which inevitably leads to the search for a new way of thinking and to the birth of a new paradigm (Kuhn 1978; Piattelli Palmarini 1984).

The revelation by the Sphere of the existence of new worlds causes A. Square acute pain—especially when the Sphere passes through it in an unlikely manner—this pain being required for a new sort of knowledge and for the benefits that will result from it, together with astonishment, rejection and then a crisis which, once it is overcome, leads A. Square to completely accept unknowable truths and to assume other truths according to a criterion of arithmetical progression. The transfer of A. Square from the Plane to the Space turns out to be a decisive moment both for a scientific reading of the text and for the epistemological approach that results from it. The confusion, that is the typical attitude of bewilderment after the sudden falling away of the obstacles fixed by rational knowledge, proper to those who live in a satisfied feeling of balance between awareness and certainty, seems to be one of the keys to the reading of the book (Longo 2002). The sense of inadequacy shown by A. Square when he explains a truth different from the truth which is prearranged in his mind is like the feeling we experience in feeling limited by the size of our world. We cannot explain Leopardi's *Infinity*: even if from a sentimental point of view we prefer to entrust it with all our hopes and wishes and we imagine it as an exciting immensity whose dimensionality is endless, we cannot think about it in a reasonable manner but as something tangible, controllable and measurable. The way in which infinity is described always conforms, from a spatial point of view, to an obstacle or to a horizon, where the view is blocked, a kind of hedge against the view.

Multidimensional tales

According to a common morphology, *Flatland* has the form of a mathematical folktale (Propp 2008), and despite the apparently dissimilar characteristics, it recalls the fantastic story *par excellence*, *Alice's Adventures in Wonderland* (Carroll 1865) which was published in London only a few years after Flatland.

The first evident comparison is set in the literary production of the two authors; *Flatland* is the earnest production of Abbott, a writer, theologian and educator, just as *Alice* is Lewis Carroll's, a famous photographer and mathematician contemporary with Abbott.

Like Abbott, Carroll imagines a surreal world where science is an instrument of explanation of the world. By a careful analysis of these fantastic tales one can infer that each text is the opposite of the other. The comparison between these two works turns on a strong opposition; indeed, the exasperation and exaggeration present in both works is equal and opposite. In *Flatland* the rationality is extreme, so that even the slightest imperfection of the figures would mean serious ethical and social infringement. *Alice* is in fact a discontinuous and fragmented work, characterised by a total lack of shared rules, a continuous transformation of the narrator and a missing structured narrative framework.

The space is a fundamental topic in both works. Such a literary space, where the fantastic is expressed in all its forms through precise but opposite language, does indeed reflect the writers' worldviews, but in *Flatland* the consistency and uniqueness of the geometric rules is applied, whereas in *Alice* the absence of any rule is stated.

The world of *Flatland* enhances movement in space but excludes any transformation, rather affirming the consistency of the geometric rules, and presenting a reality always encoded in codified, repeatable patterns. In *Alice*, change is in the nature of things; in Alice's fall into the middle of the earth a few physical laws are well explained, but exaggerated and paradoxical. Alice is subjected to a series of fast expansions and contractions, while behaving with no apparent discomfort. In such a scientific text no weight or number is envisaged, everything is upside-down and the multiplication table goes crazy. Space and time are key variables in fantastic literature, the space in *Alice* is adaptable, as if it were just one of several dimensions of reality of the story. In *Flatland*, space reveals the existence of different unperceivable worlds, mentally unreachable, cross-sections of the fantastic and reality. In both texts spaces are mental places, and the deduction of physical spaces always involves a deduction of mental spaces.

In both texts the narrative development of the plots has the same weight but is also opposite, and they both deal with the literary topos of the journey. In *Flatland* it is upside-down, the story is not told by the visitor, but by the one who gets an unexpected visit, as if the adventures of Alice were told by the Rabbit or Gulliver's travels were told by the Lilliputians. In *Alice* the journey is quite like a dream and madness is a feature of many of the characters Alice meets in her adventures. Carroll thought that one of the manifestations of madness was not being able to distinguish dream and reality. It is not surprising therefore to discover that one of the trains of thought of Alice's adventures is such a lack of distinction among fantasy and reality. The two elements are kept completely separated, until at the end Alice wakes up and discovers that she has dreamt such a dream, and tells her sister, who immediately falls asleep, in turn, and dreams of Alice dreaming her dream. The nonsense pervades the text as a metaphor of the true human condition, so that a pursuit of the real meaning of life is quite impossible (Gardner 1960). In relation to the spaces, compared to *Alice*, *Flatland* presents a proper feature of utopias, in which the political dimension is intertwined with cartography. Over the centuries the relationship between the spaces of cities and the political dimension has become very narrow, and consequently utopian literature establishes a deep connection, and the spatial organisation develops as a political metaphor.

Mapping the space

Flatland is a modern utopia, representing most of all the utopian concepts of a map in all its forms and explaining the dimensional jump. In this regard the text has two fundamental aspects: on one hand *Flatland* is itself a map, so there is no need for any mental effort to collapse solid structures, even utopian, onto a Cartesian plane; it lies already on a plane itself so that the container coincides perfectly with its content. On the other hand *Flatland* explodes into a new three-dimensionality, an unknown space as a metaphor for the contemporary space. Maps are tools of mediation between reality and the subject, by definition imperfect, approximate projections of a physical place, unfinished, partial and provisional images. In such an image the features of the territory are reduced, selected and reproduced, and refer only to some of the knowable levels of truth. There is just one case in which maps overlap and enclose the territory: in utopias, descriptions of fantastic and invented places which exist only thanks to a graphical representation. In this case there are countless levels of truth and a complete identity between place and representation. According to the definition of utopia, because it is essentially global, predictive and encompassing, the figurative representation is absolutely fundamental to ensure truthfulness, but in these texts no approximation is to be made. In the utopian maps there are no filters, interpretations or graphic conventions, because by definition there is no reality presented, only its representation (Bonaiuti 2009, 346–62). Consequently, these fantastic geographies are correct by definition, the only reality that utopias can afford is contained in their image. In this case the correspondence between maps and territories becomes a real coincidence.

In the utopian cities, the map coincides precisely with the place, as a projection of a place-that-pragmatically-does-not-exist: reality is represented in many dimensions, setting a complete identity among design and territory. Utopias, as representations of rational organisations, tend to have a positive vision of the world, as opposed to chaos. The dimensional changes have substantial weight in the geographical maps but in the transition between utopia and maps they are set apart, annulled, one being the perfect representation of the other. Invented maps produce instead of *re*producing, *de*-scribe rather than *circum*-scribe, and their imaginary geographies are by definition accurate. They are built as a possible and desirable model of perfection. Both can be multiplied and reduced, have to be conquered, identified, located and designated continuously (Farinelli 2009, 98–118). There is only a representation, which becomes in itself a territory, as a projection of a place which does not physically exist. The map itself is the territory.

The coincident relationship between utopia and representation is defined by the dimensional shift, the transition between the flat map, in which the space is represented, and the space itself.

Industrial revolution and literary implications

Yet the journey of A. Square into three-dimensional space is a cultural transition: when Abbott wrote his geometrical romance, England was the centre of a scientific and social revolution. Pure-state energy was undergoing many changes, thermal energy was turning into mechanical and electric energy, introducing a widespread use of steam engines that upset the standards of the rural life whose survival depended unconditionally on the seasonal cycles. People established a new relationship with Nature thanks to the machine, and so industrialisation led to a social revolution that upset the secular hierarchy and human relations and brought about a new picture of the world. Due to the large number of migrants moving from the country, the rural landscapes turned into big cities and the standardisation of the structures together with the synchronisation of times and behaviours were the result of the movement from the country to the factory, i.e., the place of production and work that basically corresponded to the living place. This structural change involved England in a cultural change that altered both the way in which reality was perceived and its time and space coordinates (Hobsbawm 1968); according to the observers of the century who wrote about the new urban life, the space changes represented the first, clear sign of the existence of a standardised society; the dullness of the new social life was already described in detail in the works of Dickens, Wilde and Shaw, who drew a uniform image of that new life (for a historical, cultural analysis of the Industrial Revolution see in particular Hobsbawm 1968; Ashton 1997; Williams 1985).

Abbott's work is the mirror of the contradictions of those times; in particular the perfect similarity between political life and social life which marked the industrial society is found in the geometrical correspondence of the Flatland plane. A case in point is the social pyramid of the Plane, which recalls also the organisation of the English factories of the time and their strictly hierarchical organising structure, which itself reflected a social division of both labour and employees. Taylor's factory, just like *Flatland*, is a microcosm which does not interact with the outside and is validated by scientific rules—efficiency, standardisation, planning and control—quite overlooking the human and creative aspects of the organisation. The Labour Organisation theorised by Friedrich Taylor, imposing just one model of reality, asserts the overall supremacy of the organisation over each element, and offers itself as a universal scientific theory which is valid in all organising contexts and ages. In the same way the society of Flatland proves the legitimacy of the notion of Taylor's only possible way by the rules of the plane in Euclidean geometry; and by overlooking emotional or contingent ways of thinking, it affirms the supremacy of the system over the individual (Taylor 1911; Weick 1997).

In the industrial age the notion of size gained a new value; industrial space was transferred; "space" was no longer the open, boundless space of the country, but it was closed, defined; the industrial space corresponded merely to the limited spaces of the factory departments, where the workplace corresponded to the living place. The Aristotelian unity of place, time and action of the English factory at the end of the century was the same as the utopia of the Plane kingdom.

The metaphor of the space flight means overcoming this traditionalist, industrial society.

One of the predominant certainties of the age was given by the progressive approach of man towards omniscience through an irreversible improvement made up of descriptive, explicative knowledge acquired by observing his own field of investigation from an objective, neutral point of view. The dichotomies between order and disorder, the whole and the details, what is necessary and what is possible, law and case, what is predictable and what is unpredictable, infallibility and fallibility, neutrality and implication, set natural sciences in the domain of the first of these dual concepts (which gave them the quality of being very accurate and precise), and human sciences in the domain of the second (which gave them the quality of being inaccurate).

The dimensional jump into the Space represents the loss of the Archimedean point, beyond and over reality, so that reality can be observed in a neutral way without being contaminated and contaminating, staying "at the centre of the universe and on top of reason." A necessary loss of absolute, mathematical and philosophical values and the acceptance of new categories, which involves a crisis of the truth considered as an entirety of clear, separate notions; a crisis of the possibility of establishing clear boundaries or limits between science and non-science, between subject and object, between independence and dependence. The transfer of A. Square into the Space stands for the refusal of accuracy and objectivity, and the acceptance of the relativity of phenomena regardless of detail and contingencies; and A. Square accepts complexity as being the essential tension between an old and a new epistemology, grasping it as an opportunity.

From a scientific point of view, in the "flat" world brightly described by Abbott "the cube on the fourth dimension walks on officially," and *Flatland* has been defined as "the best description of the fourth dimension"; nevertheless, the meaning of the stories thus related is not only to be seen in the divulgation of scientific theories, but above all in the coexistence of these two worlds as the cultural gap between two ages of thinking. On one hand it is like an indispensable methodological standard of scientific examination; on the other hand, it considers knowledge in a broad, but not endless, context of application. *Flatland* reveals the dimensional—but above all intellectual—relativity of every situation: through a geometrical periphrasis it distinguishes the signs of a new culture among fixed falsehoods. As a matter of fact, theories on the fourth dimension and non-Euclidean geometry have been one of the most shocking issues in the history of human thinking; literature's proper task is to elaborate and divulge the new scientific concepts, usually explaining the fourth dimension as a spatial or geometric variable.

During his imprisonment, A. Square frames long monologues while waiting for an audience with the energy and enthusiasm of those who distinguish the signs of a new culture among the prearranged falsehoods of their world, a paradigm that puts aside the previous harshness, accepts new values and longs for plurality, complexity, paradox, complementarities and the postmodern.

Concerning this, the most suitable reading key for approaching *Flatland* as a literary piece is given by the author himself:

> To The Inhabitants of SPACE IN GENERAL/ And H.C. IN PARTICULAR/ This Work is Dedicated/ By a Humble Native of Flatland/ In the Hope that/ Even as he was Initiated into the Mysteries/ Of THREE Dimensions/ Having been previously conversant/ With ONLY TWO/ So the Citizens of that Celestial Region/ May aspire yet higher and higher/ To the Secrets of FIVE FOUR OR EVEN SIX Dimensions/ Thereby contributing/ To the Enlargement of THE IMAGINATION/ And the possible Development/ Of that most rare and excellent Gift of MODESTY/ Among the Superior Races/ Of SOLID HUMANITY. (Abbott 2010, 13)

This dedication reminds us that the meaning of the stories that have been told is to be found in the urgent warning about modesty, which is an essential methodological criterion for the scientific enterprise. Knowledge can be broadly applied but human limits must be constantly evaluated in relation to an endless notion of knowledge. The incipit of the romance, which refers to a notion of generating power implicit in the text "Be patient, for the world is broad and wide," is one reading key for the work and more generally of mathematical utopian texts. Abbott's work, a multidimensional imaginary tale, is a warning to be patient, and somehow it also advises us to be far-sighted because the immensity of the world is a metaphor of both its complexity and the endless opportunities we have to pursue utopias.

NOTES

Chapter Two

[1] This discourse is surprisingly new. In the current discourse of regionalism, it is difficult to believe that identity did not belong to the vocabulary of 19th century nationalism. The dictionaries of social sciences did not identify the term in 1930s. See Gleason 1983, 910.

[2] "Sukuidentiteettiä pohditaan sukulaisia tavattaessa tai sukuyhdistyksen toimintaan osallistuttaessa. Kansallinen identiteetti tulee mieleen ja keskusteluun tiettyjen tapahtumien yhteydessä: esimerkiksi urheilukilpailuissa tai kohdattaessa kotimaan kansalaisia ulkomailla. Etninen identiteetti aktivoituu ulkomaalaisiin tai vähemmistöryhmiin kohdistettavassa syrjinnässä. Tilanteissa ei kollektiivista identiteettiä keksitä tai sepitetä tyhjästä vaan niiden jäsentämiseen käytetään olemassa olevia, kulttuuriin yleistyneitä koodeja" (my translation).

Chapter Three

[1] This is quoted in Taylor 1994, 42. Taylor, in a note, writes, "I have no idea whether this statement was actually made in this form by Saul Bellow, or by anyone else. I report it only because it captures a widespread attitude, which is, of course, why the story had currency in the first place."

[2] This meta-historical, naturalist view of history is also visible in Cohen and Kymlicka's (1988) treatment of Marx's view of history. They claim that the tendency of economic growth is independent of social structure (172); that is, it is rooted in human nature and the human situation. This implies that there is a meta-historical "human nature." However, there is no "productive force," in Marx's conception, which is independent of and external to the socio-historical conditions.

[3] Marx further adds, "Consequently Herr Bauer has no inkling that real secular Jewry, and hence religious Jewry too, is being continually produced by the present-day civil life and finds its final development in the money system. He could not have any inkling of this because he did not know Jewry as a part of the real world but only as a part of his world, theology; because he, a pious, godly man, considers not the active everyday Jew but the hypocritical Jew of the Sabbath to be the real Jew" (1975, 109).

[4] In the foreword to the *Holy Family* Engels writes, "Real humanism has no more dangerous enemy in Germany than spiritualism or speculative idealism, which substitutes 'self-consciousness' or the 'spirit' for the real individual man and with the evangelist teaches: 'It is the spirit that quickeneth; the flesh profiteth nothing.' Needless to say, this incorporeal spirit is spiritual only in its imagination. What we

are combating in Bauer's criticism is precisely speculation reproducing itself as a caricature. We see in it the most complete expression of the Christian-Germanic principle, which makes its last effort by transforming 'criticism' itself into a transcendent power" (1975, 7).

5 Habermas states, "On the one hand, a collectivity that thinks of itself as a community with its own identity attains a new level of recognition by taking the step of becoming a nation in its own right. It cannot reach level as a pre-political linguistic and ethnic community, or even as an incorporated or a fragmented "cultural nation." The need to be recognised as a nation-state is intensified in times of crisis, when the populace clings to the ascriptive signs of a regressively revitalised collective identity, as for instance after the dissolution of the Soviet empire. This kind of support offers dubious compensation for well-founded fears about the future and lack of social stability. On the other hand, national independence is often to be had only at the price of civil wars, new kinds of repression, or ensuing problems that perpetuate the initial conflicts with the signs reversed."

Chapter Four

1 The Bartlett's Test of Sphericity was used to test the appropriateness of factor analysis in this study. This test found that factor analysis was a significant technique for this study (Significance = .000).

2 To obtain the rotated factor matrix, varimax rotation technique was used.

3 Guttman-Kaiser rule was used for determining the number of factors. Guttman-Kaiser is the "eigenvalue equal or greater than 1" criteria. In this study, there were 16 Eigenvalues that were greater than 1, that is, there was a linear combination of 16 factors.

4 Tabachnick and Fidell (1989) use loadings whose absolute values are equal or greater than 0.30 In my data, the loadings vary between –0.200 and 0.923. For each of the 16 factors, I grouped the ones whose absolute values are equal or above 0.30.

Chapter Five

1 It is interesting to note that the original manuscripts of other two novels of Kafka, "The Castle" and "Amerika" were donated to the Bodleian Library at Oxford by Max Brod himself.

2 Right before submitting this article to the publisher, the verdict was finally rendered. The manuscripts should go to the National Library in Israel, which promised to put them on display as soon as possible, while stressing the need for future cooperation between the library and the German Literary Archive in Marbach.

3 Fiala-Fürst (2002) stresses that in the 1920s there were people pointing at a Sonderweg ("special path") for the Moravian Jewish literature, even when created beyond Moravian borders.

[4] The title "Friends of the world" was borrowed from the title of the first poetry collection composed by Franz Werfel (1890–1945).
[5] "Es ist wohl kaum zu bestreiten, dass die Prager deutsche Literatur den weitaus wichtigsten Komplex literarischer Werke in deutscher Sprache darstellt, das ausserhalb des geschlossenen deutschen Sprachgebiets entstanden ist."
[6] As written on its website (<www.franzkafka-soc.cz/index.php?action=view&page=uvod&lang=en>), visited in 24 June 2010. The centre works in tight cooperation with German institutions. Just for illustration: one of the latest conferences on Kafka was held in the Goethe Institute in Prague, and among the co-organisers were The Centre for Slavonic studies at the University of Regensburg, and the Centre for German Studies at the Charles University in Prague.
[7] Examples of such books where the word "German" is used in the title: Ralph Blumenau, *A History of the Jews in German-speaking Lands* (London: University of the Third Age in London, 1995); Herman Pollack, *Jewish Folkways in Germanic Lands (1648–1806): Studies in Aspects of Daily Life* (Cambridge, MA: MIT Press, 1971); Klara Pomeranz Carmely, *Das Identitätsproblem juedischer Autoren im deutschen Sprachraum: Von der Jahrhundertwende bis zu Hitler* (Scriptor, 1981); *Metzler Lexikon der deutsch-jüdischen Literatur: Jüdische Autorinnen und Autoren deutscher Sprache von der Aufklärung bis zur Gegenwart*, edited by Andreas B. Kilcher (Stuttgart: Verlag J. B. Metzler, 2000). In the book *Judentum deutschen Sprachraum*, edited by Karl E. Groezinger (Suhrkamp, 1991), the geographic scope of the articles and of the editors' research interest is not explicitly stated. According to the editor, the volume does not deal with "the history of the Jewry in the German speaking area," but rather it studies the phenomenon called Ashkenazic Jewry (p. 8).
[8] This is an example of a collection of studies *Jüdische Identitäten im Mitteleuropa: Literarische Modelle der Identitätskonstruktion*, edited by Armin A. Wallas (Tübingen: M. Niemeyer, 2002).
[9] See, for example, the rare voice of the journalist and writer Dan Hrubý, "Kafka: Čech jako poleno!" *Reflex*, 25/3/2010. He wonders why Kafka never enjoys the label "Czech writer" in the Czech milieu, although this is a commonly used collocation in other countries. To support his finding, he quotes from Israeli press. As we will see, this is not a coincidence, as in German press one would rarely find it.
[10] All the quotations and information concerning the Museum of the Czech Literature in Prague were retrieved and last accessed 5 May 2011 from <www.pamatniknarodnihopisemnictvi.cz/cs/aktualne-z-cinnosti-pnp-archiv-1-2.php>.
[11] In the aforementioned article the image next to the text is quite interesting. Besides the notoriously and widely used portrait of Franz Kafka (without a hat) the collage at the background plays a game of associations. One can see a dog, a gramophone record, and also a house in front of which grow palm trees—an image that is hardly imaginable in Kafka's "Prague" setting, but is quite natural and logical in the Israeli context; thus (1) stressing Kafka's wish to immigrate to

Palestine, and (2) understanding Israel as a natural and the only true home for every Jew, including Kafka.

[12] This is a very short notice on the back page of the edition about a new book release. Kafka is described as a "Jewish-Czech writer," with the "Jewish" in first place.

[13] The notion of the world cultural heritage (*Weltkulturerbe*) is strongly present especially in the German articles reporting on the auction of Kafka's letters to his sister Ottla. This might be explained in the context of the campaign led by German cultural institutions against the danger of selling these manuscripts to a private collector. See e.g. "Die Frau, bei der Kafka ein anderer war," *Frankfurter Allgemeine Zeitung*, 24 January 2011 (<www.faz.de>), retrieved 4 May 2011.

[14] At this place it is proper to differentiate between two proper nouns, which in English both are translated as "Czech": "Böhme" and "Tscheche." The first was used to express the connection to the Czech lands (Bohemia) mostly by liberal German-speaking individuals, while the other meant belonging to the Czech nation. The origins of this dichotomy as well as its transformation from the second half of the 18th century onwards remains beyond the limits of this study, but would deserve an individual chapter.

Chapter Six

[1] This word is here used according to the meaning given by Italo Calvino in his *Lezioni Americane* (1988 Milan, Garzanti) i.e. "writing as metaphor of the world dusty substance"; in this way it can be used by a lot of different readers.

[2] Even though the essay is anonymous, it is attributable to the mathematician William Garnett. See Thomas Banchoff, "From Flatland to Hyper-graphics: Interacting with Higher Dimensions," in *Interdisciplinary Science Reviews* 15, no. 4 (1990): 364–72, which I also refer to for some quotations taken from scientific participations and papers that were otherwise impossible to find.

BIBLIOGRAPHY

"111 mikhtavim shel hasofer hatzekhi Franz Kafka yimakhru bim'khira pumbit." 2011. *Haaretz*, 02 February 2011. Retrieved 4 May 2011. www.haaretz.co.il.

"Boker Kafkai beveyt hadin be-Ramat Gan." 2011. *Haaretz*, 18 February. Retrieved 18 March 2011. www.haaretz.co.il.

"Der Prozess gehört uns alles." 2010. *Frankfurter Allgemeine Zeitung*, 7 August. Retrieved 4 May 2011. www.faz.net.

"Die Frau, bei der Kafka ein anderer war." 2011. *Frankfurter Allgemeine Zeitung*, 24 January. Retrieved 4 May 2011. www.faz.de.

"Dopisy Franze Kafky mají být prodány v dražbě, německé kulturní instituce protestují." 2011. *Hospodářské Noviny*, 14 February. Retrieved 04 May 2011. www.life.ihned.cz.

"Dopisy Franze Kafky se po protestech dražit nebudou, koupí je univerzita v Oxfordu a archiv v Marbachu za tajnou částku." 2011. *Hospodářské Noviny*, 4 April. Retrieved 4 May 2011. www.life.ihned.cz.

"Dostane literární svět neznámou Kafkovu povídku?." 2010. *Aktuálně.cz*, 21 July. Retrieved 4 May 2011. www.aktualne.centrum.cz.

"Franz Kafka má v Izraeli svůj novodobý 'proces.'" 2011. *Aktuálně.cz*, 25 February. Retrieved 4 May 2011. www.aktualne.centrum.cz.

"Hadoch hasofi leveyt hamishpat me'asher ki kitvei yad mekori'im shel Kafka nimtz'u bakasafot." 2011. *Haaretz*, 25 February. Retrieved 18 March 2011. www.haaretz.co.il.

"Hitgalu kitvei yad shel Kafka beivrit." 2010. *Yedioth Acharonot*, 09 June. Retrieved 18 March 2011. www.ynet.co.il.

"Hoffnung auf unbekannte Texte von Franz Kafka: Literaturarchiv Marbach will Nachlass von Max Brod in Tel Aviv erwerben." 2008. Interview for the radio station Deutschlandfunk, 7 July. Retrieved 3 May 2011. www.dradio.de.

"Kafka baderekh le-Germania." 2011. *Haaretz*, 7 January.

"Kafka gehört der Welt," 2011. *Die Welt*, 5 April. Retrieved 4 May 2011. www.welt.de.

"Kafka im Banktresor – wer hat's erfunden? Eine Schweizer Tagung zur Poetik des Literaturbetriebs." 2011. *Die Welt*, 7 March 2011. Retrieved 18 March 2011. www.welt.de.

"Kafka: Čech jako poleno!." 2010. *Reflex*, 25 March.

"Kafkas letztes Geheimnis." 2010. *Tagesspiegel*, 26 January.
"Marbach und Oxford erwerben Kafka-Briefe." 2011. Die Welt, 4 April. Retrieved 6 April 2011. www.diewelt.de. "Německo a Izrael se přou o Kafkův Proces. Nejde však jen o rukopis." 2009. *Hospodářské Noviny*, 17 December. Retrieved 18 March 2011. www.kultura.ihned.cz.
"Marbach: Im Endlager der Deutschen Literatur," Die Welt, 29/12/2010, www.welt.de, retrieved 18/03/2011. Berlin.
"Nish'arim babayit." 2011. *Haaretz*, 14 March.
"Spor o rukopis Kafkova Procesu se vyhrocuje." 2009. ČTK, 19 October.
"Streit um Kafka Erbe." 2009. *NZZ Online*, 16 September.
"Streit um Prozess-Handschrift. Israel fordert von Deutschland Kafka-Manuskript." 2009. Der Spiegel, 16 October.
"Tauziehen um Kafka und Brod." 2010. *FAZ*, 22 January.
"The Greater Municipality of Ankara Metropol İmar" (nd). Retrieved March 2011. www.ankara.bel.tr/AbbSayfalari/Projeler.
"Vzpomínky na Kafku jsou na trhu. Se čtyřicetiletým zpožděním." 2011. *iDnes.cz*, 22 November. Retrieved 18 March 2011. www.kultura.idnes.cz.
"Zápas jménem psaní: nový Franz Kafka v Čechách ležící, spící." 2010. *Hospodářské Noviny*, 20 February. Retrieved 18 March 2011. www.kultura.ihned.cz.
Aaltonen, Esko. 1963. Kotiseututyön opas. [A Guide to Work for Home Site] Kolmas uudistettu painos. Forssan Kirjapaino Oy. [In Finnish only.]
Abbott, Edwin A., William F. Lindgren, Thomas F. Banchoff, 2010. *Flatland: An Edition with Notes and Commentary*. New York: Cambridge University Press.
Abbott, Edwin. Abbott. 1884. *Flatland, a Romance of Many Dimensions*. London: Seeley & Co.
Ager, Alastair, and Alison B. Strang. 2004. "Indicators of Integration: Final Report." *Home Office Development and Practice Report*, 28. London: Home Office.
Agnew, John, and Stuart Crobridge. 1994. *Mastering Space: Hegemony, Territory and International Political Economy*. London: Routledge.
Akhtar, Salman, and Steven Samuel. 1996. "The Concept of Identity: Developmental Origins, Phenomenology, Clinical Relevance, and Measurement." *Harvard Review of Psychiatry*, 3(5): 254–67.
Alba, Richard. 1999. "Immigration and the American Realities of Assimilation and Multiculturalism, Inclusion or Exclusion of Immigrants." *Demographie aktuell*, 14: 3–16.

Alexander, Jeffrey C. 2003. *The Meanings of Social Life: A Cultural Sociology*. New York: Oxford University Press.

Allen, John, Doreen Massey and Allen Cochrane. 1998. *Rethinking the Region*. London: Routledge.

Alonso González, Carmen María. 2006. "La Construcción de la Identidad de Castilla y León a través de Su Imagen Tturística." Paper presented at the 9th Congreso Iberoamericano de Comunicación - IBERCOM, Sevilla-Cádiz, Spain, 15–18 November.

Amin, Ash. 2004. "Regions Unbound: Towards a New Politics of Place." *Geografiska Annaler: Series B, Human Geography*, 86 (1): 33–44.

Ansaldi, Waldo. 2001. "La Seducción de la Cultura: Mucho Más que un Mercado." *Encrucijadas UBA*, 1 (4): 64–77.

Appadurai, Arjun. 1991. "Global Ethnoscapes: Notes and Queries for a Transnational Anthropology." In *Recapturing Anthropology: Working in the Present*, edited by Richard J. Fox, 191–210. Santa Fe, NM: School of American Research Press.

—. 1992. "Putting hierarchy in its place." In *Rereading Cultural Anthropology*, edited by George E. Marcus, 34–47. Durham, NC: Duke University Press.

—. 1996. *Modernity at Large: Cultural Dimensions of Globalization*. Minneapolis: University of Minnesota Press.

Armstrong, John Alexander. 1982. *Nations before Nationalism*. Chapel Hill, NC: University of North Carolina Press.

Aronsson, Peter. 2007. "The Old Cultural Regionalism – and the New." In *An Agenda for Regional History*, edited by Bill Lancaster, Diana Newton and Natasha Vall, 251–70. Newcastle: Northumbria University Press.

Arslanoğlu, Rana A. 1998. *Kent, Kimlik ve Küreselleşme*. Bursa: ASA Yayınları.

Ashbrook, John. 2011. "Politicization of Identity in a European Borderland: Istria, Croatia, and Authenticity, 1990–2003." *Nationalities Papers: The Journal of Nationalism and Ethnicity*, 39 (6): 871–97.

Ashton, Thomas S. 1997. *The Industrial Revolution, 1760–1830*. Oxford: Oxford University Press.

Atkinson, David, Peter Jackson, David Sibley, and Neil Washbourne, eds. 2005. *Cultural Geography. A Critical Dictionary of Key Concepts*. London: I. B. Tauris.

Azeri, Siyaves. 2013. "Multiculturalism: The ideology of the New World Order." In *Identities, Cultures, Spaces: Dialogue and Change*, edited by Fernando Kuhn, 57–81. Newcastle-upon-Thyne: Cambridge Scholars Publishing.

Azevedo, Raimondo Cagiano, and Barbara Sannino. 1997. "A European Research Project on Migrants Integration." In *Measurement and Indicators of integration, Community Relations*. Strasbourg: Directorate of Social and Economic Affairs, Council of Europe Publishing.

Baccolini, Raffaella, Vita Fortunati, and Nadia Minerva. 1996. *Viaggi in utopia*. Ravenna: Longo.

Backzo, Bronisław. 1989. *Utopian Lights: the Evolution of the Idea of Social Progress*. New York: Penguin.

—. 1979. *L'Utopia*. Turin: Einaudi.

Baldini, Massimo. 1974. *Il Linguaggio delle Utopie: Utopia e Ideologia. Una Rilettura Epistemological*. Roma: Studium.

Baldwin-Edwards, Martin. 2005. "The Integration of Immigrants in Athens: Developing Indicators and Statistical Measures." Athens: Mediterranean Migration Observatory.

Banchoff, Thomas. 1990. "From Flatland to Hyper-graphics: Interacting with Higher Dimensions." *Interdisciplinary Science Reviews*, 15 (4): 364–72.

Banerjee, Padmini, and Myna German. 2010. "Migration and Transculturation in the Digital Age: A Framework for Studying the 'Space Between.'" *Journal of Global and International Studies*, 2 (1): 22–35.

Bauböck, Rainer, Agnes Heller, and Aristide R. Zollberg, eds. 1996. *The Challenge of Diversity: Integration and Pluralism in Societies of Immigration*. Aldershot, UK: Avebury.

Baum, Fran, Catherine Palmer, Carolyn Modra, Charlie Murray, and Robert Bush. 2000. "Families, Social, Capital and Health." In *Social Capital and Public Policy in Australia*, edited by Ian Winter, 250–75. Melbourne: Australian Institute of Family Studies.

Baumann, Gerd. 1999. *The Multicultural Riddle: Rethinking National, Ethnic and Religious Identities*. London: Routledge.

Bayardo, Rubens, and Mônica Lacarrieu. 1999. "Nuevas Perspectivas sobre la Cultura en la Dinámica Global/Local." In *La Dinámica Global/Local*, edited by Rubens Bayardo and Mônica Lacarrieu, 9–24. Buenos Aires: Ciccus/La Crujía.

Bechev, Dimitar. 2004. "Contested Borders, Contested Identity: The Case of Regionalism in Southeast Europe." *Journal of Southeast European and Black Sea Studies* 4 (1): 77–95.

Benessaieh, Alef. 2010. "Multiculturalism, Interculturality, Transculturality." In *Ameriques Transculturelles - Transcultural Americas*, edited by Alef Benessaieh, 11–38. Ottawa: University of Ottawa Press.

Berkman, Gülden. 1994. *Geography of Health and Location of Health Facilities in Ankara*. Ankara: Middle East Technical University.

Berry, John. W. 1992. "Acculturation and Adaptation in a New Society." *International Migration Review* 30: 69–86.

Bhabha, Homi K. 1994. *The Location of Culture*. London: Routledge.

Bijl, Rob V., Asian Zorlu, Annet S. van Rijn, Roel P. W. van Jennissen, and Martine Blom. 2005. *The Integration Monitor 2005: The Social Integration of Migrants Monitored over Time: Trend and Cohort Analyses – Cahier 2005-16a*. The Hague: WODC. Retrieved 11 April 2010. www.wodc.nl.

Binder, Jana. 2003. "Travellerscapes: Tourism Research and Transnational Anthropology." Paper presented at the conference "Alltag der Globalisierung: Perspektiven einer Transnationalen Anthropologie," Frankfurt am Main, 16–18 January.

Bishop, Peter. 2011. "Eating in the Contact Zone: Singapore Foodscape and Cosmopolitan Timespace." *Continuum: Journal of Media & Cultural Studies*, 25 (5): 637–52.

Blum, Lawrence. 1998. "Recognition, Value, and Equality: A Critique of Charles Taylor's and Nancy Fraser's Accounts of Multiculturalism." In *Theorizing Multiculturalism: A Guide to the Current Debates*, edited by Cynthia Willett, 73–99. Malden, MA: Blackwell.

Blumenau, Ralph. 1995. *A History of the Jews in German-speaking Lands*. London: London University of the Third Age.

Boas, Franz. 1930. "Anthropology." in *Encyclopedia of the Social Sciences*, 2: 79.

Bolin, Göran. 2006. "Visions of Europe – Cultural Technologies of Nation-States." *International Journal of Cultural Studies*, 9 (2): 189–206.

Bonaiuti, Gianluca. 2009. "L'utopia come scienza escatologica." *Morus, Utopia e Renascimento*, 6: 345–63.

Bookman, Milica Z. 1997. *The Demographic Struggle for Power: The Political Economy of Demographic Engineering in the Modern World*. London: Frank Cass.

Bourdon, Jérôme. 2007. "Unhappy Engineers of the European Soul: The EBU and the Woes of Pan-European Television." *International Communication Gazette* 69 (3): 263–80.

Boyarin, Jonathan. 1997. "A Response from New York: Return of the Repressed." In *Grasping Land: Space and Place in Contemporary*

Israeli Discourse and Experience, edited by Eyāl Ben-Arî, Yoram Bilu, 217–29. Albany, New York: State University of New York Press.

Braman, Sandra. 1996. "Interpenetrated Globalization: Scaling, Power, and the Public Sphere." In *Globalization, communication and transnational civil society*, edited by Sandra Braman and Annabelle Sreberny-Mohammadi, 21–36. Cresskill, NJ: Hampton Press.

Brancato, Sabrina. 2006. "'Glocality' and Cultural identity." *This Century's Review*, 1 (4). http://history.thiscenturysreview.com/gloacality.html.

Brenner, Neil, Bob Jessop, Martin Jones, and Gordon MacLeod, eds. 2003. *State/Space: A Reader*. Oxford: Blackwell.

Brubaker, Rogers and Frederick Cooper. 2000. "Beyond 'identity.'" *Theory and Society*, 29: 1–47.

Buzzi, Peter, and Claudia Megele. 2011. "The Social Networking and Hyper-reality on Global Impact of Migration." In *Migration, Technology and Transculturation: A Global Perspective*, edited by Myna German, and Padmini Banerjee, 30–55. St Charles, MO: Lindenwood University Press.

Caldeira, Jorge. 1997. "O Mercosul para além da economia." In *O Mercosul e a Integração Sul-Americana: Mais do que a Economia, Encontro de Culturas*. Brasília: Fundação Alexandre de Gusmão.

Calderón G, Fernando, and Alicia Szmuckler B. 1999. "Aspectos Culturales de las Migraciones en el Mercosur." In *UNESCO/MOST Discussion Papers*. Paris: Unesco, retrieved 10 June 2008. www.unesco.org/most/calderon.htm.

Caldo, Costantino. 1996. *Geografia Umana*. Firenze: Palumbo.

Caldo, Costantino, and Vincenzo Guarrasi, eds. 1994. *Beni Culturali e Geografia*. Bologna: Pàtron.

Calvino, Italo. 1988. *Lezioni Americane*. Milan: Garzanti.

Carmely, Klara Pomeranz. 1981. *Das Identitätsproblem juedischer Autoren im deutschen Sprachraum: Von der Jahrhundertwende bis zu Hitler*. Königstein, Germany: Scriptor.

Cars, Göran, Mats Johansson, Ola Nygren, and Friedrich Schindegger. 1999. "Theme 1.3: Indicators for Social Integration & Integration." Stockholm: The European Commission Study Programme in European Spatial Planning.

Casero, Andreu. 2001. "European-wide television and the construction of European identity: The case of Euronews." Formats, 3. www.iua.upf.edu/formats/formats3/menu_art_a.htm.

Castells, Manuel. 2009. *Communication Power*. New York: Oxford University Press.

Cayton, Andrew R. L. 2001. "The Anti-Region: Place and Identity in the History of the American Midwest." In *The Identity of the American Midwest: Essays in Regional History*, edited by Andrew R. L. Clayton and Susan E. Gray, 140–59. Bloomington, IN: Indiana University Press.

Cellucci, Carlo. 2002. *Matematica e Filosofia*. Bari: Laterza.

Chalaby, Jean K. 2005. "Deconstructing the Transnational: A Typology of Cross-Border Television Channels in Europe." *New Media and Society*, 7 (2): 155–75.

Clifford, James. 1993. "On Collecting Art and Culture." In *The Cultural Studies Reader*, edited by Simon During, 57–76. London: Routledge.

—. 1997. *Routes: Travel and Translation in the Late Twentieth Century*. Cambridge, MA: Harvard University Press.

Collins, Richard. 1998. "Supper with the devil – a Case Study in Private/Public Collaboration in Broadcasting: The Genesis of Eurosport." *Media Culture Society*, 20 (4): 653–63.

Conversi, Daniele. 2010. "The Limits of Cultural Globalization?" *Journal of Critical Globalisation Studies*, 3: 36–59.

Conzen, Kathleen Neils. 2001. "Pi-ing the Type: Jane Gray Swisshelm and the Contest of Midwestern Regionality." In *The Identity of the American Midwest. Essays in Regional History*, edited by Andrew R. L. Clayton and Susan E. Gray, 91–110. Bloomington, IN: Indiana University Press.

Coussey, Mary, and Elisabeth Sem Christensen. 1997. "Indicators of Integration." In *Measurement and Indicators of Integration*, 19–27. Strasbourg: Council of Europe Publishing.

Cox, Robert W. 2005. "Global Perestroika." In *The Global Governance Reader: Concepts and Issues*, edited by Rorden Wilkinson, 140–55. Abingdon, UK: Routledge.

Craith, Mairèad Nic. 2004. "Local Cultures in a Global World." In *Communicating Cultures*, edited by Ullrich Kockel and Mairèad Nic Craith, 279–99. Münster: Lit Verlag Münster.

Crang, Philip, Claire Dwyer, and Peter Jackson. (2003). "Transnationalism and the Spaces of Commodity Culture." *Progress in Human Geography*, 27 (4): 438–56.

Cusack, Tricia. 2007. "Introduction: Riverscapes and the Formation of National Identity." *National Identities*, 9 (2), 101–104.

Dagevos, Jaco. 1997. "Equivalency And Equal Access as Standards or Ethnic Minority Policy in The Netherlands." In *Measurement and Indicators of integration*, 89–97. Strasbourg: Council of Europe Publishing.

Dahl, Øyvind. 2008. "The Dynamics of Communication." In *The Intercultural Perspective in a Multicultural World 11th NIC Conference*, edited by Eilef Gard and Birte Simonsen, 27–46. Kristiansand, Denmark: Universitetet I Agder.

Davies, David W. 1978. *Introduction to Flatland, by Edwin Abbott*, Pasadena. Grant Dahlstrom, pp. 4–6.

De Certeau, Michel. 1984. *The Practice of Everyday Life*. Berkeley, CA: University of California Press.

De Jager, Thomas Thijs. 2009. "Imagining the European Union: A Geo-historical Overview of Dominant Metaphors on the EU's Political Geography." Master thesis. Radboud University Nijmegen, 2009.

Deas, Iain. 2004. "From a New Regionalism to An Unusual Regionalism? Mapping the Emergence of Non-Standard Regional Configurations in Europe." Paper presented at the 100th annual meeting for the Association of American Geographers, Philadelphia, 18 March 2004.

Delanty, Gerard. 2007. "Peripheries and Borders in a Post−Western Europe." *Eurozine*, 29 August 2007, retrieved 7 May 2010. www.eurozine.com/articles/2007-08-29-delanty-en.html.

Dematteis, Giuseppe. 1994. "Nodi e Reti nello Sviluppo Locale." In *Il Territorio dell'Abitare: Lo Sviluppo Locale come Alternativa Strategica*, edited by Alberto Magnaghi, 249–68. Milano: Franco Angeli.

Döring Jörg, and Tristan Thielmann. 2009. *Spatial Turn: Das Raumparadigma in den Kultur-und Sozialwissenschaften*. Bielefeld: Transcript.

Drakulić, Slavenka. 2011. "Euroskansen." *Eurozine*, 3 February 2011, retrieved 12 August 2011. www.eurozine.com/articles/2011-02-03-drakulic-en.html.

Dündar, Özlem. 1998. "Two Different Approaches To The Renewal Of Squatter Housing Areas in Turkey." Paper presented at the conference for the European Network for Housing Research – ENHR. Cardiff, 7–11 September.

Duruz, Jean, Susan Luckman, and Peter Bishop. 2011. "Bazaar Encounters: Food, Markets, Belonging and Citizenship in the Cosmopolitan City." *Continuum: Journal of Media & Cultural Studies*, 25 (5): 599–604.

Eddington, Arthur. 1987. *Space, Time, and Gravitation: An Outline of the General Relativity Theory*. Cambridge: Cambridge University Press.

Eder, Klaus. 1995. "Remembering National Memories Together: The Formation of a Transnational Identity in Europe." In *Collective Memory and European Identity: The Effects of Integration and*

Enlargement, edited by Klaus Eder, and Willfried Spohn, 197–220. Aldershot, UK: Ashgate.

Edwards, R. W. 2004. "Measuring Social Capital: An Australian Framework and Indicators." Information Paper. Canberra: Australian Bureau of Statistics.

Eke, E. Feral. 1981. "The Absorption of Low Income Groups in Ankara." Ekistics 286: 64–70.

Ekholm, Elina. 1997. "Experience in Measuring Refugees' Integration in Finland." In *Measurement and Indicators of integration*, 179–86. Strasbourg: Council of Europe Publishing.

Emmer, Michele. 2004. *Mathland: Dal mondo piatto alle ipersuperfici.* Turin: Testo & Immagine.

Enzinger, Han. 2003. "The Rise and Fall of Dutch Multiculturalism." Paper presented at the conference "Migration – Citizenship –Ethnos: Incorporation Regimes in Germany, Western Europe and North America." Toronto: University of Toronto and the Heinrich Böll Foundation, 2–4 October.

Erder, Sema. 1996. *İstanbul'a Bir Kent Kondu: Ümraniye*. İstanbul: İletişim Yayınları.

Eriksen, Thomas Hylland. 1993. *Kulturterrorismen: Et Oppgjør med Tanken om Kulturell Renhet*. Oslo: Spartacus.

Eriksson, Erik. 1968. *Identity: Youth and Crisis*. New York: W. W. Norton.

Erman, Tahire. 1998. "Farklılaşan Kırsal Kökenli Cemaat, Değişen Gecekondu: Bir Etnografik Araştırmanın Gösterdikleri." *Sosyoloji Araştırmaları Dergisi*, 1 (1–2): 47.

—. 2001. "The Politics of Squatter (Gecekondu) Studies in Turkey: The Changing Representations of Rural Migrants in the Academic Discourse." *Urban Studies* 38 (7): 983–1002.

—. 2004. "Gecekondu Çalişmalarinda 'Öteki' Olarak Gecekondulu Kurgulari." *European Journal of Turkish Studies*, Thematic Issue 1, Gecekondu, Retrieved 14 January. www.ejts.org/document85.html.

Ersoy, Melih. 1985. *Göç ve Kentsel Bütünleşme* [Migration and Urban Integration]. Ankara: Türkiye Gelişme Araştırmaları Vakfı Yay.

Esser, Hartmut. 2003. *Does the New Immigration Require a New Theory of Intergenerational Integration?* Mannheim: MZES.

Fainstein, Susan S., and Dennis R. Judd. 1999. "Global Forces, Local Strategies, and Urban Tourism." In *The Tourist City*, edited by Dennis R. Judd, and Susan S. Fainstein, 1–20. New Haven, CT: Yale University Press.

Farinelli, Franco. 2009. *L'invenzione della Terra*. Palermo: Sellerio.

Fearon, James D. 1999. "What Is Identity (as We Now Use the Word)?" Mimeo, Stanford, CA: Stanford University, November.

Featherstone, Mike. 2006. "Genealogies of the Global." *Theory, Culture and Society*, 23 (2–3): 387–419.

Featherstone, Mike, and Scott Lash.1999. "Introduction." In *Spaces of Culture: City, Nation, World*, edited by Mike Featherstone, and Scott Lash, 1–13. London: Sage.

Ferguson, Niall. 2005. "Sinking Globalization." *Foreign Affairs*, 84 (2): 64–77.

Fernández Manjón, Desiderio. 2010. *La Identidad Humana y los Territorios. El caso de Castilla y León*. Madrid: Vision Libros.

Fiala-Fuerst, Ingeborg. 2002. "Mähren – ein Sonderweg der deutschgeschriebenen jüdischen Literatur?" In *Jüdische Identitäten im Mitteleuropa: Literarische Modelle der Identitätskonstruktion*, edited by Armin A. Wallas, 123–24. Tübingen: M. Niemeyer.

Fitzgerald, Marian. 1997. "Measurements and Indicators of Integration." In *Measurement and Indicators of integration*, 65–78. Strasbourg: Council of Europe Publishing.

Forleo, Marianna. 2010. "Metafore Geometriche e Riflessioni Utopiche." *Rivista di Studi Utopici*, 8: 45–57.

—. 2004. "Matematica e Livelli di Realtà." *Prometeo*, 12.

—. 2013. "Science and Society in a Utopian Map." In *Identities, Cultures, Spaces: Dialogue and Change*, edited by Fernando Kuhn, 125–41. Newcastle-upon-Thyne: Cambridge Scholars Publishing.

Fortunati, Vita, and Raymond Trousson. 2000. *Dictionary of Literary Utopias*. Paris: Champion.

Franklin, Adrian, and Mike Crang. 2001. "The Trouble with Tourism and Travel Theory?" *Tourist Studies*, 1 (1): 5–22.

Fraser, Nancy. 1998. "From Redistribution to Recognition: Dilemmas of Justice in a Post-Socialist Age." In *Theorizing Multiculturalism: A Guide to the Current Debates*, edited by Cynthia Willett, 19–49. Malden, MA: Blackwell.

Gardner, Martin. 1960. *The Annotated Alice*. New York: Bramhall House Clarkson Potter.

Geertz, Clifford. 1973. *The Interpretation of Cultures*. New York: Basic Books.

—. 2000. *Available Light: Anthropological Reflections on Philosophical Topics*. Princeton, NJ: Princeton University Press.

Georgalou, Mariza.2009. "Scoring a Hat Trick: Nation, Football and Critical Discourse Analysis." *Rice Working Papers in Linguistics*, 1: 108–41.

Gere, Charlie. 1997. "Museums, Contact Zones and the Internet." In *Museum Interactive Multimedia 1997: Cultural Heritage Systems Design and Interfaces*, edited by David Bearman, and Jenifer Trant, 59–68. Le Havre: Archives & Museum Informatics.

Giddens, Anthony. 1990. *The Consequences of Modernity*. Stanford, CA: Stanford University Press.

Glasgow, Nina, and Andrew J. Sofranko. 1980. "Migrant Adjustment and Integration in the New Residence." In *Rebirth of Rural America: Rural migration in the Midwest*, edited by Andrew J. Sofranko and James D. Williams, 87–104. Ames, IA: North Central Regional Center for Rural Development.

Gleason, Philip. 1983. "Identifying Identity: A Semantic History." *Journal of American History*, 69 (4): 910–31.

Glick Schiller, Nina, Linda Basch, and Cristina Szanton Blanc. 1995. "From Immigrant to Transmigrant: Theorising Transnational Migration." *Anthropological Quarterly*, 68 (1): 48–63.

Gökçe, Bahadır, ed. 1993. *Gecekondulularda Ailelerarasi Geleneksel Dayanişmanin Çağdaş Organizasyonlara Dönüşümü*, Ankara: Secretariat of Women and Social Services.

Gold, John R., and Stephen Victor Ward, eds. 1994. *Place promotion: The use of publicity and marketing to sell towns and regions*. Chichester, UK: Wiley.

Gold, Thomas, Doug Guthrie and David Wank. 2002. "An Introduction to the Study of Guanxi." In *Social Connection in China: Institutions, Culture, and The Changing The Nature of Guanxi*, edited by Thomas Gold, Doug Guthrie and David Wank, 3–20. Cambridge: Cambridge University Press.

Goldstücker, Eduard, ed. 1967. *Weltfreunde: Konferenz über die Prager deutsche Literatur*. Prague: Academia.

Goldstücker, Eduard, František Kautman and Paul Reiman (eds). 1965. *Franz Kafka aus Prague Sicht 1963*. Prague: Verlag der Tschechoslowakischen Akademie der Wissenschaften.

Gordon, Miltom M. 1964. *Assimilation in American Life: The Role of Race, Religion and National Origin*, New York: Oxford University Press.

Göschel, Albrecht. 2001. "Integration and the City." *German Journal of Urban Studies*, 40 (1), Retrieved 8 June 2007. www.difu.eu/publikationen/dfk.

Graham, Brian G. 2002. "Heritage as Knowledge: Capital or Culture?" *Urban Studies*, 39: 1003–1017.

Graham, Brian G., John Gregory Ashworth and John E. Tunbridge (eds). 2000. *A Geography of Heritage: Power, Culture and Economy*. London: Arnold.

Grillo, Ralph. D. 2003. "Cultural Essentialism and Cultural Anxiety." *Anthropological Theory* 3 (2): 157–73.

Gripsrud, Jostein. 2007. "Television and the European Public Sphere." *European Journal of Communication*, 22 (4): 479–92.

Groezinger, Karl E., ed. 1991. *Judentum deutschen Sprachraum*. Frankfurt am Main: Suhrkamp.

Grundy, Sue, and Lynn Jamieson. 2007. "European Identities: From Absent-Minded Citizens to Passionate Europeans." *Sociology* 41 (4): 663–80.

Guest, Avery M., and Keith R. Stamm. 1993. "Paths of Community Integration." *The Sociological Quarterly*, 34: 581–95.

Gupta, Akhil, and James Ferguson. 1997. "Culture, Power, Place: Ethnography at the End of an Era." In *Culture, Power, Place: Explorations in Critical Anthropology*, edited by Akhil Gupta and James Ferguson, 1–29. Durham, NC: Duke University Press.

Gutmann, Amy. 1994. "Introduction." In: *Multiculturalism: Examining the Politics of Recognition*, edited by Amy Gutmann, 3–24. Princeton, NJ: Princeton University Press.

Habermas, Jürgen. 1994. "Struggle for Recognition in the Democratic Constitutional State." In: *Multiculturalism: Examining the Politics of Recognition*, edited by Amy Gutmann, 107–48. Princeton, NJ: Princeton University Press.

Haines, Valerie A., Jeanne S. Hurlbert, and John J. Beggs. 1996. "Exploring the Determinants of Support Provision: Provider Characteristics, Personal Networks, Community Contexts, and Support Following Life Events." *Journal of Health and Social Behavior*, 37: 252–64.

Hair, Joseph. F., Rolph E. Anderson, Ronald L. Tatham, William C. Black. 1995. *Multivariate Data Analysis with Readings*. Upper Saddle River, NJ: Prentice Hall.

Hall, Stuart. 1990. "Cultural Identity and Diaspora." In *Identity*, edited by Jonathan Rutherford, 222–37. London: Lawrence & Wishart.

—. 1992. "The Question of Culture Identity." In *Modernity and its Futures*, edited by Stuart Hall, David Held and Tony McGrew, 273–326. Cambridge: Polity Press.

—. 1996. "Introduction: Who Needs Identity?" In *Questions of Cultural Identity*, edited by Stuart Hall, and Paul du Gay, 1–17. London: Sage.

—. 1996b. "When Was the 'Post-Colonial'?: Thinking at the Limit." In *The Post-Colonial in Question*, edited by Lidia Curti and Iain Chambers, 242–60. London: Routledge.

—. 1997. "Introduction." In *Representation: Cultural Representation and Signifying Practices*, edited by Stuart Hall, 1–12. Milton Keynes, UK: The Open University.

Hannerz, Ulf. 1990. "Cosmopolitans and Locals in World Culture." In *Global Culture: Nationalism, Globalization and Modernity*, edited by Mike Featherstone, 237–51. London: Sage.

—. 1996. *Transnational Connections: Cultures, People, Places*. London: Routledge.

Harris, Anthea, ed. 2007. Incipient Globalization? Long-Distance Contacts in the Sixth Century. Oxford: Archaeopress.

Hauck, Jan David. 2007. "Mercosur Im Wandel: Von einer Kultur der Desintegration zu einer Kultur der Integration." In *Mercosul / Mercosur: Dynamic der Grenzen und Kulturelle Integration*, edited by Ligia Chiappini, and Jan David Hauck, 269–84. Mettingen: Brasilienkunde Verlag.

Häyrynen, Maunu. 2000. "The Kaleidoscopic View: The Finnish National Landscape Imagery." *National Identities*, 2: 5–19.

Heckmann, Friedrich, and Dominique Schnapper, eds. 2003. *The Integration of Immigrants In European Societies*. Stuttgart: Lucius and Lucius.

Hekmat, Mansoor. 2001/2006. *The World after September 11*. London: WCPI Publication.

Held, David. 1995. *Democracy and the Global Order: From the Modern State to Cosmopolitan Governance*. Stanford: Stanford University Press.

Held, David, and Anthony G. McGrew. 2007. "Introduction: Globalization at Risk?" In *Globalization Theory: Approaches and Controversies*, edited by David Held and Anthony G. McGrew, 1–11. Cambridge: Polity.

Heller, Wilfried. 2011. "Identities and Conceptions of Border Area Populations in East-Central and South-East Europe – Thematic Aspects and Questions of an Actual Research Field." Journal of Urban and Regional Analysis, 3 (1): 5–12.

Hepburn, Eve. 2007. "The Rise and Fall of a 'Europe of the Regions': The Territorial Strategies of Substate Political Parties 1979–2006." Paper presented at the 10th biennial conference for the European Union Studies Association – EUSA, Montreal, 17–19 May 2007.

Hirst, Paul, and Grahame Thompson. 1996. *Globalization in Question: The International Economy and the Possibilities of Governance*. Cambridge: Polity Press.

Hobsbawm, Eric J. 1968. *Industry and Empire*. London: Penguin.

Hobsbawm, Eric, and Terence Ranger, eds. 1983. *The Invention of Tradition*. Cambridge: Cambridge University Press.

Hollinshead, Keith. 1998. "Tourism, Hybridity, and Ambiguity: The Relevance of Bhabha's 'Third Space' Cultures." *Journal of Leisure Research*, 30 (1):121–56.

Holmes, David. 2001."Virtual Globalization: An Introduction." In *Virtual Globalization: Virtual Spaces/Tourist Spaces*, edited by David Holmes, 1–64. London: Routledge.

Hopper, Paul. 2007. *Understanding Cultural Globalization*. Cambridge,: Polity Press.

House, James S., Karl R. Landis, and Debra Umberson. 1988. "Social Relations and Health." *Science*, 241: 540–45.

Hume, David. 1826. *Treatise on Human Nature*. [original 1739] In *The Philosophical Works of David Hume in Four Volumes. Vol 1*, 5–347. Edinburgh: Adam Black and William Tait.

Hurt, R. Douglas. 2001. "Midwestern Distinctiveness." In *The Identity of the American Midwest: Essays in Regional History*, edited by Andrew R. L. Clayton and Susan E. Gray, 160–79. Bloomington, IN: Indiana University Press 2001.

Jack, Gavin, and Alison M. Phipps. 2005. *Tourism and Intercultural Exhange: Why Tourism Matters*. Channel View Publications: Clevedon, UK.

Jamieson, Lynn. 2002. "Theorising Identity, Nationality and Citizenship: Implications for European Citizenship Identity." *Sociológia*, 34 (6): 507–32.

Jann, Rosemary. 1985. "Abbott's Flatland: Scientific Imagination and Natural Christianity." *Victorian Studies*, 473–90.

Jenkins, Brian, ed. 1996. *Nation and Identity in Contemporary Europe*. London: Routledge.

Jessop, Bob, Neil Brenner, and Martin Jones. 2008. "Theorizing Sociospatial Relations." *Environment and Planning D: Society and Space* 26: 389–401.

Joachimsthaler, Jürgen. 2002. "Kulturraumformung durch Sprach-und Literaturpolitik." *Orbis Linguarum*, 21: 109–29.

Johnston, Ronald John. 1985. "Places Matter." *Irish Geography*, 18: 59–63.

Kahraman, Z. Ezgi Haliloğlu. 2013. 2008. "The Relationship between Squatter Housing Transformation and Social Integration of Rural Migrants into Urban Life: A Case Study in Dikmen." Phd diss. Ankara: Middle East Technical University.
—. 2011. "Urban Integration as A Multi-Dimensional Process in The Ethnically Diverse City." In *Future Urban Research in Europe Series*, edited by Frank Eckardt and John Eade, 25–47. Berlin: BWW Berliner Wissenschats-Verla Publishing.
—. "Defining Urban Integration through Active Participation of Rural Migrants." In *Identities, Cultures, Spaces: Dialogue and Change*, edited by Fernando Kuhn, 83–106. Newcastle-upon-Thyne: Cambridge Scholars Publishing.
Kaplan, David H., and Guntram H. Herb. 2011. "How Geography Shapes National Identities." *National Identities* 13: 349–60.
Karp, Ivan, Christine Mullen Kreamer, and Steven D. Lavine, eds. 1992. *Museums and Communities*. Washington: Smithsonian Institute Press.
Karpat, Kemal. 1976. *The Gecekondu: Rural Migration and Urbanization*. Cambridge: Cambridge University Press.
Kartal, Kemal. 1978. *Kentleşme ve İnsan* ["Urbanisation and Human Beings"], TODAİ Yayınları, No. 5. Ankara: Doğan Basımevi.
Kaunismaa, Pekka. 1998. "Mitä on kollektiivinen identiteetti?" ["What Is Collective Identity?"] In *Puheenvuoroja identiteetistä: Johdatusta yhteisöllisyyden ymmärtämiseen*, 37–54. Jyväskylä: Atena. [In Finnish only.]
Kearney, Michael. 1995. "The Local and the Global: The Anthropology of Globalization and Transnationalism." *Annual Review of Anthropology*. 24: 547–65.
Kearns, Gerald, and Chris Philo, eds. 1993. *Selling Places: The City as Cultural Capital, Past and Present*. Oxford: Pergamon.
Kennedy, Paul, and Victor Roudometof. 2001. *Communities across borders under globalising conditions: New immigrants and transnational cultures*. Working Paper Transnational Communities. Oxford: University of Oxford.
Kilcher, Andreas B., ed. 2000. *Metzler Lexikon der deutsch-jüdischen Literatur: Jüdische Autorinnen und Autoren deutscher Sprache von der Aufklärung bis zur Gegenwart*. Stuttgart: Verlag J. B. Metzler.
—. 2011. "Der Kafka-Nachlass als Streitobjekt des Literaturbetriebs: Literatur als/statt Betrieb." Lecture presented at the confererence Zur Poetik des Literaturbetriebs, Zürich, 3–5 March.
King, Anthony D. 1990. *Global Cities: Post-Imperialism and the Internationalization of London*. London: Routledge.

Kıray, Mübeccel B. 1972. *Örgütleşemeyen Kent* ["Unorganised City"], Ankara: Sosyal Bilimler Derneği.

Kirshenblatt-Gimblett, Barbara. 1998. *Destination Culture: Tourism, Museums, and Heritage*. Berkeley, CA: University of California Press.

Klusáková, Lud'a, and Laure Teulières. 2008. "Conclusion: Frontiers and Identities on Urban, Regional and National Scales." In *Frontiers and Identities. Cities in Regions and Nations*, edited by Lud'a Klusáková and Laure Teulières, 323–27. Pisa: Pisa University Press.

Kongar, Emre. 1973-a. "Altındağ'da Kentle Bütünleşme." *Amme İdaresi Dergisi*, 6 (3): 58–84.

—. 1973-b. "Altındağ Gecekondu Bölgesi." *Amme İdaresi Dergisi*, 6 (4): 108–38.

Kotler, Philip, Christer Asplund, Irving Rein and Donald Haider. 1999. *Marketing Places Europe: How to Attract Investments, Industries, Residents and Visitors to Cities, Communities, Regions and Nations in Europe*. London: Financial Times/Prentice Hall.

Kotler, Philip, Donald H. Haider, and Irving J. Rein. 2002. *Marketing Places*. New York: The Free Press (Simon and Schuster).

Kuhn, Fernando. 2008. "Mercosur in the Media of Mercosur Countries." *The Global Studies Journal*, 1 (3): 111–22.

—. 2009. "Internet: A 'Glocal' Medium for Brazilian Small Football Clubs." Paper presented at the 1st "International Media Readings," Moscow, 8–10 October.

—. 2012. "Regional Spatialities, Regional Identities: Challenges and Opportunities for Regional Media." Paper presented at the 13th conference for the International Society for the Study of European Ideas – ISSEI. Nicosia, 2–6 July.

Kuhn, Thomas. 1978. *La Struttura delle Rivoluzioni Scientifiche*. Turin: Einaudi.

Kuperminc, Jean-Claude, and Rafaële Arditti, eds. 2001. *Preserving Jewish Archives as Part of the European Cultural Heritage: Proceedings of the Conference on Judaica Archives in Europe, for Archivists and Librarians, Potsdam, 1999, 11–13 July*. Paris: Nadir de l'Alliance Israëlite Universelle.

Kuzio, Taras. 2001. "Identity and Nation-Building in Ukraine." *Ethnicities*, 1 (3): 343–65.

Kymlicka, Will. 1992. "The Rights of Minority Cultures: Reply to Kukathas." *Political Theory*, 20 (1): 140–6.

—. 2009. "Categorizing Groups, Categorizing States: Theorizing Minority Rights in a World of Deep Diversity." *Ethics and International Affairs*, 23 (4) 371–88.

Kymlicka, Will, and Gerald Allan Cohen. 1988. "Human Nature and Social Change in the Marxist Conception of History." *The Journal of Philosophy*, 85 (4): 171–91.

Lähdesmäki, Tuuli. 2010. "European Capitals of Culture as Cultural Meeting Places: Strategies of Representing Cultural Diversity." *Nordisk Kulturpolitisk Tidskrift*, 01/2010: 27–43.

Lamb, Sarah. 2000. *White Saris and Sweet Mangoes: Aging, Gender, and Body in North India*. Berkeley. CA: University of California Press.

Lancaster, Bill. 2007. "The North East, England's Most Distinctive Region?" In *An Agenda for Regional History*, edited by Bill Lancaster, Diana Newton and Natasha Vall, 23–42. Newcastle: Northumbria University Press.

Larson, John Lauritz. 2001. "Pigs in Space: or, What Shapes America's Regional Cultures?" In *The Identity of the American Midwest: Essays in Regional History*, edited by Andrew R.L. Clayton and Susan E. Gray, 69–77. Bloomington, IN: Indiana University Press.

Leggewie, Claus. 2009. "Battlefield Europe: Transnational Memory and European Identity." *Eurozine*, (Trans. Simon Garnett from the German original "Schlachtfeld Europa Transnationale Erinnerung und Europäische Identität," in *Blätter für Deutsche und Internationale Politik*, 28 April 2009), 4 December 2010, retrieved 12 August 2011. www.eurozine.com/articles/2009-04-28-leggewie-en.html.

Leitmann, Josef, and Deniz Baharoğlu. 1999. "Reaching Turkey's Spontaneous Settlements: The Institutional Dimension of Infrastructure Provision." *International Planning Studies*, 4 (2): 95–212.

Lejeune, Philippe. 1975. *Le Pacte Autobiographique*. Paris: Seuil.

Levine, Ned. 1973. "Old Culture-New Culture: A Study of Migrants in Ankara, Turkey." *Social Forces*, 51 (3): 355–68.

Lewis Carroll. 1865. *Alice's Adventures in Wonderland*. London: Macmillan & Co.

Lie, Rico. 2002. "Spaces of Intercultural Communication." Paper presented at the 23rd conference for the International Association for Media and Communication Research - IAMCR, Barcelona, 21–26 July.

Locke, John. 1976 [original 1690]. *An Essay Concerning Human Understanding (Everyman's Library)*. London: Dent.

Logan, Joy. 2005–6. "Transculturation and Affect in the L2 Classroom: Teaching English and Ethnography in Yucatan." *Estudios de Lingüística Inglesa Aplicada*, 6: 41–62.

Longo, Giuseppe O. 2002. "Il Disorientamento nella Scienza." Paper presented at the 18th meeting Seminario d'Estatef, Ravello, Italy, 30 June - 3 July.

Lowenthal, David. 1998. *The Heritage Crusade and the Spoils of History*. Cambridge: Cambridge University Press.

MacDonald, George F. 1992. "Change and Challenge: Museums in the Information Society." In *Museums and Communities - The Politics of Public Culture*, edited by Ivan Karp, Christine Mullen Kreamer, and Steven. D. Lavine, 158–81. Washington: Smithsonian Institution Press.

Mäkinen, Minna. 1996. "Kuvia kotiseudusta: Lempääläisnuorten kotiseutumielikuvia piirustusten ja kirjoitusten valossa." [Images of Homely Landscapes. Mental Images of Homely Landscapes Illustrated by the Drawings and Writings of the Juvenile in Lempäälä] Jyväskylä: Jyväskylän yliopisto, Etnologian laitos. Joulukuu. [In Finnish only.]

—. 2009. "Kotikunta kaupunginosaksi: Säynätsalon kunnan ja Jyväskylän kaupungin kuntaliitos kulttuurisena ilmiönä." ["From Home Municipality to Part of a City: The Fusion of Säynätsalo and Jyväskylä as a Cultural Phenomenon"] Jyväskylä: Jyväskylän kaupungin raportit. [In Finnish only.]

Mann, Michael. 1986. *The Sources of Social Power*. Cambridge: Cambridge University Press.

Martell, Luke. 2007. "The Third Wave in Globalization Theory." International Studies Review, 9: 173–96.

Martín-Barbero, Jesús. 1999. "Las Transformaciones del Mapa: Identidades, Industrias y Culturas." In *América Latina: Un Espacio Cultural en un Mundo Globalizado*, edited by Manuel Antonio Garretón, 296–331. Bogotá: Convenio Andrés Bello.

Marx, Karl. 1996. "Capital: A Critique of Political Economy. Vol. 1." In: *MECW, Vol. 35*. Moscow: Progress Publishers.

Marx, Karl, and Friedrich Engels. 1975. "The Holy Family, or Critique of Critical Criticism." In *MECW, Vol. 4*, 5–211. Moscow: Progress Publishers.

Matteucci, Nicola. 1982. *L'Utopia e le sue Forme*. Bologna: Il Mulino.

Medina-Lopez-Portillo, Adriana, and John H. Sinnigen. 2009. "Interculturality x Intercultural Competencies in Latin America." In *The Sage Handbook of Intercultural Competence*, edited by Darla K. Deardorff, 249–63. Thousand Oaks, CA: Sage.

Meredith, Paul. 1998. "Hybridity in the Third Space: Rethinking Bycultural Politics in Aotearoa – New Zealand." Paper presented at the Te Oru Rangahau Maori Research and Development Conference, Palmerston North, New Zealand, 7–9 July.

Metropol İmar. 1994. *Dikmen Vadisi Projesi ve Yildiz-Oran Aksi Revizyon İmar Plani Raporu*, Ankara.

Moore, Jerry D. 2004. *Visions of Culture: An Introduction to Anthropological Theories and Theorists*. Walnut Creek, CA: Altamira.

Morley, David, and Kevin Robins. 1995. *Spaces of Identity: Global Media, Electronic Landscapes and Cultural Boundaries*. Abingdon, UK: Routledge.

Movius, Lauren. 2010. "Cultural Globalisation and Challenges to Traditional Communication Theories." *PLATFORM: Journal of Media and Communication*, 2 (1): 6–18.

Nederveen Pieterse, Jan. 2004. *Globalization and Culture: Global Mélange*. Boulder, CO: Rowman and Littlefield.

—. 2009. *Globalization and Culture: Global Mélange*. Lanham, MD: Rowman & Littlefield.

Neumann, Iver B. 1993. "Russia as Central Europe's Constituting 'other'." *East European Politics and Society*, 7(2): 349–69.

Nijman, Jan. 1999. "Cultural Globalization and the Identity of Place: The Reconstruction of Amsterdam." *Ecumene*, 6 (2): 146–65.

Nora, Pierre. 1989. "Between Memory and History: Les Lieux de Mémoir. " *Representations*, 26 (Special Issue: Memory and Counter-Memory): 7–24.

Norusis, Marija J. 1990. *The SPSS Guide to Data Analysis for Release 4*. Chicago: SPSS.

Öncü, Ayşe. 1976. *Örgüt Sosyolojisi*. Ankara: Sosyal Bilimler Derneği.

Oring, Elliott. 1994. "The Arts, Artifacts, and Artifices of Identity." *The Journal of American Folklore*, 107 (424): 211–33.

Ortiz, Fernando. 1995. *Cuban Counterpoint: Tobacco and Sugar*. Durham, NC: Duke University Press. Translated by Harriet de Onís. (Original Spanish edition published in 1940. Original translation by Onìs published in 1947, New York: Knopf).

Osterhammel, Jurgen, and Niels P. Peterson. 2005. *Globalization: A Short History*. Princeton: Princeton University Press.

Paasi, Anssi. 1986. Neljä maakuntaa. Maantieteellinen tutkimus aluetietoisuuden kehittymisestä. [Four Regions. Geographical Research Concerning the Development of Regional Consciousness] Joensuu: Joensuun yliopisto, yhteiskuntatieteellisiä julkaisuja 8. Joensuu. [In Finnish only.]

—. 2000. "Territorial Identities as Social Constructs." *Hagar – International Social Science Review,* 1 (2): 91–113.

—. 2002. "Place and Region: Regional Worlds and Words." *Progress in Human Geography*, 26 (6): 802–11.

—. 2003. "Region and Place: Regional Identity in Question." *Progress in Human Geography*, 27: 475–85.

Painter, Joe. 2008. "European Citizenship and the Regions." *European Urban and Regional Studies*, 15 (1): 5–19.

Palmer, Catherine. 1999. "Tourism and the Symbols of Identity." *Tourism Management*, 20: 313–21.

Parekh, Bhikhu. 2005. "Dialogue between Cultures." In *Democracy, Nationalism, and Multiculturalism*, edited by Ramón Máiz and Ferran Requejo, 13–24. London: Frank Cass.

Patterson, Sheila. 1963. *Dark Strangers: A Sociological Study Of The Absorption of A Recent West Indian Migrant Group in Brixton, South London*. London: Tavistock.

Penninx, Rinus. 2004. "Integration Policies for Europe's Immigrants: Performance, Conditions and Challenges." Paper presented at the Sachverstängenrat für Zuwanderung und Integration, Gouda, 26 February.

Phythian-Adams, Charles. 2007. "Differentiating Provincial Societies in English History: Spatial Contexts and Cultural Processes." In *An Agenda for Regional History*, edited by Bill Lancaster, Diana Newton and Natasha Vall, 3–22. Newcastle: Northumbria University Press.

Piattelli Palmarini, Massimo. 1984. *Livelli di realtà*. Milan: Feltrinelli.

—. 2003. *I Linguaggi della Scienza*. Milan: Mondadori.

Picard, Michel. 2008. "Balinese Identity as Tourist Attraction." *Tourist Studies*, 8 (2): 155–73.

Pillemer, Karl, Phyllis Moen, Elaine Wethington, and Nina Glasgow, eds. 2000. *Social Integration in the Second Half of Life*. Baltimore: Johns Hopkins University Press.

Pollack, Herman. 1971. *Jewish Folkways in Germanic Lands (1648–1806): Studies in Aspects of Daily Life*. Cambridge, MA: M.I.T. Press.

Pollice, Fabio. 2003. "The Role of Territorial Identity in Local Development Processes." In *The Cultural Turn in Geography, Proceedings of the Conference 18–20th of September 2003 - Gorizia Campus*, edited by Paul Claval, María Paola Pagnini, and Maurizio Scaini. Trieste: Università di Trieste / International Geographical Union. www.openstarts.units.it/proceedings/.

Pooley, Colin G. 2007. "The Role of Migration in Constructing Regional Identity." In *An Agenda for Regional History*, edited by Bill Lancaster, Diana Newton and Natasha Vall, 63–81. Newcastle: Northumbria University Press.

Popper, Karl. 1969. *Filosofia e Scienza*. Turin: Einaudi.

Prato, Giuliana B. 2009. "Introduction." In *Beyond Multiculturalism: View from Anthropology*, edited by Giuliana B. Prato, 1–19. Farnham, UK: Ashgate Publishing Company.

Pratt, Mary Louise. 1991. "Arts of the Contact Zone." *Profession*, 91: 33–40.

—. 1992. *Imperial Eyes: Travel Writing and Transculturation*. London: Routledge.

Pred, Allan. 1984. "Place as Historically Contingent Process: Structuration and the Time-Geography of Becoming Places." *Annals of the Association of American Geographers*, 74: 279–97.

Propp, Vladimir. 2008. *Morphology of Folktale*. Austin, TX: University of Texas Press.

Putnam, Robert. D. 1995. "Bowling Alone: America's Declining Social Capital," *Journal of Democracy*, 6: 65–78.

Raffestin, Claude. 1983. *Per una Geografia del Potere*. Milano: Unicopli.

Raheja, Gloria Goodwin, and Ann Grodzins Gold. 1994. *Listen to Heron's Words: Reimagining Gender and Kinship in North India*. Berkeley, CA: University of California Press.

Rex, John. 2003. "Integration Policy in Great Britain." In *The integration of immigrants in European societies*, edited by Friedrich Heckmann, and Dominique Schnapper, 79–104. Stuttgart: Lucius and Lucius.

Richeri, Giuseppe. 1994. *La Transición de la Televisión*. Barcelona: Editorial Bosch.

Riemann, Bernhard. 1994. *On the Hypotheses which Lie at the Foundation of Geometry* (edited by Renato Pettoello). Turin: Bollati-Boringhieri.

Riukulehto, Sulevi. 2010a. "The Three Stages of Landscapes as a Basis for Regional Identity." Paper presented in NORSA 2010. June 21st–23rd 2010, Seinäjoki. Abstract in The Search: Future Dynamics of Regional Development, 49–50. Elina Pulliainen and Kirsi Siltanen (eds.). Tampere: University of Tampere.

—. 2010b: "Reforming Regional Identities between Local and National. Experiencies from Western Finland." Paper presented at the 12th international conference for the International Society for the Study of European Ideas – ISSEI. Ankara, 2–6August 2010.

—. 2013. "Homely Sites and Landscapes as Elements of Regional Identity." In *Identities, Cultures, Spaces: Dialogue and Change*, edited by Fernando Kuhn, 41–56. Newcastle-upon-Thyne: Cambridge Scholars Publishing.

Robertson, Roland. 1992. *Globalization: Social Theory and Global Culture*. London: Sage.

—. 1995. "Glocalisation: Time-Space and Homogeneity-Heterogeneity." In *Global Modernities*, edited by Mike Featherstone, Scott Lash, and Roland Robertson, 25–44. London: Sage.

Robinson, Williams I. 2007. "Theories of globalization." In *The Blackwell Companion to Globalization*, edited by George Ritzer, 125–43. Malden, MA: Blackwell.

Rosaldo, Renato. 1993. *Culture and Truth: The Remaking of Social Analysis*. London: Routledge.

Rosenberg, Justin. 2005. "Globalization Theory: A Post-Morten." *International Politics*, 42: 2–74.

Rubešová, Markéta P. 2013. "Territorializing Spiritual Values: Notions of 'Belonging' and 'Possessing' in the Context of the Controversy over Max Brod's Legacy." In *Identities, Cultures, Spaces: Dialogue and Change*, edited by Fernando Kuhn, 107–24. Newcastle-upon-Thyne: Cambridge Scholars Publishing.

Rucker, Rudolf. 1984. *The Fourth Dimension: A Guided Tour of the Higher Universes*. Boston: Houghton Mifflin.

Russell, Bertrand. 1970. *Introduzione alla Filosofia Matematica*. Roma: Newton Compton.

Sadhu Swati, and Kumar Chattopadhway. 2006. "A Note on Multidimensional Study of Social Integration in a Rural Society." *Bangladesh e-Journal of Sociology* 3 (1): 1–15.

Salzer, Mark, and Richard C. Baron. (2006) *Community Integration and Measuring Participation*. Philadelphia, PA: University of Pennsylvania Collaborative on Community Integration.

Sandkühler, Hans Jörg. 2004. "Pluralism, Cultures of Knowledge, Transculturality, and Fundamental Rights." In *Transculturality: Epistemology, Ethics, and Politics*, edited by Hans Jörg Sandkühler, 79–100. Peter Lang: Frankfurt.

Saul, John Ralston. 2005. *The Collapse of Globalism*. London. Atlantic Books.

Schlesinger, Philip. 1996. "El Contradictorio Espacio Comunicativo de Europa." *Voces y Culturas*, 9: 7–27.

Schlögel, Karl. 2004. "Europe tests its Boundaries: A Searching Movement." *Eurozine*, 24 November 2011, retrieved 13 April 2012. www.eurozine.com/articles/2004-11-24-schloegel-en.html.

Schrenk, Lisa D. 1999. "From Historic Village to Modern Pavillion: The Evolution of Foreign Architectural Representation at International Expositions in the 1930s." *National Identities*, 1: 287–312.

Schuerkens, Ulrike. 2003. "The Sociological and Anthropological Study of Globalisation and Localisation." *Current Sociology*, 51 (3/4): 209–22.

Sen, Amartya. 2005. *The Argumentative Indian: Writings on Indian Culture, History and Identity*. London: Penguin Books.

Sencer, Yakut I. 1979. *Türkiye'de Kentleşme, Kültür Bakanlığı Yayınları (345)*. Ankara: Ongun Kardeşler Matbaacılık.

Şenyapılı, Önder. 1981-b. *Kentleşemeyen Ülke, Kentlileşen Köylüler*. Ankara: ODTÜ Mimarlık Fakültesi Ara Yayınları (R-1 09 81).

Şenyapılı, Tansi. 1978. *Bütünleşmemiş Kentli Nüfus Sorunu* ["Non Integrated Urban Population"], Ankara: ODTÜ Mimarlık Fakültesi Yayını (27), Ankara.

—. 1979. "A Proposal for A Framework for Marginal Sector and Squatter Housing." *METU Studies in Development* 6: 24–25.

—. 1981-a. *Gecekondu-Çevre İşçilerin Mekanı*. Ankara: ODTÜ.

—. 1982. "Economic Change and The Gecekondu Family." In *Sex Roles, Family and Community in Turkey*, edited by Çiğdem Kağıtçıbaşı, 237–48. Bloomington, IN: University Turkish Studies.

—. 2004. "Charting the 'Voyage' of Squatter Housing in Urban Spatial 'Quadruped.'" *European Journal of Turkish Studies,* Thematic Issue No1, Gecekondu. Retrieved 22 January 2011. www.ejts.org/document142.html.

Seweryn, Olga. 2007. "Identity Change as a Consequence of Migration Experience." In *Imagining Frontiers, Contesting Identities*, edited by Ann Katherine Isaacs, and Gudmundur Halfdanarson. Pisa: Università di Pisa.

Shaw, Stephen, Susan Bagwell, and Joanna Karmowska. 2004. "Ethnoscapes as Spectacle: Reimaging Multicultural Districts as New Destinations for Leisure and Tourism Consumption." *Urban Studies*, 41 (10): 1983–2000.

Shevchenko, Andriy, and David van Reybrouck. 2011. "Splitting up? The Re-Nationalization of Europe (debate)." *Eurozine*, 14 March 2011, retrieved 12 August 2011. www.eurozine.com/articles/2011-03-14-lviv-en.html.

Shome, Raka, and Radha Hedge. 2002. "Culture, Communication, and the Challenge of Globalisation." *Critical Studies in Media Communication*, 19 (2): 172–89.

Short, John R., and Yeong-Hyun Kim. 1999. *Globalization and the City*. Essex: Addison Wesley Longman.

Sinclair, John, Elizabeth Jacka, and Stuart Cunningham. 1996. "Peripheral Vision." In *New Patterns in Global Television: Peripheral Vision*, edited by John Sinclair, Elizabeth Jacka, and Stuart. Cunningham, 1–32. Oxford: Oxford University Press.

Sklair, Leslie. 1999. "Competing Conceptions of Globalization." *Journal of World-Systems Research*, 2: 143–63.

Song, Sarah. 2007. *Justice, Gender, and the Politics of Multiculturalism*. New York: Cambridge University Press.

Spencer, Herbert. 1851. *Social Statistics: Or the Conditions Essential to Human Happiness Specified, and the First of Them Developed*. Reprint, New York: D. Appleton and Co, 1865.

Spoehr, John, Lou Wilson, Kate Barnett, Tania Toth, and Amanda Watson-Tran. 2007. "Measuring Social Inclusion and Exclusion in Northern Adelaide." Report for the Department of Health. Adelaide: Australian Institute for Social Research, University of Adelaide.

Sreberny-Mohammadi, Annabelle. 1996. "Globalization, Communication and Transnational Civil Society: Introduction." In *Globalization, Communication and Transnational Civil Society*, edited by Sandra Braman and Annabelle Sreberny-Mohammadi, 1–19. Cresskill, NJ: Hampton Press.

Steingress, Gerhard. 2010. "Globalizing Cultures: A Challenge for Contemporary Cultural Sociology." *Eurasian Journal of Anthropology*, 1 (1): 1–10.

Stocking Jr., George W. 1982. *Race, Culture, and Evolution: Essays in the History of Anthropology*. Chicago: Chicago University Press.

Stolle-McAllister, John. 2007. "Constructing Interculturality in Ecuador: Challenges to the Humanities." *International Journal of the Humanities*, 5 (6): 163–69.

Straubhaar, Joseph. 1997. "Distinguishing the Global, Regional and National Levels of World Television." In *Media in Global Context: A reader*, edited by Annabelle Sreberny-Mohammadi, Dwayne Winseck, Jim McKenna, and Oliver Boyd-Barrett, 284–98. London: Edward Arnold.

Street, Brian V. 1993. "Culture is a Verb: Anthropological Aspects of Language and Cultural Process." In *Language and Culture*, edited by David Graddol, Linda Thompson and Michael Byram, 23–43. Clevedon, UK: British Association for Applied Linguistics in association with Multilingual Matter.

Suárez-Orozco, Carola. 2004. "Formulating Identity in a Globalized World." In *Globalization: Culture and Education in the New Millennium*, edited by Marcelo M. Suárez-Orozco, and Desiree Qin-Hilliard, 173–202. Berkeley, CA: University of California Press & Ross Institute.

Suzuki, Peter. 1964. "Encounters with Istanbul: Urban Peasants and Village Peasants." *International Journal of Comparative Sociology*, 5: 208–15.

—. 1966. "Peasants Without Plows: Some Anatolians in Istanbul." *International Journal of Comparative Sociology*, 31 (4): 428–38.

Tabachnick, Barbara G., and Linda S. Fidell. 1996. *Using Multivariate Statistics*. New York: Harpercollins College Publishers.

Taylor, Charles. 1994. "Politics of Recognition." In *Multiculturalism: Examining the Politics of Recognition*, edited by Amy Gutmann, 25–77. Princeton, NJ: Princeton University Press.

Taylor, Friedrich. 1911. *Principles of Scientific Management*. New York: Harper & brothers.

Taylor, Peter J. 1994. "The State as Container: Territoriality in the Modern World-System." *Progress in Human Geography*, 18: 151–62.

The American Heritage Dictionary of the English Language. 2009. Fourth Edition. Boston: Houghton Mifflin Company.

The European Commission. 2002. *Migration and Social Integration of Migrants, Valorization of research on migration and immigration funded under 4th and 5th European Framework Programmes of Research*. Brussels.

The European Foundation for the Improvement of Living and Working Conditions. 2006. *Integration of immigrants: Contribution of local and regional authorities*. Dublin. Retrieved August, 2007. www.eurofound.eu.int.

Thorsten, Marie. 2005. "Silk Road Nostalgia and Imagined Global Community." *Comparative American Studies*, 3 (3): 301–17.

Thrift, Nigel. 1998. "Towards a New New Regional Geography." *Berichte zur deutschsen Landeskunde*, 72 (1): 37–46.

Tomlinson, John. 1999. *Globalization and Culture*. Chicago: University of Chicago Press.

—. 2003. "Globalization and Cultural Identity." In *The Global Transformations Reader*, edited by David Held and Anthony McGrew, 269–72. Cambridge: Polity.

Triandafyllidou, Anna, and Ruth Wodak. 2003. "Conceptual and Methodological Questions in the Study of Collective Identity: An Introduction." *Journal of Language and Politics*, 2 (2): 205–23.

Trousson, Raymond. 1992. *Viaggi in nessun Luogo: Storia del Pensiero Utopico*. Ravenna: Longo.

Tuomi-Nikula, Outi. 2009. "Kotiseutu kulttuuriperintökokemuksena – saksalainen kokemus." [Home site (Heimat) as an Experience of

Cultural Heritage – German Experience] *Elore*, 16 (1). Suomen Kansantietouden Tutkijain Seura ry.

Türker-Devecigil, Pinar. 2003. "An Agent-oriented Approach to the Analysis of Urban Transformation Process: Ankara-Dikmen Valley within the Context of Sustainable Urban Development." PhD Thesis, Ankara, Middle East Technical University.

—. 2005. "Urban Transformation Projects as a Model to Transform Gecekondu Areas in Turkey: The Example of Dikmen Valley – Ankara." *European Journal of Housing Policy* 5 (2): 211–29.

Türksoy, Ömü. 1983. "An Attempt to Understand Urban Integration through The Evaluation of Mental Maps: Cognitive Maps of Ankara Constructed by High School Students." Master Thesis, Ankara, Middle East Technical University.

Turner, Victor Witter. 1977. "Variations on a Theme of Liminality." In *Secular Ritual*, edited by Sally Falk Moore, and Barbara G. Myerhoff, 36–52. Amsterdam: Van Gorcum.

—. 1982. *From Ritual to Theatre: The Human Seriousness of Play*. New York: Performing Arts Journal Publications.

Tylor, Edward Burnett. 1871. *Primitive Culture*. New York: J.P. Putnam's Sons.

UNWTO Tourism Highlights, 2012 Edition. 2012. Press release. Madrid: World Tourism Organisation (UNWTO), retrieved 30 April 2012. http://mkt.unwto.org/en/publication/unwto-tourism-highlights-2012-edition.

Uzun, Nil. 2003. "The Impact of Urban Renewal and Gentrification of Urban Fabric: Three Cases in Turkey." *Tijdschrift Voor Economische en Sociale Geografie*, 94 (3): 363–75.

Vermeulen, Hans. 1999. "Immigration, Integration and the Politics of Culture." *The Netherlands' Journal of Social Sciences*, 35: 6–22.

Wallas, Armin A., ed. 2002. *Jüdische Identitäten im Mitteleuropa: Literarische Modelle der Identitätskonstruktion*. Tübingen: M. Niemeyer.

Wallerstein, Immanuel. 1974. *The Modern World System – I*. New York: Academic Press.

Ward, Stephen Victor. 1998. *Selling Places: The Marketing and Promotion of Towns and Cities, 1850–2000*. Routledge: London.

Waters, Malcolm. 1995. *Globalization*. London: Routledge.

Weatherford, Jack McIver. 2004. *Genghis Khan and the Making of the Modern World*. New York: Crown.

Weick, Karl. 1997. *Senso e Significato nell'organizzazione*. Milan: Raffaello Cortina.

Weigert, Andrew J. 1983. "Identity: Its Emergence within Sociological Psychology." *Symbolic Interaction*, 6 (2): 183–206.

Welsch, Wolfgang (1999). "Transculturality – the Puzzling Form of Cultures Today." In *Spaces of Culture: City, Nation, World*, edited by Mike Featherstone, and Scott Lash, 194–213. London: Sage.

Wendt, Alexander. 1994. "Collective Identity Formation and the International State." *American Political Science Review*, 88 (2): 384–96.

Werner, Heinz. 1997. "Measurements and Indicators of Integration." In *Measurement and Indicators of integration*, 163–78. Strasbourg: Council of Europe Publishing.

Williams, Raymond. 1895. *The Country and the City*. London: Hogarth Press.

Yasa, İbrahim. 1970. "The Gecekondu Family: A Family Typology in Transition." *The AÜSBF Journal*, 25: 9–18.

Young, Iris Marion. 1998. "Unruly Categories: A Critique of Nancy Fraser's Dual Systems Theory." In *Theorizing Multiculturalism: A Guide to the Current Debates*, edited by Cynthia Willett, 50–67. Malden, MA: Blackwell.

CONTRIBUTORS

Siyaves Azeri has a Ph.D. in Philosophy from the University of Ottawa and is currently a postdoctoral researcher at the University of Queens, Ottawa. He has taught as an assistant professor at Koç University in Istanbul, and has also taught at the University of Ottawa and as a guest lecturer at Istanbul Technical University. His major field of interest is the problem of personal identity and the metaphysics of the self. Other areas include modern and contemporary philosophy and the application of particular philosophical theories to literature and film.

Marianna Forleo has a Ph.D. in History and Politics from Florence University and is a researcher at the Institute for the Development of Vocational Training ISFOL, in Rome. She also collaborates with the Faculty of Political Sciences of Romatre University, as well as contributing to the journals of the field. Her main areas of interest are utopia and distopia across the nineteenth and twentieth centuries.

Z. Ezgi Haliloğlu Kahraman has an M.S.E. and Ph.D. in City Planning from the Middle East Technical University in Ankara, and is currently working as Assistant Professor and Head of the Department of City and Regional Planning at Çankaya University, also in Ankara. Her research and teaching interests focus on participatory design and planning processes, user-centered design approach, rural migrants in cities, urban integration and urban transformation.

Fernando Kuhn graduated in journalism and worked as a reporter and editor for Brazilian newspapers and magazines. He has a master's degree in multimedia from the Brazilian Universidade Estadual de Campinas (Unicamp) and a Ph.D. in social communication from the Universidade Metodista de São Paulo (Umesp), also in Brazil (where he was twice awarded with a fellowship of The State of São Paulo Research Foundation Fapesp); he was also a researcher at the University of London's School of Oriental and African Studies (SOAS) as part of his doctoral research. He coordinated the implementation of the digital media course in the Faculdades Integradas Alcantara Machado (FIAM) in Sao Paulo, and took part in the Global Media research group, based in Umesp. He is currently a researcher at the Community and Local Communication research group of the same university, and has been chairing the "Maps of Dialogue" working group of the International Society for the Study of European Ideas ISSEI. His other areas of interest are international communication, globalisation, diasporas, regional media, ethnic media, intercultural communication, media and sport, media and environment, popular culture and journalism.

Sulevi Riukulehto works in the University of Helsinki, Ruralia Institute as Research Director in Regional History and Adjunct Professor (Economic History). His position is part of a multidisciplinary research network (Epanet) in Seinäjoki. The main topics for research in Ruralia Institute are rural policy, innovation systems and the interaction between towns and rural areas. He leads the research group of Regions, History, and Culture, which is focusing on the origin and development processes of regions and structures, homely landscapes, home territories and cultural phenomena in rural context. His publications deal with the history of economic thought, and the history of forestry.

Markéta P. Rubešová is a Ph.D candidate in General History at the Charles University in Prague, and is a cataloguer at The Art Museum Yad Vashem. Her fields of interest include the social and cultural history of the Ottoman Empire in the Early Modern Period, translation and interpretation of Hebrew texts (Rabbinical and modern Hebrew) and its problems and methods, Jewish historical experiences in different cultural settings, and stereotypes, identities, the individual and society in historical perspective.

INDEX

L

M

N

O

P

R

S

T

U

V